TCP/IP and Related Protocols

Uyless Black

Third Edition

McGraw-Hill

New York   San Francisco   Washington, D.C.   Auckland   Bogotá
Caracas   Lisbon   London   Madrid   Mexico City   Milan
Montreal   New Delhi   San Juan   Singapore
Sydney   Tokyo   Toronto

Library of Congress Cataloging-in-Publication Data

Black, Uyless D.
   TCP/IP and related protocols
  Uyless Black.—3rd ed.
     p.   cm.—(McGraw-Hill series on computer communications)
  Includes index.
  ISBN 0-07-913282-0
  1. TCP/IP (Computer network protocol) 2. Computer network
protocols. I. Title. II. Series.
TK5105.585.B54 1998
004.6'2—dc21   97-33278
                                                CIP

McGraw-Hill

A Division of The McGraw·Hill Companies

1 2 3 4 5 6 7 8 9 0 DOC/DOC 9 0 2 1 0 9 8 7

ISBN 0-07-913282-0

*The sponsoring editor for this book was Steven M. Elliot, the editing
supervisor was Paul R. Sobel, and the production supervisor was Tina
Cameron. It was set in Century Schoolbook by Donald A. Feldman of
McGraw-Hill's Professional Book Group composition unit.*

Printed and bound by R. R. Donnelley & Sons Company.

McGraw-Hill books are available at special quantity discounts to use
as premiums and sales promotions, or for use in corporate training programs. For more information, please write to the Director of Special
Sales, McGraw-Hill, 11 West 19th Street, New York, NY 10011. Or
contact your local bookstore.

This book is printed on recycled, acid-free paper containing a
minimum of 50% recycled, de-inked fiber.

Contents

To Ross Black, my brother and role model

Preface

This third edition of *TCP/IP* reflects changes that have occurred in this protocol suite during the past few years, as well as changes that have occurred in other parts of the industry that have a bearing on TCP/IP. The changes deal with (a) the release of a new verison of IP, called IPv6, (b) the growth of Frame Relay networks and the need to run on Frame Relay systems, and (c) the entry of ATM into the data communications area, and the potential need to interwork IP with ATM.

As with the first two editions, this book remains as a user guide, and a general tutorial on the TCP/IP protocol suites.

The title of this book for the first two editions included a subtitle, *Related Protocols*. Although no longer in the book's title, the book maintains the same approach of explaining, not just TCP/IP, but other complementary protocols that make up the TCP/IP protocol suite.

I hope you find this book a useful addition to your library. If you have questions, or would like to communicate with me, I can be reached at 102732.3535@compuserve.com.

Uyless Black

Acronyms

AAL	ATM adaptation layer
ABM	asynchronous balanced mode
ACK	positive acknowledgment
ACSE	association control service element
AFI	authority format identifier
ARP	address resolution protocol
AS	autonomous system
ASN.1	Abstract Syntax Notation One
ATM	Asynchronous transfer mode
AUI	attachment unit interface
BECN	backward explicit congestion notification
BER	basic encoding rules
BGP	border gateway protocol
B-ISDN	broadband ISDN
BIU	bus interface unit
BOOTP	bootstrap protocol
CATV	coaxial cable TV
CDIR	Classless Inter-Domain Routing
CEF	congestion encountered forward
CEI	Connection endpoint identifier
CLNP	connectionless network protocol
CLP	cell loss priority
CMIP	common management information protocol
CMOT	common management information services and protocol over TCP/IP
CRC	cyclic redundancy check

CSMA/CD	carrier sense, multiple access collision detection
DA	destination address
DE	discard eligibility
DIC	data network identification code
DLCI	data link connection identifier
DNS	domain name system
DPA	destination physical address
DQDB	distributed-queue-dual-bus
DSAP	destination service access point
DSP	domain-specific part
DSU	digital service unit (also data service unit)
DTE	data terminal equipment
DTP	data transfer protocol
EGP	external gateway protocol
EOT	end of transmission
FCS	frame-check sequence
FDDI	fiber distributed data interface
FNC	Federal Networking Council
FTAM	file transfer and access management
FTP	file transfer protocol
GGP	gateway-to-gateway protocol
GOES	geosynchronous orbiting environmental satellite
GOSIP	U.S. Government OSI Profile
HDLC	high-level data link control
HMP	host monitoring protocol
I	information (field)
I/G	individual/group (address bit)
IAC	interpret as command
ICI	intercarrier interface
ICMP	internet control message protocol
IDI	initial domain identifier
IDP	initial domain part

IEEE	Institute of Electrical & Electronics Engineers
IETF	Internet Engineering Task Force
IGMP	Internet group management protocol
IGP	internal gateway protocol
IMIB	Internet Management Information Base
IMP	interface message processor
INOC	Internet Network Operations Center
IP	internet protocol
IPDU	internetwork PDU
IPX	Internet packet exchange protocol
IRTF	Internet Research Task Force
ISDN	integrated services digital network
ISO	International Standards Organization
ISS	initial send sequence
ITU-T	International Telecommunication Union—Telecommunication Standardization Sector
IVD	integrated voice/data
IWU	internetworking unit
LAN	local area network
LAPB	link access protocol, balanced
LCN	Logical channel number
LCP	link control protocol
LLC	logical link control
LPP	lightweight presentation protocol
LSAP	link service access point
LSDU	link service data unit
MAC	media access control
MAN	metropolitan area network
MAU	medium attachment unit
MCF	MAC convergence function
MDI	medium dependent interface
MIB	Management Information Base
MTU	maximum transmission unit
MX	mail exchange
NAK	negative acknowledgment

TTL	time-to-live
TUBA	TCP & UDP with bigger addresses
U/L	universal/local (bit)
UDP	user datagram protocol
UI	unnumbered frame
ULP	upper layer protocol
UNI	user-network-interface
UT	Universal Time
VCI	virtual circuit identifier
VCI	virtual channel identifier
VPI	virtual path identifier
WAIS	wide area information servers
WAN	wide area network
WEB	worldwide web
XDR	external data representation
XID	exchange identification
XNS	Xerox network system

TCP/IP and the Internet

Data communication networks were developed to allow users to share computer and information resources as well as a common communication system. As organizations have brought the computer into almost every facet of business, it has become obvious that a single network, while very useful, is inadequate to meet the information needs of businesses and individuals. A user of one network, for example, often needs to access and share the resources of computers and databases that "belong" to another network. Merging all resources into one network, however, is prohibitively complex and expensive.

In the late 1960s and early 1970s, networks were built so users residing on different networks could not share resources. Network administrators also were reluctant to allow users to tap into resources because of concerns about security as well as excessive usage of network resources. As a result, it was difficult for a user to extend the use of an information system to another user across networks. The networks were either incompatible with each other or were not allowed to communicate because of administrative problems.

During this time, many people began to think about sharing resources among user applications. To do so, however, network administrators had to agree upon a set of common technologies and standards so the networks could communicate with each other. Applications such as electronic mail and file transfer also needed to be standardized to permit interconnections of end-user applications.

In the early 1970s, several groups around the world began to address network and application compatibility. At that time the term *internetworking*, which means interconnecting computers and/or networks, was coined. The concepts of internetworking were pioneered by the International Telecommunication Union, Telecommunications Standardization Sector (ITU-T), the International Standards Organization (ISO), and especially the original designers of the

ARPANET. *ARPA* refers to the Advanced Research Projects Agency, which is a U.S. Department of Defense (DOD) organization.

In fairness to the pioneers of internetworking concepts (and layered protocols, discussed later in this chapter), the ARPA protocols were well in existence before the ISO and ITU-T took an interest in this important subject. The procurement for ARPANET took place in 1968, and the machines selected for this procurement were Honeywell 316 interface message processors (IMPs). The initial effort was contracted through Bolt Bernak & Newman (BBN), and the ARPANET nodes were initially installed at UCLA, University of California at San Bernardino; the Stanford Research Institute (SRI); and the University of Utah. The well-known request for comments (RFCs) resulted from this early work.

After the pioneer work of a group of talented and dedicated engineers, these initial efforts were organized through the ARPANET Network Working Group. The group was disbanded in 1971, and the Defense Advanced Project Research Agency (DARPA) assumed the work of the earlier organization. DARPA's work in the early 1970s led to the development of an earlier protocol, the network control program, later the Transmission Control Protocol and the Internet Protocol (TCP/IP). Two years later, the first significant parts of the Internet were placed into operation. At about this time, DARPA started converting some of its computers to the TCP/IP suite of protocols. DARPA required that all computers connected to ARPANET had to use TCP/IP by January 1, 1983.

TCP/IP was initially used to connect ARPANET, the Packet Radio Net (PRNET), and the Packet Satellite Net (SATNET). Most user computers were large mainframes with terminals attached through terminal access servers. As ARPANET grew, the Department of Defense decided to split it into two networks. The other network was named MILNET and was set up for military purposes. ARPANET continued to be used for its original intent: a network to support R&D (research and development) applications. By the mid-1980s, the "ARPA Internet" was called simply "the Internet." In 1990, the last original ARPANET node was taken out of commission.

Perhaps one of the most significant developments in TCP/IP was DARPA's decision to implement TCP/IP around the UNIX operating system. Of equal importance, the University of California at Berkeley was selected to distribute the TCP/IP code. Some implementors have said that releasing such complex and functionally rich code was a "license to steal." Whatever one's view on the matter, it was a very significant and positive move in the industry. Because the TCP/IP code was nonproprietary, it spread rapidly among universities, private companies, and research centers. Indeed, it has become the standard suite of data communications protocols for UNIX-based computers.

During this period, other networks using TCP/IP were being created, based on funding from the U.S. government and other research agencies. The NSFnet was established as a high-capacity network by the National Science Foundation and is still in existence. NSF has played a key role in the development of the Internet, both in funding and strategic guidance.

The National Science Foundation (NSF) operation was managed by the joint efforts of MCI, Sprintlink, and IBM by forming Advanced Network Services (ANS). Access to the Internet was provided at network access points (NAPs), which connected to other networks, both private and public.

In November 1994, the NSF informed colleges and other institutions to look for another feed into the Internet because the U.S. government was getting out of the public Internet business. Most of the feeds were existing networks that had interconnected into the NSF backbone. NSF announced it would provide some funding for a few more years, and in 1995 it started disconnecting its NAPs.

Today, the Internet is commercial, with the ISPs charging a fee for its customers to use the ISP access to the other ISPs and the many files and data bases available (many of which are free to use) throughout the world.

Organization of the Internet

As the Internet grew, its organization and management were delegated to the Internet Advisory Board, or IAB (see Figure 1.1). Originally, the IAB consisted of a number of subsidiary organizations, but their main function was to coordinate the Internet task forces. In 1989, the task forces were placed into two major groups within the IAB: Internet Research Task Force (IRTF) and the Internet Engineering Task Force (IETF). The IRTF is responsible for ongoing research activities. The IETF concerns itself with tactical issues, such as implementation and engineering problems.

Request for comments (RFCs)

The request for comments (RFCs), briefly mentioned earlier in this chapter, are technical notes on an internet protocol. They represent the documentation of the Internet.

Some RFCs are de facto standards for TCP/IP, others are published for informational purposes, and still others are the result of research and might eventually become future standards. Presently, over 1000 RFCs are in existence, although quite a number of these specifications have been superseded.

and NAKs, respectively) and sequencing. In practice, most connectionless systems do not provide these services. By its very nature, connectionless service can achieve the following:

- A high degree of independence from specific protocols within a subnetwork
- A considerable degree of independence of the subnetworks from each other
- A high degree of independence of the subnetwork(s) from the user-specific protocols.

A connectionless network is likely more robust than its connection-oriented counterpart because each PDU is handled as an independent entity. Therefore, data units can take different routes to avoid failed nodes or congestion at a point in the network(s). Connectionless protocols do, however, consume more overhead in relation to the length of the headers and in proportion to the amount of user data in the PDU than their connection-oriented counterparts. The characteristics of connectionless networks are summarized in Figure 1.4.

Before leaving the subject of connectionless and connection-oriented protocols, note that the practical network manager recognizes the benefits of both connection-oriented and connectionless layers within a system. The choice depends on the type of service needed by the end user, as well as the cost and overhead to obtain it. Because most vendors provide for a variety of connection-oriented and connectionless products, it is a matter of deciding which type of service and which options you want. But let there be no mistake, if you care for your data, you must have a protocol residing somewhere in the system that accounts for the proper reception of all traffic.

Evolution of connectionless and connection-oriented systems

Many internets are connectionless, with little or no support for sequencing and acknowledgment. Most local area networks fit into this category, as does IP. In contrast, TCP is connection-oriented and

- No end-to-end mapping
- Full addressing with data unit
- May use alternate routing
- Limited or no accountability

Figure 1.4 Connectionless Service.

provides several data-integrity support functions. (I will examine the rationale for these combinations later in the book.) For now, it is useful to note that some newer technologies are using connection-oriented techniques, such as Frame Relay and Asynchronous Transfer Mode (ATM). One of the main reasons for this evolution is the ability to use short headers, such as the abbreviated identifier (a virtual circuit ID), in the PDU. Thus overhead bits are few, which translates into more efficient operations. Later in the book, I will examine Frame Relay and ATM in relation to IP in more detail.

Internet Layers

Both software and hardware operating on TCP/IP networks typically consist of a wide range of functions to support the communications activities. The network designer is faced with an enormous task in dealing with the number and complexity of these functions. To address these problems, a designer structures an internet by *layering* the functions.

Although modern networks are now described as being divided into seven conceptual layers, internet architecture is based on four layers. Figure 1.5 depicts the internet layer architecture. The bottom layer of the internet model contains subnetworks, and is thus called the *subnetwork* layer; it includes the subnetwork interfaces. These subnetworks allow data to be delivered within each network. Examples of subnetworks are X.25, Frame Relay, ATM, and an Ethernet local area network (LAN). Although this layer includes a subnetwork, in actual implementations the data link and physical layers are required in all machines communicating with a subnet or gateway. Figure 1.5 is abstract, therefore, because this layer must also include the data link and physical layers. Later figures will show this lower layer in more detail.

The next layer is the *internetwork* layer. This layer provides the functions necessary for connecting networks and gateways into one

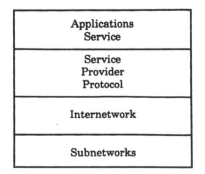

Figure 1.5 Internet Layers.

coherent system. This layer is responsible for delivering data from the source to the final destination. It contains the IP and internet control message protocol (ICMP). As discussed later, other supporting protocols for route discovery and address mapping also reside with IP at this layer.

The third layer is known as the *service provider protocol* layer. This layer is responsible for end-to-end communications. If the communication is connection-oriented, it provides reliability measures and has mechanisms that account for all traffic flowing through an internet. This layer contains the TCP and user datagram protocol (UDP).

Finally, the upper layer is called the *application service* layer. This layer supports the direct interface to an end-user application. Internet applications are responsible for functions such as file transfer, remote terminal access, remote job execution, and electronic mail. This layer contains several widely used protocols, such as the File Transfer Protocol (FTP).

Example of Layer Operations

Figure 1.6 shows the relationship of subnetworks and gateways to layered protocols. The layers depicted in Figure 1.5 are changed to show the lower data link and physical layers, and the upper layers are renamed with terms more widely used in the industry.

In this figure, assume that the user application in host A sends an application PDU to an application layer protocol in host B, such as a file transfer system. The file transfer software performs a variety of

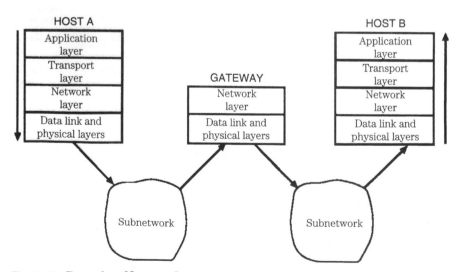

Figure 1.6   Examples of Internet Layer Operations.

functions and sends file records to the user data. In many systems, the operations at host B are known as *server* operations and the operations at host A are known as *client* operations.

As indicated by the downward arrows in the protocol stack at host A, this unit is passed to the transport layer protocol. This layer performs a variety of operations (discussed in later chapters) and adds a header to the PDU passed to it. The unit of data is now called a *segment*. The PDU from the upper layers is considered to be data to the transport layer.

Next, the transport layer passes the segment to the network layer, also called the *IP layer*, which again performs specific services and appends a header. This unit (now called a *datagram* in internet terms) is passed down to the lower layers. Here, the data link layer adds its header as well as a trailer, and the data unit (now called a *frame*) is launched into the network by the physical layer. Of course, if host B sends data to host A, the process is reversed and the direction of the arrows is changed.

Internet protocols are unaware of what goes on inside the network. The network manager is free to manipulate and manage the PDU in any manner necessary. In some instances, however, the internet PDU (data and headers) remains unchanged as it is transmitted through the subnet. In Figure 1.6, it emerges at the gateway where it is processed through the lower layers and passed to the IP (network) layer. Here, routing decisions are made based on the destination address provided by the host computer.

After these routing decisions have been made, the PDU is passed to the communications link connected to the appropriate subnetwork (consisting of the lower layers). The PDU is re-encapsulated into the data link layer frame and passed to the next subnetwork. As before, this unit is passed through the subnetwork transparently (usually), where it finally arrives at the destination host.

The destination (host B) receives the traffic through its lower layers and reverses the process that transpired at host A; it de-encapsulates the headers by stripping them off in the appropriate layer. The header is used by the layer to determine the actions it is to take; the header therefore governs the layer's operations.

The PDU created by the file transfer application in the application service layer is passed to the file transfer application residing at host B. If host A and B are large mainframe computers, this application is likely an exact duplicate of the software at the transmitting host. The application might, however, perform a variety of functions, depending on the header it receives. It is conceivable that the data could be passed to another end-user application at host B, but in many instances the user at host A merely wants to obtain the services of a server protocol, such as a file transfer or e-mail. If this is the case, it

is not necessary for an end-user application process to be invoked at
host B.

To return the retrieved data from the server at host B to the client
at host A, the process is reversed. The data is transferred down
through the layers in the host B machine, through the network,
through the gateway, to the next network, and up the layers of host A
to the end user.

Device Drivers

One reason that TCP/IP is not concerned with the underlying layers
(layers two and one, and especially layer one) is due to an intricate,
low-level piece of software call a *device driver*. Its purpose is to isolate
upper-layer protocols (and the operating system) from the physical
interface on a communications link. Every hardware device on a
machine must operate with a device driver. The device driver is
responsible for manipulating the hardware for which it is responsible.

A networking device driver manages networking hardware and
operates at the MAC layer (described in Chapter 2), so it is often
called a MAC driver. Thus, IP can operate over one of these drivers
and not be concerned with all the details of the hardware. For more
detail, you can study the Packet Driver, which was developed by FTP
Software (FTP Software, Inc., 2 High Street, North Andover, MA).

The TCP/IP Model: A Closer Look

Figure 1.7 depicts an architectural model of TCP/IP and several of the
major related protocols. The choices in the stacked layers of this
model vary, depending on the needs of network users and the decisions made by network designers. For the present, you will see some

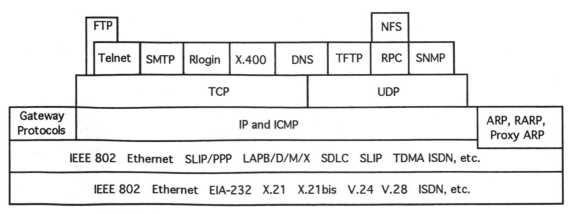

Figure 1.7 The TCP/IP Suite (Not All-Inclusive).

of the protocols explained in the previous material, specifically IP and TCP. The protocols that rest over TCP (and UDP) are examples of the application service layer protocols, also called *application service* in Figure 1.5. The lower two layers represent the data link and physical layers and, as the figure depicts, are implemented with a wide choice of standards and protocols. This figure will be used later in the book to explain the layer operations in more detail.

Ports and Sockets: An Introduction

Each application layer process using the TCP/IP protocols must identify itself by a *port number*. This number is used between the two host computers to identify which application program is to process the incoming traffic. The use of port numbers also provides a multiplexing capability by allowing multiple user programs to communicate concurrently with one application program, such as TCP. The port numbers identify these application entries. The concept is quite similar to a service access point (SAP) in the OSI Model.

In addition to ports, TCP/IP-based protocols use an identifier called a *socket*. The socket was derived from the network input/output operations of the 4.3 BSD UNIX system. It is quite similar to UNIX file access procedures in that it identifies an endpoint communications process.

In internets, some port numbers are preassigned. These are called *well-known ports* and identify widely used applications, called *well-known services*. The well-known port numbers occupy values ranging from 1 to 1023. Organizations should not use the numbers within these ranges because they are reserved; if you need to assign a port number to a specific application, use a number above 1023. Later discussions will examine ports and sockets in more detail.

Challenges of Internetworking

Armed with this background information, we can now examine the issues and problems a network administrator encounters in providing internetworking services. Regarding TCP/IP specifically, these issues are discussed throughout the book. For now, however, I will keep the discussion general.

Different networks might use different length sizes for PDUs. If different length sizes are used, the networks or gateways must provide for the fragmentation of data units. In doing so, the identity of the data units must not be lost. The varying-length sizes of the data units do not eliminate the requirement of maintaining a sequence number relationship on an end-to-end basis, either. In Chapter 5, we will

Figure 1.8d depicts two LAN configurations. Notice that two interconnected gateways are attached to an Ethernet-type topology (network 128.1) and a token ring topology (network 128.2). This configuration is common within office buildings that have a number of interconnected LANs. Figure 1.8e shows one gateway (G) (router or bridge) connecting two Ethernet-type networks. This approach is also quite common. Note that Figures 1.8d and 1.8e are drawn without the network cloud.

Finally, Figure 1.8f shows several network clouds. From the perspective of an internet user, the outer cloud represents the user's virtual network. The user is not concerned with the fact that user data might need to traverse four networks (128.1, 11.1, 11.2, and 128.2) and three gateways (A, B, and C) to reach its final destination.

I have used the term *gateway* to describe all internetworking functions. Chapter 3 expands this description to include gateways, bridges, and routers.

Summary

Internet protocols are designed to permit and facilitate the sharing of computer resources across different networks. Because these protocols were initially sponsored by the U.S. government and because their operations are simple yet effective, they have become the most widely used set of data networking protocols in existence. Although internet protocols are called TCP/IP, these two standards represent only a small part of a wealth of standardized internet data network standards.

2

Introduction to Networks, Bridges, Gateways, and Routers

TCP/IP has been implemented on both wide area and local area networks (WANs and LANs). This chapter describes several prominent types of WANs and LANs and explains their primary operating characteristics. I will also examine routing schemes used to relay traffic between networks (internetworking) and examine bridges, routers, and gateways. I will finish by introducing source routing and spanning tree protocols and discussing their relationship to TCP/IP. This chapter also introduces internet routing and route discovery protocols, which are further discussed in Chapter 8, and the IP routing algorithm, discussed further in Chapters 3 and 5.

A General Taxonomy

Communication systems on many WANs employ switches to route traffic from multiple users on a limited number of links. The stations attached to the network use the switch to share the links. Without the switch, each station would need multiple lines to communicate with the other stations. Indeed, a fully meshed network requires many lines, which is clearly an impossible task if many stations are involved. An alternative to a switched network for sharing links is a broadcast network, in which only one link is used. Multiple stations copy all the data units and discard those that are not addressed to a particular station. Most LANs use some type of broadcast protocol.

Figure 2.1 depicts the layers of WANs and LANs from the context of the seven-layer OSI model. As the figure reveals, WANs reside in the lower three layers and LANs in the lower two layers of the OSI model. Does this mean that you do not need to be concerned with the upper layers of the model when dealing with TCP/IP? Indeed not; the TCP/IP protocol control information (PCI) headers placed around them and they are routed through the network as independent entities.

A packet-switching network contains multiple switches, which allows the network load to be distributed to multiple switching sites (see Figure 2.2). Additional communication lines are also attached to the switches. The arrangement allows alternate routing, which avoids failed or busy nodes and channels. For example, in Figure 2.2, a packet switch can route the packets of one message to more than one packet switch.

Packet switching works well with data communication traffic because many devices, such as keyboard terminals, transmit traffic in bursts. The data is sent on the channel, which is then idle while a terminal user inputs more data into the terminal or pauses to think about a problem. The idle channel time could translate into wasted line capacity, but a packet switch interleaves multiple transmissions from several terminals onto one channel. In effect, packet switching achieves statistical time- division multiplexing (STDM) across the communications line. This approach provides better use of the expensive communications channel.

Packet switching goes one step further than the simple multiplexing of communication lines. It can also multiplex multiple user ses-

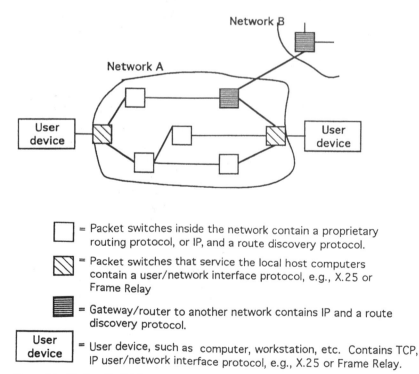

= Packet switches inside the network contain a proprietary routing protocol, or IP, and a route discovery protocol.

= Packet switches that service the local host computers contain a user/network interface protocol, e.g., X.25 or Frame Relay

= Gateway/router to another network contains IP and a route discovery protocol.

User device = User device, such as computer, workstation, etc. Contains TCP, IP user/network interface protocol, e.g., X.25 or Frame Relay.

Figure 2.2 Packet Switching.

sions onto a single communications port on the computer. Instead of dedicating one port to one user, the system interleaves the bursts of traffic from multiple users across one port.

Packet switching also provides an attractive feature for connecting terminals and computers together for a session. In a circuit-switched telephone structure, connect time is often slow. A switched telephone call requires that a number be dialed and that all resources be set up before the call can be routed to the destination. With a packet-switching system, however, dedicated leased lines are available for multiple users to transmit and receive their data traffic. The lines do not require any circuit setups because they are permanently connected through the system. This technique can improve the slow connect time associated with multiple telephone circuit switches. Of course, leased lines are very expensive and are used only for applications that cannot tolerate dialing delays.

Figure 2.2 also shows the relationship of some of the TCP/IP protocols to the packet-switching components. Note that it shows only one of several configurations that exist in the industry; it is not meant to be all-inclusive. Typically, the user device (host) interfaces into a packet-switched network with a user/network interface protocol. The most widely used network interface protocols in the industry today are X.25 and Frame Relay. IP is also stored at the host machine because the gateways rely on the IP header to be created by the host computer. Additionally, the transmission control protocol (TCP) resides at the host machine to provide end-to-end integrity for the transmission between the two end-user devices. Inside the network, the packet switches might contain a vendor's proprietary routing protocol; in some instances, IP is employed with a companion route discovery protocol. (IP is a routing protocol but not a route discovery protocol.)

The gateways in this figure could be configured with IP as in the case of an internet. In a number of public packet networks, the gateway protocol is often X.75. The X.75 protocol, although a gateway protocol, is quite different from IP because it is connection-oriented and does not perform routing.

Choosing the packet route

Packet-switched networks route user traffic based on a variety of criteria, generally referred to as *least-cost routing* (also called the *cost metric*), which is examined in Chapter 8. The name does not mean that routing is based solely on obtaining the least-cost route in the literal sense. Other factors are often part of the routing algorithm:

- Capacity of the link
- Number of packets waiting for transmission onto the link

tion. Thus far, optical fiber paths have seen limited application, but their positive attributes ensure their continued use.

The *physical interface* between the path and the user station can take several forms. It could be a single CATV tap, infrared diodes, microwave antennas, or laser-emitting semiconductors for optical fibers. Some LANs provide regenerative repeaters at the interface; others use the interface as buffers for data flow.

The *protocol control logic* component controls the LAN and provides for the end user's access onto the network. The LAN protocols employ methods and techniques discussed later in this chapter.

The last major component is the *user workstation*. It can be anything from a word processor to a mainframe computer. Several LAN vendors provide support for other vendors' products, and several layers of the OSI model are also supported by some LANs.

Types of LANs

These types of LANs are prominent today:

- Carrier sense/collision detection, with CSMD/CD and IEEE 802.3
- Token ring
- Token bus

In the following subsections, broadcast technology implemented in Ethernet and token networks is emphasized for each type of LAN, as it is the prevalent approach to switching in LANs.

Carrier Sense/Collision Detection

Carrier sense/collision detection is widely used in LANs. Many vendors use this technique with Ethernet and the IEEE 802.3 specification. A carrier sense LAN considers all stations as peers; the stations contend for the use of the channel on an equal basis. Before transmitting, the stations monitor the channel to determine if the channel is active (that is, if another station is sending data on the channel). If the channel is idle, any station with data to transmit can send its traffic onto the channel. If the channel is occupied, the stations must defer to the station using the channel.

Figure 2.3 depicts a carrier sense/collision detection LAN. Stations A, B, C, and D are attached to a channel (such as coaxial cable) by bus interface units (BIU). Assume stations A and B want to transmit traffic. Station D, however, is currently using the channel, so the BIUs at stations A and B "listen" and defer to the signal from station D that is occupying the channel. When the line becomes idle, A and B then attempt to acquire the channel.

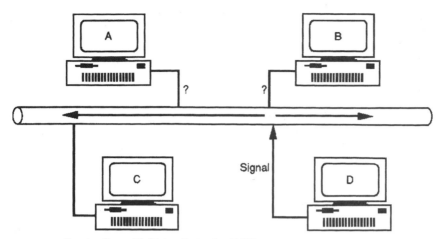

Figure 2.3   Carrier Sense/Collision Detection LAN.

Because A's transmission requires time to propagate to other stations, these other stations might be unaware that A's signal is on the channel. In this situation, A could transmit its traffic even if another station seized the channel. This problem is called a *collision window*, which is caused by the propagation delay of the signal and the distance between two competing stations (*propagation delay* is the delay that occurs before the stations know that another one is transmitting).

Carrier sense networks are usually implemented on short-distance LANs because the collision window lengthens as the channel gets longer. Longer channels provide the opportunity for more collisions and can reduce throughput in the network. Generally, a long propagation delay coupled with short frames and high data transfer rates gives rise to a greater incidence of collisions. Longer frames can mitigate the effect of a long delay, but they reduce the opportunity for competing stations to acquire the channel.

Each station is capable of transmitting and listening to a channel simultaneously. When two signals collide, they create voltage irregularities on the channel, which are sensed by the colliding stations. The stations then turn off their transmission and, through an individually randomized wait period, attempt to seize the channel again. Randomized waiting decreases the chances of another collision because it is unlikely that the competing stations will generate the same wait time.

CSMA/CD and IEEE 802.3

The best-known scheme for controlling a LAN on a bus structure is carrier sense multiple access with collision detection (CSMA/CD). The most widely used implementation of CSMA/CD is found in the

Ethernet specification. Xerox Corporation was instrumental in providing the research for CSMA/CD and in developing the first baseband commercial products. The broadband network was developed by MITRE. In 1980, Xerox, Intel Corporation, and Digital Equipment Corporation jointly published a specification for an Ethernet LAN. This specification was later introduced to the IEEE 802 committees and, with several modifications, has found its way into the IEEE 802.3 standard. (The Ethernet and 802.3 interfaces do differ in formatting conventions.)

CSMA/CD Ethernet is organized around the concept of layered protocols (refer back to Figure 2.1). The user layer is serviced by the two CSMA/CD layers, the data link layer, and the physical layer. Each of the bottom two layers consists of two separate entities. The data link layer provides the actual logic to control the CSMA/CD network. It is medium-independent, so the network could be broadband or baseband. The 802 standard includes both broadband and baseband options.

Token ring

Token-ring topology is another LAN protocol offered by a number of vendors, and it is published as the standard IEEE 802.5. IBM has based many of its LAN products around the token ring, which is illustrated in Figure 2.4. The stations are connected to a concentric ring through a ring interface unit (RIU). Each RIU is responsible for monitoring the data passing through it, as well as regenerating the signal and passing it to the next station. If the address in the header of the transmission indicates that the data are destined for a station, the RIU copies the data and passes the information to the user device.

If the ring is idle (that is, if no user data occupies the ring), a "free" token is passed around the ring from node to node. This token indicates that the ring is available and that any station with data to transmit can use the token to transmit traffic. The control of the ring is passed sequentially from node to node around the ring.

When a station has the token, it controls the ring. Upon acquiring the token (i.e., marking the token as busy), the transmitting station inserts data behind the token and passes the data through the ring. As each RIU monitors the data, it regenerates the transmission, checks the address in the header of the data, and passes the data to the next station. When the data arrives at the transmitting station, this station frees the token and passes it to the next station on the ring, preventing one station from monopolizing the ring. If the token passes completely around the ring without being used, back to the station that just transmitted, that station can once again use the token and transmit data.

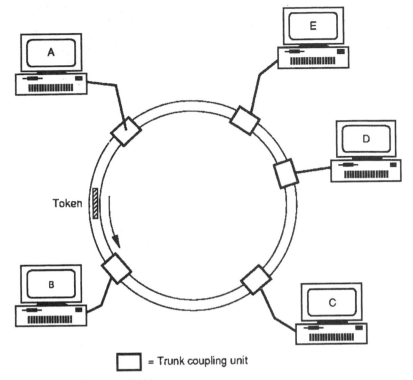

= Trunk coupling unit

Figure 2.4 Token Ring LAN.

Many token-ring networks use priority schemes. The object of the priority scheme is to give each station an opportunity to reserve the use of the ring for the next transmission. As the token and data circle the ring, each node examines the token, which contains a reservation field. If a node's priority is higher than the priority number in the reservation field, it raises the reservation field number to its level, thus reserving the token on the next round. If another node does not make the reservation field higher, the station uses the token and channel on the next pass around the ring.

The station with the token must store the previous reservation value in a temporary storage area. Upon releasing the token, the station restores the network to its previous lowest-priority request. In this manner, once the token is freed for the next round, the station with the highest reservation can seize the token.

The LLC Sublayer

Figure 2.1 introduced the LLC protocol. This section examines it in more detail, as many LANs use it to interface with the network layer (including the IP). The IEEE 802 standards split the data link layer into two sublayers: MAC and LLC. As discussed earlier in this chapter and illustrated in Figure 2.1, MAC encompasses 802.3, 802.4, 802.5, and others. LLC includes 802.2. This sublayer was implemented to make the LLC sublayer, independent of specific LAN access methods. The LLC sublayer also provides an interface into or out of the specific MAC protocol.

The MAC/LLC split provides several attractive features. First, it controls access to the shared channel among the autonomous user devices. Second, it provides for a decentralized (peer-to-peer) scheme that reduces the LAN's susceptibility to errors. Third, LLC is independent of specific access methods, while MAC is protocol-specific, giving an 802 network a flexible interface with upper-layer protocols (ULPs) such as IP or the OSI's connectionless network protocol (CLNP), discussed in Chapter 5.

Classes of service

The 802 LAN standards include four types of service for LLC users:

Type 1.   Unacknowledged, connectionless service

Type 2.   Connection-oriented service

Type 3.   Acknowledged, connectionless service

Type 4.   All of the above services

All 802 networks must provide unacknowledged, connectionless service (Type 1). Optionally, connection-oriented service can be provided (Type 2). Type 1 networks provide no acknowledgments (ACKs), flow control, or error recovery. Type 2 networks provide connection management, ACKs, flow control, and error recovery. Type 3 networks provide no connection setup or disconnect, but they do provide for the acknowledgment of data units.

Most Type 1 networks use a higher-level protocol (i.e., TCP in the transport layer) to provide connection management functions. IP can reside over LLC as well. Therefore, a LAN-layered model could be as follows: Physical, MAC, LLC, IP, TCP, and an application layer. Chapter 5 discusses the relationship of TCP/IP and LLC in more detail.

Repeaters, Bridges, Routers, Brouters, and Gateways

Networks were originally conceived to be fairly small systems consisting of relatively few machines. As the need for data communication services has grown, networks must be connected together to share resources and distribute functions and administrative control. In addition, some LANs, by virtue of their restricted distance, often need to be connected together through other devices. These devices have numerous names in the industry; this section will explain and define each.

Figure 2.5 shows the relationships of these devices using a layered model. A *repeater* connects the media on a LAN, typically called *media segments*. The repeater has no upper-layer functions; its principal job is to terminate the signal on one LAN segment and regenerate it on another. So a repeater has no internetworking capabilities.

The term *bridge* is usually associated with an internetworking unit (IWU). It operates at the data link layer (always at the MAC sublayer and sometimes at the LLC sublayer). Typically, it uses MAC physical addresses to perform its relaying functions. As a general rule, it is a fairly low-function device and connects homogeneous networks (for example, IEEE-based networks).

A *router* operates at the network layer using network layer addresses (for example, IP, X.121, and E.164). It usually contains more capabilities than a bridge and can offer flow control mechanisms as well as source routing or nonsource routing features, which are discussed in the next section.

Gateway describes a machine or software module that not only performs routing capabilities but can also act as a protocol conversion or mapping facility (also called a *convergence function*). For example, such a gateway could relay traffic and also provide conversion between two different types of mail transfer applications. Unfortunately, the term *gateway* is used in many ways in the data communications industry. Some people use it to describe any internetworking device. I use the terms *gateway* and *router* interchangeably.

Yet another term that has entered the market is *brouter* (as if there were not enough terms already.) A *brouter* is a machine that combines the features of a router and a bridge. At first glance it might

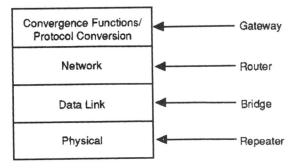

Figure 2.5 Placement of Internetworking Operations.

seem redundant, but the brouter is a powerful and flexible addition to internetworking products. Most high-end routers can perform bridging and routing operations.

To avoid any confusion, some people use the term introduced earlier in this section: *internetworking unit*. An IWU is a generic term that describes a router, gateway, bridge, or anything else that performs relaying functions between networks.

Source routing and nonsource routing

How internetworking PDUs or datagrams or packets are routed between networks can be a source of confusion. The two major methods of performing routing are source routing and nonsource routing. *Source routing* derives its name from the fact that the transmitting device (the source) dictates the route of the PDU through an internet. The source (host) machine places the addresses of the "hops" (the intermediate networks or IWUs) in the PDU. Such an approach means that the internetworking units need not perform address maintenance; they simply use an address in the routing field to determine where to route the frame. In contrast, *nonsource routing* makes decisions about the route and does not rely on the PDU to contain information. Spanning tree routing is usually associated with nonsource routing and bridges, and is quite prevalent in LANs.

An example of source routing on a LAN is illustrated in Figure 2.6. The routing information field contains the LAN and bridge identifiers for each intermediate hop through the LAN network. Routing is accomplished by each bridge that examines successive LAN and bridge numbers in the routing information field and makes a routing decision accordingly. For example, bridge 5 might receive a frame from LAN 3. Based on the routing information in the routing field, LAN 5 might need to route the frame out of its port to LAN 6 or out of another port to LAN 2. Again, under these conditions, the bridge has no control over how the frame is routed.

Figure 2.7 depicts the operations of nonsource routing with a spanning tree bridge. The bridge processor forwards frames based on an examination of the destination address. The bridge processor compares this address to its bridge and routing information database. If the destination address is found in the forwarding table of its database, it determines the direction of the frame. If the frame is not intended for the port from which it came, it is forwarded on the correct port to the address indicated in the database. Otherwise, it is discarded. If the source address in the frame is not contained in the database, this address is then added with the appropriate port on which it was received and a timer is started. The purpose of the timer is to keep the forwarding database updated in as timely a manner as possible.

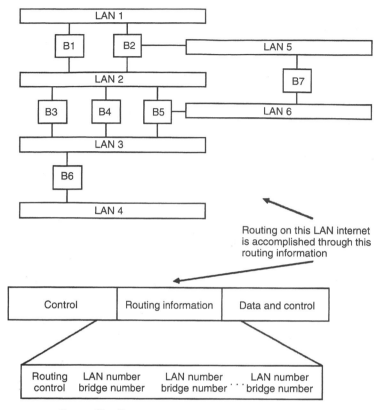

Figure 2.6 Source Routing.

For example, assume that a frame is received at port A on the LAN in Figure 2.7. The source MAC address in this frame is 1234. The bridge checks if this address is in the forwarding database. If not, it stores address 1234 with a notation that it can be found at port A. Now assume that a frame arrives at port B at destination address 1234 in the frame. The bridge processor examines its forwarding table and determines that station 1234 can be found at port A; consequently, it forwards this frame to the network attached to port A.

The IP is not aware of these operations on the LAN because the IP PDU resides in the I (information) field of the LAN frame. The bridge does not process the I field, but treats it transparently. Consequently, the bridge is concerned only with MAC source and destination addresses. Any higher-level addresses (such as a network address) that reside in the IP PDU are not acted on by the spanning tree bridge. As you will see in later chapters, however, these network addresses become vital for processing PDUs across WANs because the MAC addresses are stripped away before the frame is sent through a

This chapter introduces the issues of naming and addressing, as well as the concepts of physical and network address resolution (mapping). Chapter 4 then continues with naming and describes the domain name system (DNS). I will also introduce Internet Protocol (IP) routing in this chapter when discussing the relationship of addresses and routing. IP is explained further in Chapter 5.

Upper Layer, Network, Data Link, and Physical Names and Addresses

Communication between users through a data network requires several forms of names and addressing. Typically, two or three addresses are required; a physical address, data link address, and network address are used on some systems, but a more common approach is to use only the physical and network address. With this approach, the physical and data link address are the same. Practically speaking, other identifiers are needed for unambiguous end-to-end communications between two users, such as upper-layer names and/or port numbers.

Physical addresses

Each device (such as a computer or workstation) on a communications link or network is identified with a physical address, often called the *hardware address*. Many manufacturers place the physical address on a communications board within the device or in an interface unit connected directly to the device. Two physical addresses are employed in a communications dialogue: one address identifies the sender (source) and the other address identifies the receiver (destination).

The length of the physical address varies; most systems use two 48-bit addresses, but other address sizes can be used. The 48-bit address structure is considered too long by some designers, but both the Ethernet and IEEE protocols use it, so it is widespread. This address is also called the *media access control* (MAC) address, which was briefly discussed in the previous chapter.

From the context of a layered data communications model, the physical address is used at the physical or data link layers. The receiving device examines the destination address of an incoming PDU. If the address matches the physical address of the device, it is passed to the next upper layer. If the address does not match the device's address, it is ignored. Thus, address detection at a lower layer prevents the data from being passed needlessly to upper layers.

Physical address detection on a LAN is illustrated in Figure 3.1. Device A transmits a frame onto the channel, which is received by all other stations attached to the channel stations B, C, and D. Assume

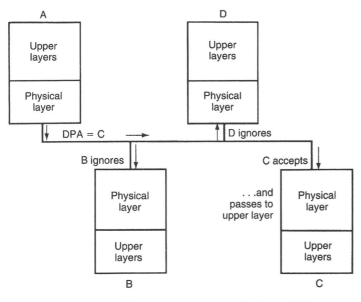

(DPA = C) = Destination physical address is C.

Figure 3.1 Physical Address Detection.

that the destination physical address (DPA) contains the value C. Consequently, stations B and D ignore the frame. Station C accepts it and passes the PDU to the next upper layer.

Universal physical addresses and protocol identifiers

Several years ago, IEEE assumed the task of assigning universal LAN physical addresses and protocol identifiers. This work was previously performed by the Xerox Corporation, who administered what were known as *block identifiers* (block IDs) for Ethernet addresses. The Xerox Ethernet administration office assigned these values, which were three octets (24 bits) in length. The organization who received this address could use the remaining 24 bits of the Ethernet address any way it chose.

Based on the IEEE 802 project, IEEE assumed the task of assigning these universal identifiers for all LANs, not just carrier sense/multiple access with collision detection (CSMA/CD) networks. IEEE, however, continues to honor the assignments made by the Ethernet administration office, although it now calls the block ID an *organization unique identifier* (OUI).

Each OUI provides an organization with the 24-bit address space, although the true address space is actually 22 bits because the first two bits are used for control purposes (described shortly). Thus the address space is 2^{22}.

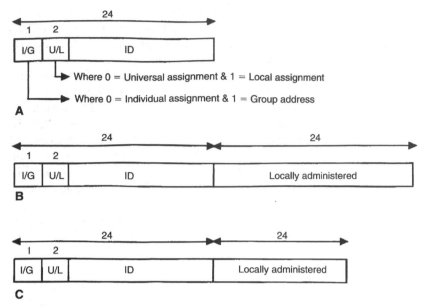

Figure 3.2 Universal Addresses and IDs: (a) Organization-Unique ID (Block ID), (b) Universal MAC Addresses, and (c) Protocol ID.

The format for the OUI is shown in Figure 3.2. The least significant bit of the address space corresponds to the individual/group (I/G) address bit. The I/G address bit, if set to a 0, means that the address field identifies an individual address. If the value is set to 1, the address field identifies a group address, which identifies more than one station connected to the LAN. If the entire OUI is set to all 1s, it signifies a broadcast address, which identifies all stations on the network.

The second bit of the address space is known as the *universal* or *local bit* (U/L). When this bit is set to a 0, it has universal assignment significance—for example, from IEEE. If it is set to a 1, it is a locally assigned address. Bit position two must always be set to 0 if administered by the IEEE.

The OUI is extended to include a 48-bit universal LAN address (designated as the *MAC* address), also shown in Figure 3.2. The 24 bits of the address space are the same as the OUI assigned by the IEEE. The second part of the address space, consisting of the remaining 24 bits, is locally administered and can be set to any value an organization chooses.

The locally administered 24 bits allow an organization to develop approximately 16 million unique and unambiguous addresses. In the event that this address space is exhausted, the IEEE will assign an additional OUI, but not additional OUIs until an organization uses all the values in the original 24-bit address space. Is the 48-bit address space sufficient for the future? Forty-eight bits provide for a 2^{48} value, which can identify approximately 281.475 trillion unique addresses, so it should be sufficient for a while.

The IEEE 802 project also administers a *protocol identifier*. This value is not a physical address, but is discussed here because of its relationship with the other IEEE addressing schemes. The format for the identifier is shown in Figure 3.2c. The first 24 bits are for the OUI, which was discussed earlier in the chapter. The remaining 16 bits are locally administered by an organization; however, in some instances these values are reserved for well-known protocols. The idea of the protocol ID is discussed further in the following sections of this chapter.

If you are interested in obtaining more information about any of these formats, contact the IEEE Standards Office, 445 Hoes Lane, Piscataway, NJ 08855-1331.

The CSMA/CD frame and MAC physical addresses

The MAC level CSMA/CD frame for 802.3 is shown in Figure 3.3. The *preamble* is transmitted first to achieve medium stabilization and synchronization. The *start frame delimiter* (SFD) follows the preamble and indicates the start of the frame. The 16- or 48-bit physical address fields contain the MAC addresses of the *destination* and *source stations*. The destination address identifies an individual workstation on the network or a group of stations. The *data length* field indicates the length of the logical link control (LLC) and data fields. If the *data* field is less than a maximum length, the *packet assembly and deassembly* (PAD) field is added to make up the difference. The *cyclic redundancy check* (CRC) value is contained in the *frame-check sequence* (FCS) field.

The Ethernet frame is shown in Figure 3.4. The formats of the Ethernet and the 802.3 frames differ. First, the 802.3 frame contains an SFD, which in actual practice becomes part of the 64-bit preamble. The 802.3 standard allows 16- or 48-bit length addresses. The next 16 bits are used differently by the two protocols. The *type* field in

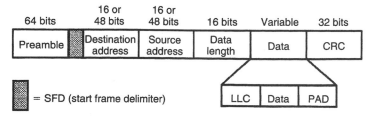

Figure 3.3 802.3 Frame.

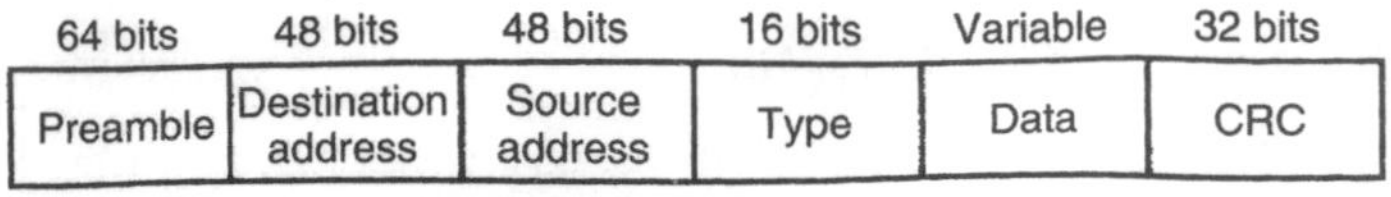

64 bits	48 bits	48 bits	16 bits	Variable	32 bits
Preamble	Destination address	Source address	Type	Data	CRC

Figure 3.4 Ethernet Frame.

Ethernet identifies different protocols running on the network; the same set of bits is used in the 802.3 frame to determine the length of the data field.

The issue of compatibility naturally arises when you look at the formats. The older versions of Ethernet (e.g., version 1.0) are not compatible with the 802 standard. Newer releases of Ethernet have made these two standards compatible at the physical layer, but they remain incompatible at the data link (LLC) layer.

RFC 894 establishes the rules for interworking Ethernet and 802.3, which can be summarized as follows:

- A machine must be able to send and receive frames using Ethernet encapsulation (RFC 894).

- A machine should be able to receive frames with either RFC 894 or RFC 1042 encapsulation.

- A machine might be able to send frames with RFC 1042 encapsulation, but it must be configurable and default to RFC 894.

Check with vendors for details on how these operations are handled. Fortunately, none of the valid 802 length fields are the same as any EtherType values, so they are distinguishable from each other. Question LAN vendors on how their LAN products support the IEEE 802.3 and the Ethernet frame formats.

Link layer addresses (LSAPs)

The IEEE 802 standards make use of yet another identifier, called the LSAP. Its purpose is to identify the specific protocol (or a specific instance of a protocol invocation) being used above the MAC layer. Table 3.1 lists some IEEE LSAP assignments and provides a brief description of the protocol. An 802 protocol must carry both a source and destination LSAP.

IEEE also specifies a code to identify the EtherType assignments. These codes are shown in Table 3.2. They identify the protocol that is running on top of Ethernet.

Extension to the LSAP header (SNAP)

Because of the separate evolution of Ethernet, TCP/IP, and IEEE LAN standards, additional requests for comments (RFCs) had to be

TABLE 3.1   The Link Service Access Point (LSAP).

IEEE binary	Internet decimal	Description
00000000	0	Null LSAP
01000000	2	Individual LLC sublayer management
11000000	3	Group LLC sublayer management
00100000	4	SNA path control
01100000	6	DOD Internet protocol
01110000	14	Proway-LAN
01110010	78	EIA-RS511
01110001	142	Proway-LAN
01010101	170	Subnetwork access protocol (SNAP)
01111111	254	ISO DIS 8473
11111111	255	Global DSAP

TABLE 3.2   EtherType Assignments (Examples).

Ethernet decimal	Hex	Description
1536	0600	XEROX NS IDP
2048	0800	DOD Internet protocol (IP)
2049	0801	X.75 Internet
2050	0802	NBS Internet
2051	0803	ECMA Internet
2052	0804	Chaosnet
2053	0805	X.25 level 3
2054	0806	Address resolution protocol (ARP)
2055	0807	XNS compatibility
4096	1000	Berkeley trailer
21000	5208	BBN Simnet
24577	6001	DEC MOP dump/load
24578	6002	DEC MOP remote console
24579	6003	DEC DECnet Phase IV
24580	6004	DEC LAT
24582	6005	DEC
24583	6006	DEC
32773	8005	HP probe
32784	8010	Excelan
32821	8035	Reverse ARP
32824	8038	DEC LANBridge
32823	8098	Appletalk

defined to provide guidance on using IP datagrams (and other protocol traffic) over Ethernet and IEEE networks. Figure 3.5 shows the approach recommended by RFC 1042, which is a standard for the transmitting IP datagrams over IEEE 802 networks. The LLC destination and source service access points (DSAP and SSAP, respectively) are each set to a decimal value of 170. (The LLC control field is not affected by this standard.) The SNAP control field can identify a specific protocol ID, and can be set to an organization-unique ID.[1] As one option, the EtherType field describes the type of protocol running on

---

[1]This field is treated differently in systems that are running IP with Frame Relay and ATM (see Chapter 14).

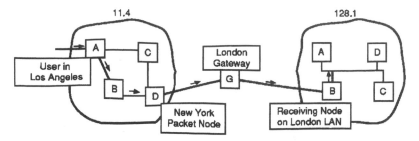

Figure 3.7   Network-Level Addressing.

This important concept is illustrated in Figure 3.7. Assume that a user (a host computer) in Los Angeles transmits packets to a packet network to be relayed to a workstation on a LAN in London. The network in London has a network address of 128.1 (This address scheme will be explained shortly). The packets are passed through the packet network (using the network's internal routing mechanisms, discussed in Chapter 2) to the packet switch in New York. The packet switch in New York routes the packet to the gateway located in London. This gateway examines the destination network address in the packet and determines that the packet is to be routed to network 128.1. It then transmits the packet onto the appropriate communications link to the node on the LAN that communicates with the London gateway. In Figure 3.7, this node is labeled B in network 128.1.

Notice that this operation did not use the destination physical addresses in these routing operations. The packet switches and gateway were concerned only with the destination network address. Physical addresses are still being used, but they identify the next machine on the respective link to receive the traffic and not the final destination machine.

Physical and network address resolution

You might wonder how the London LAN can pass the packet to the correct device (host). As explained earlier, a physical address prevents every packet from being processed by the upper-layer network-level protocols residing in every machine attached to the network. Therefore, the answer is that the final destination network (or gateway) must be able to translate a higher-layer network destination address to a lower-layer physical destination address.

Figure 3.8 explains how this task is accomplished. Node B on the LAN is tasked with address resolution. Assume that the destination address contains a network address, such as 128.1, *and* a host address, say 3.2. The two addresses could therefore be joined (or concatenated) to create a full internet network address, which would

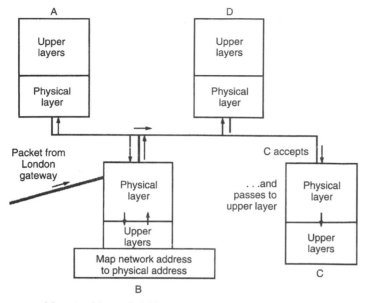

Figure 3.8 Mapping Network Addresses to Physical Addresses.

appear as 128.1.3.2 in the destination address field of the IP PDU (datagram).

Once the LAN node receives the datagram from the gateway, it must examine the host address and either look up the address in the table that contains the local physical address for the network address, or query the station for its physical address. Upon obtaining the correct physical address, the node then encapsulates the user data into the physical layer frame, places the appropriate physical layer address in the destination address of the frame, and transmits the frame onto the LAN channel. All devices on the network examine the physical address. If this address matches the device's address, the PDU is passed to the next upper layer; otherwise, it is ignored.

It is conceivable that the host address 3.2 also could be the actual physical address, but it is more common to assign different address values to a host address and its hardware physical address. For example, the value of 128.1.3.2 could be mapped into an IEEE MAC 48-bit physical address.

Are two addresses necessary?

A number of people have complained about having to use both physical- and network-level addresses. After all, an address space for a MAC address of 2^{48} provides over 281 trillion unique identifiers. From their perspective, it seems reasonable that this address space is sufficient to provide unique addressing without requiring them to use additional address fields. Several reasons do exist for different levels of addressing schemes in any network.

Historically, the address spaces for LANs and internet networks were developed by separate groups. First, each group recognized the need for unique identifiers and devised them. The evolution of LANs and the Internet was such that the identifiers remained separate. Second, link capacity is still important in networks and will be for many years. Using a large address identifier, such as a 48-bit rather than a slightly smaller 32-bit network address, saves 50 percent of addressing bits transmitted. Third, under the present scheme, if the hardware interface (the board) of a computer station on a LAN becomes faulty, the board is replaced. If these addresses were used for network routing, each board replacement would require changing the network routing tables. Finally, designers believe it efficacious to hide lower-layer physical addresses from upper-layer software. It provides for cleaner interfaces and gives network administrators more flexibility in configuring network resources in various parts of the network.

All these arguments have merit. On a more general level, I think I speak for many people who support a common-sense application of the multiplication principle. For example, a nine-digit number such as a social security number is more than adequate to distinguish any entity in the United States ($10^9 = 1$ billion). As another example, if you wanted to identify something with, say, a more user-friendly six-letter sequence in the English alphabet, you could still obtain unique identifiers for more than 300 million things with a 26^6 notation. It is quite easy to lose patience with different companies, department stores, etc., who construct long and complex identifiers for passwords, account numbers, etc.

Upper-layer protocol (ULPs) identifiers and names

Physical, data link, and network layer addresses are insufficient to move a packet to its final destination inside the host machine; other higher-layer identifiers are needed. For example, a packet might be destined for a specific software application, such as an electronic mail or a file transfer system. Because both applications reside in the same upper layer (the application layer), some means must be devised to identify the application that is to process the packet. The host machine, therefore, uses a ULP identifier to determine which application receives the data.

Upper-layer identifiers are identified by a variety of terms. Internet convention is to use the terms *protocol ID*, *port*, and *socket*. The Open Systems Interconnection (OSI) model convention is to use the terms *service access point* (SAP) and *selector*. Internet terms are explained later in the next section.

Complete naming, addressing, and identification operation

Figure 3.9 shows an example of the names, addresses, and identifiers used in the internet layers, both at a sending and receiving computer. The left part of the figure shows that a sending computer creates various names, addresses, and identifiers at different layers that are used by the peer layer of the receiving computer (the right part of the figure) to identify the destination, the protocols to invoke, and the functions to perform.

The user application at the sending computer (such as a JAVA or C application) is responsible for creating its own user name. Typically, user names are created in accordance with an organization's specific

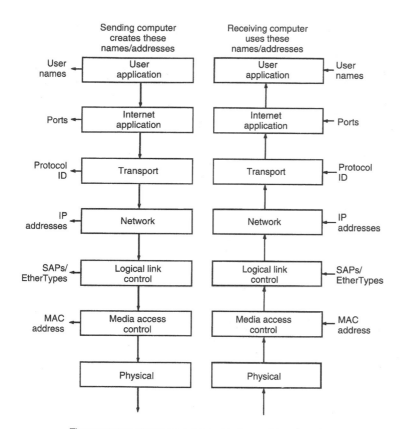

Figure 3.9   Relationship of Names and Addresses to Internet Layers.

protocols, or, in some instances, standards define user names. The user name is then passed along with data to the internet application layer.

The specific internet application (such as file transfer or electronic mail) is identified with a port number. Frequently used applications have reserved port numbers and are called *well-known ports*. Consequently, if the sending computer wants to invoke the internet application concerning file transfer, for example, it would code a port number of 20 in the destination port field.

The user name created by the user application might actually be identified with the port number. A source port number could be used in lieu of a user name to identify the end-user application. Check the specific installation to find out how specific upper-layer conventions are handled.

Next, the traffic is passed to the transport layer entity, which typically is either the transmission control protocol (TCP) or the user data protocol (UDP). In either case, this transport entity is identified by a *protocol ID*. At the receiving machine, the protocol number identifies the transport entity that is to receive the traffic. Consequently, the transport protocol ID identifies UDP, TCP, OSI's TP4, etc. After the transport layer entity, the traffic is passed down to the network layer, which handles the network addresses, also called *IP addresses*. These addresses are used in the network layer to determine where the traffic is to be routed through an internet.

After processing at the IP module, the traffic is passed to LLC. As discussed earlier, LLC works with destination and source SAPs. The concept of the SAP is quite similar to that of the port at the upper layer. The source SAP identifies the entity operating above LLC that is sending the traffic, and the destination SAP identifies the entity operating above LLC that is to receive the traffic. Ordinarily, this entity would be the IP residing at the network layer, but as shown in Table 3.1 the destination SAP could identify other entities, such as SNA's path control or the ISO's IP equivalent (IS 8473). It is important to emphasize that, for Ethernet, the EtherType field is used instead of the destination LSAP.

The last set of addresses used are the IEEE 48-bit MAC addresses. MAC receives the traffic from LLC and then creates the destination and source MAC addresses. As shown at the bottom of Figure 3.9, these names and addresses are sent to the receiving computer if it is on the same LAN or LAN segment as the sending machine. If the PDU is sent across a WAN, the MAC addresses are stripped off before the unit is transmitted.

At the receiving end, the destination MAC address is used by MAC to determine if the traffic is to be received at this station. Remember from Figure 3.7 that this MAC address might be retrieved from a table at a local machine. If so, MAC accepts the traffic and passes it (after stripping off the MAC fields) to LLC. LLC, in turn, uses the destination SAP to determine the proper protocol at the network layer. Ethernet uses the EtherType field.

Once the traffic is passed to the network layer, the IP address is used by gateways or routers to determine a route through the network. If the traffic has arrived at the receiving host computer, the IP address is used in conjunction with the port number to provide a unique and unambiguous connection between the two machines, known as the *socket*. I will examine the socket in more detail in Chapter 7, along with TCP and UDP. The protocol identifier (PID) determines which transport layer protocol is to receive the traffic, which is then passed up to an internet application. The destination port number then determines which internet application entity is to receive the traffic.

Finally, the traffic might be passed to an end-user application at the receiving machine, although today the end-user application often resides only at the originating computer. This approach means that the internet application (such as the file transfer example) receives the data, services it, and perhaps returns a reply. This approach is quite common in a client-server relationship, where the sending computer contains the client and the receiving computer contains the server, but not an actual end-user application.

The process can of course be reversed. In Figure 3.9, the direction of the arrows could be changed to represent data moving from the computer on the right side of the figure to the computer on the left.

The actual PDU transmitted on the channel contains considerable overhead just in names and addresses. The situation suggested at the bottom part of the figure, however, is not quite as onerous as it might appear because the destination and source MAC addresses are not transported across a WAN. As discussed earlier, they are inserted at the destination network or computer using a process called *address mapping*. This topic will be discussed shortly.

In summary, the internet standards (in conjunction with IEEE LANs) use the names, addresses, and identifiers at each layer, as shown in Table 3.3.

The IP Address Structure

This section describes the original format for the IP address, which is still in use. It also introduces some changes made in 1993 to improve the IP address. These changes are described in more detail in Chapter 5.

TCP/IP networks use a 32-bit address to identify a host computer and the network to which the host is attached. The structure of the IP

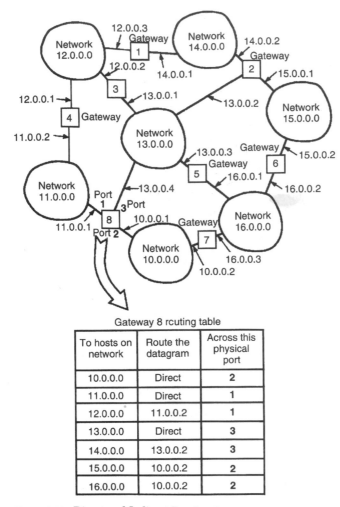

To hosts on network	Route the datagram	Across this physical port
10.0.0.0	Direct	2
11.0.0.0	Direct	1
12.0.0.0	11.0.0.2	1
13.0.0.0	Direct	3
14.0.0.0	13.0.0.2	3
15.0.0.0	10.0.0.2	2
16.0.0.0	10.0.0.2	2

Figure 3.11   Direct and Indirect Destinations.

networks and the relevant router to reach the network as well as the physical port to that router.

It is obvious that routing tables do not need to contain a full address. Nonetheless, Figure 3.11 shows the awkward nature of the IP address structure. Notice that router 8 has three IP addresses: 11.0.0.1, 13.0.0.4, and 10.0.0.1. While these addresses are certainly manageable, they do point out the need to carefully administer IP addresses.

This problem stems from the fact that the IP address is an interface address. Therefore, every port on a machine must have an IP address. IP relies on a route discovery protocol to find the routes through an internet. For example, network 14.0.0.0 is reached from router 8 through a connection to network 13.0.0.0 out of the router's port 3 with an internet address of 13.0.0.2. If the communications link at 13.0.0.4 fails, however, IP does not know that alternate routes are available on other interfaces.

Of course, most vendor's products today approach this problem in one of two ways. Some systems build secondary routes into the routing tables. In the previous example, the column "Route the Datagram" would have a second dimension (or even a third) that describes alternate routes in case the first route fails. Again, this approach works well enough, but it can produce some fairly complex routing tables. Some systems perform a spontaneous route discovery process as soon as it determines that a route has failed.

IP routing logic

The preceding discussion of direct and indirect routing implies that a gateway needs only the network part of an IP address to perform routing. Figure 3.12 shows a logic flow chart of the IP routing algorithm. Each machine maintains a routing table containing destination network addresses and the specified "next hop" machine. The table is used to perform three types of routing:

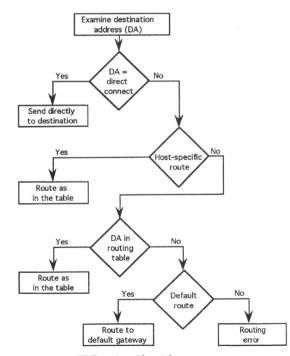

Figure 3.12 IP Routing Algorithm.

- Direct routing to locally attached machines
- Indirect routing for networks that must be reached via one or more routers
- Default routing to the destination network if the first two types of routing are unsuccessful

Relationship of IP and MAC Addresses

The IP datagram contains both the source and destination address of the sender and receiver. These two addresses do not change. They remain intact, end to end. The destination address is used at each IP module to determine which node is to receive the datagram next. It is matched against the IP routing table to find the physical interface for this next node.

In contrast, the MAC source and destination addresses change as the frame is sent across each link. After all, MAC addresses are significant only at the link layer.

In Figure 3.13, the IP source address of 172.16.1.1 and destination address of 172.18.1.2 stay the same throughout the journey through an internet. The MAC addresses change at each link. (I have abbreviated the MAC addresses in this example.) It is necessary for the destination MAC address to contain the MAC address of the machine on the respective LAN that is to receive the frame. Otherwise, the frame cannot be delivered.

Multihomed hosts

As mentioned earlier in the chapter, routers and hosts can have multiple physical connections to other networks throughout an internet,

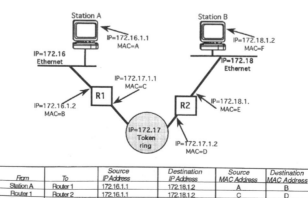

From	To	Source IP Address	Destination IP Address	Source MAC Address	Destination MAC Address
Station A	Router 1	172.16.1.1	172.18.1.2	A	B
Router 1	Router 2	172.16.1.1	172.18.1.2	C	D
Router 2	Station B	172.16.1.1	172.18.1.2	E	F

Figure 3.13 Relationship of IP and MAC Address.

and are called *multihomed hosts*. Multihomed hosts must have a unique IP address for each of their physical connections. Multihomed hosts can provide flexible routing, but often create problems in managing traffic.

Multihomed hosts were originally intended to allow one physical interface to be identified by one IP address. In practice, however, some vendors allow combinations of multiple internet addresses across one physical interface. In addition, some interfaces are known as *logical hosts*. Logical host interfaces occur when a host has more than one IP address, but the addresses have the same network number or the same subnetwork number. Such a logical host interface could share one or several physical interfaces.

As a practical matter, it is a good idea to keep the host out of the routing business. If the host routing table has no information for the destination IP address, it simply chooses a default routing by selecting an entry in the routing table. The router should forward the datagram based on its routing table and return a message to the host stating that this event has indeed occurred. As you will see, this message should entail a redirect message issued through the Internet Control Message Protocol (ICMP). The host computer should then update its default entry to the appropriate designation returned by the router.

Address Resolution Issues

As discussed earlier, each device attached to a single physical LAN is identified by a physical hardware address. Other identifiers are also assigned, including network addresses. The vast majority of physical addresses are assigned by the manufacturer before the LAN product (a network interface card, or NIC) is shipped to the customer or when the product is installed at the customer's site.

The approach creates an interesting problem, which we have begun to address: how can we relate the physical address to a network address, and vice versa? For example, if host A wants to send a datagram to host D, it might not know the physical address of host D. To compound the problem, the higher-layer network address might also be unknown to host A. Therefore, some method must be devised to relate different levels of addresses to each other.

The Address Resolution Protocol (ARP)

The IP protocol stack provides a tool for resolving addresses. The address resolution protocol (ARP) handles the translation of IP addresses to physical addresses and hides these physical addresses from the upper layers.

ARP works with mapping tables, referred to as the *ARP cache*. The table provides mapping between an IP address and a physical address. In a LAN (such as an Ethernet or IEEE 802 network), ARP takes the target IP address and searches for a corresponding target physical address in a mapping table. If ARP finds the address, it returns the physical address back to the requester, which could be a router, a server on a LAN, or any other device (such as a work-station).

If the necessary address is not found in ARP cache, the ARP module sends a broadcast onto the network. The broadcast is called the *ARP request*, which contains an IP target address. Consequently, if one of the machines receiving the broadcast recognizes the IP address in the ARP request, it returns an ARP reply back to the inquiring host. This reply contains the physical hardware address of the queried host. Upon receiving the reply, the inquiring host places the address into the ARP cache. Thereafter, datagrams sent to this particular IP address can be translated into the physical address by accessing the cache. The ARP system thus allows an inquiring host to find the physical address of another host by using the IP address.

The concepts of ARP requests and replies are shown in Figure 3.14. Host A wants to determine C's physical address. It broadcasts datagrams to B, C, and D. Only C responds because it recognizes its IP address in the incoming ARP request datagram. Host C places its address into an IP datagram in the form of the ARP reply.

In addition to mapping IP addresses to physical addresses, ARP allows the designation of specific hardware types. Therefore, when an ARP datagram is received by the queried host, it can use a field in the datagram to determine if the machine is using a particular type of hardware, such as an Ethernet interface or packet radio.

The ARP packet format is shown in Figure 3.15. It is encapsulated into the physical-layer PDU. For example, the physical-layer PDU could be an Ethernet frame, described in Chapter 2. The EtherType field is set to 8035_{16} (or 32821_{10}) to identify an ARP frame, which is part of the field labeled "physical layer header" in Figure 3.15. Table 3.2 provides the EtherType values. The following is a brief description of each field:

Physical layer header.   The header for the physical layer packet.

Hardware.   Specifies the type of hardware interface in which the inquiring host seeks a response. Examples are Ethernet and packet ratio (Table 3.7 lists some assigned values).

Protocol.   Identifies the type of protocol the sender is using; typically it is IP.

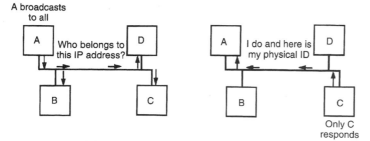

Figure 3.14 ARP Request and Reply.

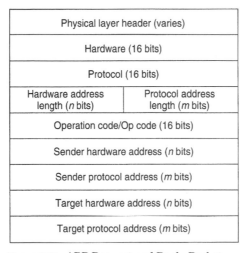

Figure 3.15 ARP Request and Reply Packet.

TABLE 3.7   ARP Hardware Type Examples.

Type	Description
1	Ethernet (10 Mb)
2	Experimental Ethernet (3 Mb)
3	Amateur radio X.25
4	Proteon ProNET token ring
5	Chaos
6	IEEE 802 networks
7	ARCNET

Hardware address length. Specifies the length in bytes of each hardware address in the packet.

Protocol address length. Specifies the length in bytes of the protocol addresses in the packet (for example, the IP address).

	ifIndex	Physical address	IP address	Mapping type
Address entry 1				
Address entry 2				
Address entry *n*				

Figure 3.17 Address Translation Table.

ifIndex. Contains the interface (physical port) of the specific interface for this address.

Physical address. This entry contains the media-dependent address (for example, a MAC address).

IP address. This entry contains the IP address, which corresponds to the physical address.

Mapping type. This entry is set to one of four values: other = 1 (none of the following), invalid = 2 (the mapping for this row entry is no longer valid), dynamic = 3 (the mapping could change), and static = 4 (entry does not change).

Proxy ARP

Another protocol, called *proxy ARP* or *promiscuous ARP*, is used in a number of ways. One implementation allows an organization to use only one IP address (the network portion of an address) for multiple networks. In essence, proxy ARP maps a single IP network address into multiple physical addresses. The concept is illustrated in Figure 3.18.

Gateway 1 (G1) hides network X from network Y and vice versa. Thus, if host A wants to send traffic to host D, host A might first form an ARP message in order to obtain the physical address of host D on network Y. The ARP message, however, does not reach host D. The gateway intercepts the message, performs the address resolution, and sends an ARP reply back to host A with the gateway's physical

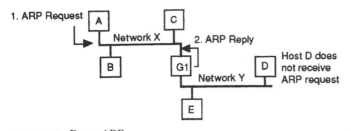

Figure 3.18   Proxy ARP.

address in the ARP target hardware address field. Host A then uses the ARP response to update its ARP table, and the ARP operation is complete. The example can also be reversed; the hosts on network X can be serviced by the gateway, as discussed for host A.

Proxy ARP is quite flexible, and nothing precludes mapping different IP address prefixes to the same physical address. Some ARP implementations, however, have diagnostic procedures that display alarms to network control if multiple addresses are mapped to the same physical address. This problem is called *spoofing* and alerts network control of possible problems.

Proxy ARP works only if the organization has installed ARP. ARP is quite simple and does not work with complex topologies, such as those with more than one gateway servicing more than one network. You can use ARP without changing routing tables in other parts of an internet. As mentioned at the start of this discussion, ARP hides physical networks through its mapping functions.

The Reverse Address Resolution Protocol (RARP)

The ARP protocol is a useful technique for determining physical addresses from network addresses. Some workstations, however, do not know their own IP address. For example, diskless (dataless) workstations do not have any IP address knowledge when booted to a system. The diskless workstations know only their hardware address.

The *reverse address resolution protocol* (RARP) works similarly to ARP except, as the name suggests, in reverse. The process is illustrated in Figure 3.19. The inquiring machine broadcasts an RARP request. This request specifies that machine A is the target machine, in contrast to the ARP protocol, which identifies the receiving machine as the target. The RARP packet contains the physical address of the sending machine and sends the transmission out as a broadcast; therefore, all machines on this physical network receive this request. Only the RARP servers are allowed to reply, however.

The servers reply by filling in the target protocol address field. They also change the operation code in the RARP message from a

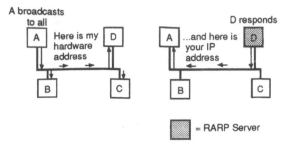

Figure 3.19 RARP Operations.

request to a reply (3 signifies a request and 4 signifies a reply) The packet is sent back to the inquiring station, which is then able to use the information in the frame to derive its IP address. The EtherType field in the frame is coded as 8035_{16} (32821_{10}) to identify the I field as an RARP packet (see Table 3.2).

Primary and secondary RARPs

RARP can be used on LANs to boot the machines to the network. These types of networks experience low failure rates; the RARP messages are rarely lost, mishandled, or otherwise corrupted. In some networks, however, more than one RARP server is required because of workload conditions. Some LANs use transmit timers and time-outs to ensure that the user stations obtain expeditious service from the RARP server. They evoke retransmissions of the RARP messages upon a time-out.

Other systems, in addition to using timeouts and retransmissions, designate an RARP server as a primary or backup server. If the primary RARP server is down or unable to fulfill a request, the request can be serviced by a designated backup server. Of course, on the down side, if the request is sent to multiple servers, these servers could create redundant traffic when they respond. Indeed, for an Ethernet type network, the replies from multiple servers increase the chances of collisions, which results in reduced throughput.

The solution to this problem is simple. In many networks, a secondary server cannot respond until it ascertains that the primary server has not responded. The secondary station thus monitors the channel to check for the reply from the primary RARP. If the reply is not detected within a set time, the secondary server times-out and assumes the role of the primary RARP. Another approach does not allow the secondary server to use the time-out function. Rather, if the requesting machine does not receive the reply from the primary server, it times-out and reissues the message. The secondary RARPs note this as a rebroadcast of the same request. At this time, a secondary

RARP or RARPs service the message. Note that not all vendors implement RARP operations. Check with your vendors to determine how or if RARP is used.

BOOTP

Although widely used, RARP has some disadvantages. Since it is intended to operate at the hardware level, it is cumbersome to obtain and manage the routine from an application. It also contains limited information. Its purpose is to obtain an IP address, but not much other information is provided. It would be useful for the reply of a message to contain information about other protocols supported by the machine, such as the gateway address and server host names. Due to these problems, the Internet now supports the Bootstrap Protocol, also known as BOOTP (see Figure 3.20).

BOOTP uses an IP datagram to obtain an IP address. This approach seems somewhat circuitous at first glance, but the destination address in the IP datagram is a limited broadcast value (all 1s yielding 255.255.255.255). A machine that chooses to use BOOTP sends out an IP limited broadcast. A designated server on the network receives the BOOTP message and sends a proper answer back to the inquirer in the form of yet another broadcast.

Operation (8)
Hardware Type (8)
Hardware Length (8)
Hops (8)
Transaction ID (32)
Seconds (16)
Client IP Address (32)
Your IP Address (32)
Server IP Address (32)
Gateway IP Address (32)
Client Hardware Address (128)
Server Host Name (512)
Boot File Name (1024)
Vendor Specific Area (512)

Figure 3.20 BOOTP Message Format.

BOOTP uses UDP at the transport layer, so the operation is connectionless. The UDP uses a checksum to check for corruption of data. BOOTP performs some transport layer functions by sending a request to the server, then a timer is started. If no reply is received within a defined period, BOOTP attempts a retransmission.

All PDU fields are of fixed length and the replies and requests have the same format. The operation field is set to 1 to denote a request and 2 to denote a reply. The next two fields are identical to the ARP protocol. The hops field must be set to a 0 in a request message. The server is allowed to pass a BOOTP message to another machine, perhaps in another network; if so, it must increment the hop count by one. The transaction ID field is used to coordinate requests and response messages. The seconds field is used to determine (in seconds) the time since the machine has started to establish the BOOTP procedure. The next four fields contain the IP addresses of the client address, as well as the requester's address, server address, and gateway address. The client hardware address is also available. The message also contains the client server and the boot filenames. The vendor-specific area is not defined in the standard.

Internet Service Providers (ISPs)

Many Internet users obtain services through an ISP by using dial-up modems and conventional telephone line (see Figure 3.21). In some of these arrangements, it is not necessary for the user to have a regis-

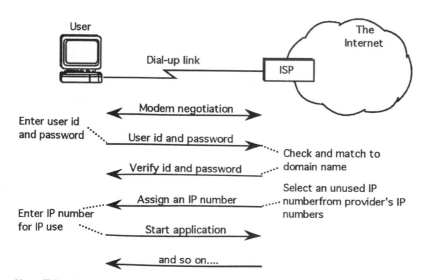

Note: This example is one of many offered by different access providers.

Figure 3.21   Connecting to an Internet Service Provider (ISP).

tered Internet address. The ISP has a block of numbers, and assigns one of these addresses to the user during the log-on process. Thereafter, this address identifies the user to the Internet.

A name server can also correlate the user to a domain name. In some access arrangements, the user must have a domain name registered with the Internet. This name is used by the ISP's name server to match the user's domain name to the respective Internet address.

Other access arrangements use a non-Internet address. For example, Compuserve uses its own specific address. In this situation, the user's Compuserve address becomes part of the Internet domain-naming system. For example, a hypothetical Compuserve address of 12345.6789 is made known to the Internet by Compuserve as 12345.6789@compuserve.com. When users want to send traffic to the Internet via this type of provider, they must enter an Internet address with a preface value that alerts the Compuserve software that an Internet (not a Compuserve address) is to be interpreted.

IP and X.121 Address Mapping

The ITU-T X.121 specification is widely used throughout the world and the majority of public packet networks employ X.121 as a network address. RFC 1236 provides guidance for mapping IP and X.121 addresses, as depicted through the DDN X.25/IP addressing conventions. Before discussing this standard, however, I will provide a brief tutorial on X.121.

International numbering plan for data networks (X.121)

X.121 uses a *data network identification code* (DNIC) based on the format DCCN, where DCC is a three-digit country code and N is the network digit identifying a specific network within a country. Figure 3.22 shows the structure for X.121. Some countries, however, have more than 10 networks; in this situation, multiple DCCs are assigned to the country. For example, the United States is assigned DCC values 310 through 316.

X.121 also defines a *network terminal number* (NTN). This 10-digit value identifies the computer, terminal, etc. within the network.

Figure 3.22 X.121 Address Format.

address coming to gateway 1, an IP gateway, contains address 128.11.1.2. From the perspective of the networks attached to gateway 1, the other networks know only about the gateway address of 128.11. Gateway G1 must resolve the local address values with either 1.0, 2.0, or 3.0, depending on which subnet is to receive the datagram.

Figure 3.24 also shows a subnet gateway, G2. This gateway is concerned with mapping the address 3.0 to the host address attached to the subnetwork. In this example, the gateway must establish the host addresses for hosts F and H. Ordinarily, this is done by accessing a look-up table in which the value of 3.0 is replaced with 3.n1 and 3.n2, which identify hosts F and H, respectively.

Figure 3.25 shows the structure of the slightly modified IP address. All that has occurred is the division of the local address (host address) into the subnet address (in this example, 1.0, 2.0, 3.0) and the host address (in this example, the addresses for hosts F and H). It is evident that both the initial internet address and the subnet address take advantage of hierarchical addressing and routing. This concept fits well with the basic gateway functions inherent in the Internet. Referring once again to Figure 3.24 and taking it from the top down, An external network is concerned only with the first half of the internet address. G1 is concerned only with the subnet address and G2 is concerned only with what is now called the host address. Taking it from the bottom up, hosts F and H are not concerned with any of the higher-layer addresses. They can communicate with each other and their gateway, G2, with physical addresses, or, if necessary, with a ULP address.

Choosing the assignments of the "local address" is left to individual network implementors. A prudent designer is careful to keep the numbering and identification consistent through the entire local subnetwork. Notwithstanding, the chosen values can vary. For example, one byte can be used as a subnet address and the second byte can be used as a host address. Alternately, the first 12 bits can be used for the subnet address and a half byte can be used as a host address. Many other choices exist in defining the local address. As mentioned previously, it is a local matter, but it does require considerable

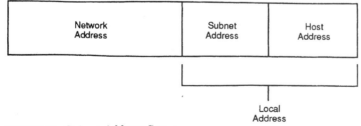
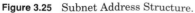

Figure 3.25 Subnet Address Structure.

thought. It requires following the same theme of the overall internet address: how many subnets must be identified in relation to how many hosts that reside on each subnet.

Subnet masks

To support subnet addressing, the IP routing algorithm was modified to support a subnet mask. The purpose of the mask is to determine which part of the IP address pertains to the subnetwork and which part pertains to the host. The convention used for subnet masking is to use a 32-bit field in addition to the IP address. The contents of the field (the mask) are set as follows:

Binary 1s. Identify the network address portion of the IP address.

Binary 0s. Identify the host address portion of the IP address. The example in Figure 3.24 would use the following mask for subnets 128.11.1, 128.11.2, and 128.11.3:

```
11111111 11111111 11111111 00000000
```

A *bitwise AND* function is performed on the IP address and the subnet mask to extract the fields of the IP address. The results of this operation are matched against a destination address in a routing table. If the results are equal, the next hop IP address (relative to this destination address) is used to determine the next hop on the route. Therefore, the last octet of all 0s identifies the host on the subnet.

The mask becomes part of the routing algorithm's conditional statement: "If the destination IP address and subnet mask equal my IP address and subnet mask, then send the datagram to the local network; otherwise, send the datagram to the gateway corresponding to the destination address." Indeed, the use of masks handles routes to direct conventions, host-specified routes, and default routes. An implementor should note the following guidelines for subnetting:

- The IP algorithm must be implemented on all machines in a subnet.
- Subnet masks should be the same for all machines.
- If one or more machines do not support masks, proxy ARP can be used to achieve subnetting.

Mask examples

Table 3.8 shows how the mask is interpreted, on a bit-by-bit basis. To use this table, imagine that a mask is coded as 255.255.240.0. Table 3.8 reveals that the binary mask is 11111111 11110000 00000000.

TABLE 3.8   Binary and
Decimal Equivalents in the
Mask.

00000000	0
10000000	128
11000000	192
11100000	224
11110000	240
11111000	248
11111100	252
11111110	254
11111111	255

Thus, the lower-order 12 bits of the IP address are to be used for a host address. As another example, imagine that a mask is coded as 255.255.255.224. Table 3.8 reveals that the binary mask is 11111111 11111111 11111111 11100000, and the lower-order five bits of the IP address are to be used for a host address.

As yet another example, assume a class B IP address of 128.1.17.1, with a mask of 255.255.240.0. To discover the subnet address value, you can perform a bitwise AND operation on the mask with the destination address, as shown in Figure 3.26.

As this example shows, when the subnet mask is split across octets, the results can be a bit confusing. In this case, the actual value for the subnet address is 0001_2 or 1_{10}, even though the decimal address of the "host" space is 17.1. The software does not care about octet alignment; it is looking for a match of the destination address in the IP datagram to an address in a routing table. Therefore, each destination network and subnetwork address in the routing table is compared to the destination network and subnetwork address of 10000000 00000001 0001. If a match is found, the datagram is routed to the entry in the routing table designated as the next node for the destination address. Otherwise, the datagram is either discarded or sent to a default next node.

Figure 3.27 shows one more example of the subnetwork mask operation (for simplicity, only two table entries are shown in the example). Each destination network and subnetwork address in the routing

IP address	10000000	00000001	0001	0001	00000001
Mask	11111111	11111111	1111	0000	00000000
Result	10000000	00000001	0001	don't care	
Logical address	128	1	1	don't care	
		network	sub net	host	

Figure 3.26   Destination Address for Mask with Bitwise AND Performed.

Step 1.
Apply mask to
dest. IP, to
compute logical
address = n

	IP address	10000000	00000001	0001	0001	00000001
	Mask	11111111	11111111	1111	0000	00000000
Bitwise and result		10000000	00000001	0001	don't care	
	Logical address	128	1	1	don't care	

network   sub net   host

Step 2.
Access table &
find closest match
of n to a logical
address in table

Destination address	Mask	Next node	On port#
128.1.129.1	255.255.240.0	56.1.22.78	4
128.1.17.1	255.255.240.0	47.1.43.56	6

n is 10000000   00000001   0001   or 128.1.1

128.1.129.1   255.255.240.0   is 128.1.8   no match
128.1.17.1   255.255.240.0   is 128.1.1   match & next node is
                                             47.1.43.56 on port # 6

Note:
First address in table above: address   10000000   0000001   1000
                                 mask   11111111   1111111   1111
                                 result   10000000   0000001   1000
                                 or 128.1.8

Next address in table above: address   10000000   0000001   0001
                                mask   11111111   1111111   1111
                                result   10000000   0000001   0001
                                or 128.1.1

Figure 3.27   One Method of Using the Routing Table.

table is compared to the destination network and subnetwork address in the IP datagram. This operation is achieved by applying the route mask to both the destination IP address in the datagram and the destination addresses in the routing table. If a match is found (which is the case in this example), the datagram is routed to the entry in the routing table designated as the next node for the destination address. Otherwise, it is either discarded or sent to a default next node. If several matches are found (not shown here), other criteria are used to determine the next node (this is explained in Chapter 5).

The value of this approach is that the local router is the only machine that has to be aware of multiple networks and addresses in the IP address. Other machines in an internet route as if the traffic were going to one network address. In other words, indirect networks do not need to know about the details of the local addressing scheme.

As a general rule, it is simpler if all stations use the same network mask. If different masks are used, then (as this example shows) a router must know the mask before it can determine the subnet address. Also, most network administrators set up addresses wherein a group of subnets or hosts are associated with one physical location. For example, subnets 1–43 could be one part of an organization's internet, and 44–77 could be in another part. This approach is important, because it allows an efficient table look-up for the addresses. It is useful to keep the subnets contiguous within a given IP address.

Keep in mind that, in this example, the address of 128.1.17.1 would be interpreted differently if the mask were different. For example, if the mask were 255.255.255.000, the third octet of 17_{10} would be interpreted as just that: 17_{10} and not 1_{10}. Obviously, masks that align on octet boundaries makes things simpler, but might not reflect reality.

Broadcast and other unique addresses

Now that you've examined the subnet mask, I will summarize the permissible formats for broadcast and other addresses.

Directed broadcast. This address allows broadcasts to all hosts on a specified network. It is used only in the destination address and its format is [*network number*, 255]. Once the datagram reaches the destination network, it is broadcasted to all hosts on that network.

Limited broadcast. The destination IP address is formatted so that every host on a physical network receives the datagram. This format will not allow the datagram to be routed outside the one physical network. Its format is [255,255].

Subnet directed broadcast. With the use of the subnet address mask value, an internet can also direct a broadcast to all hosts on a specified subnetwork. Again, this format should be used only in the destination address field, and its format is [*network number*, *subnetwork number*, 255].

All subnetworks directed broadcast. This address format (again, only in the destination field) allows a datagram to be broadcast to all subnetworks on a specified subnetted network. Its format is [*network number*, 255, 255]. As a note of caution, make sure to read RFC 1812; it describes some problems with this operation.

Internal host loopback address. This address is for internal routing within a host, and is not sent onto the network. It is used when two applications reside inside the same host. Its format is [127, *any value*]

Vendors vary with how they support broadcasting in their products. Some machines have not been programmed to understand subnetting, which can cause some problems if you use a subnet mask. Additionally, some machines do not understand the relationship of a link layer broadcast address and the IP broadcast address. The link layer and IP destination addresses should complement each other. If one has a broadcast address, so should the other. At a minimum, if a link layer contains a broadcast address, the destination address field and the IP datagram should be an IP multicast address or an IP broadcast address.

It is also possible to build the address mask with noncontiguous 1s. For example, this option is permissible: 0100110001100000. Because the operation simply does bitwise AND functions, any combination of the 1s identifies the subnet. While this mask is possible, however, it is not a very good idea because it makes things unnecessarily complex.

Before leaving subnet addresses, I want to emphasize that selecting subnet address space is strictly up to the user. For example, if a class B address is used in which the host address space is 16 bits, the subnet address might be 8 bits and the host address might be the other 8 bits, which allows the network administrator to configure 254 subnets with 254 hosts to each subnet (0 and 256 are not available). Or, using 6 bits for the subnet address space would offer the capability of identifying 64 networks ($2^6 = 64$), which is equivalent to 10 bits for the host's identification attached to these networks, resulting in a maximum number of 10^{24} hosts for each network ($2^{10} = 1024$).

One scheme for assigning masks is to partition the subnet and host spaces (RFC 1219 provides further guidance). Assuming the use of a class C network with 8 bits available for the subnet and host addresses, assigning a number takes the form *ssgghhh* (where *s* = subnet, *g* = growth bits, and *h* = host bits). The mask for this address space is 11110000. If it becomes necessary to add hosts to the subnet and enlarge the host's address space, the address space could be changed to *ssgghhhh* (an additional *h*) and the mask would still be 11110000. Suppose the internet grows and needs more bits for subnet addresses. The address space could be changed to *sssghhhh* and the mask would remain the same. Of course, if the hosts on this internet grew to the extent that the final *g* bit had to be used (*ssshhhhh*), then the mask would be changed to 11100000.

Table 3.9 contains a complete list of the possible subnetwork mask values for binary, hex, and decimal notations.

Classless Interdomain Routing (CIDR)

In order to extend the limited address space of an IP address, Classless Interdomain Routing (CIDR) is now used in many systems. It permits networks to be grouped together logically and to use one entry in a routing table for multiple class C networks.

The following example shows how the concept works. The first requirement for CIDR is for multiple networks to share a certain number of bits in the high-order part of the IP address. Say the first

TABLE 3.9   IP Subnet Mask Values.

Binary Values				Hex Values				Decimal Values			
1111 1111	1111 1111	1111 1111	1111 1111	FF	FF	FF	FF	255	255	255	255
1111 1111	1111 1111	1111 1111	1111 1110	FF	FF	FF	FE	255	255	255	254
1111 1111	1111 1111	1111 1111	1111 1100	FF	FF	FF	FC	255	255	255	252
1111 1111	1111 1111	1111 1111	1111 1000	FF	FF	FF	F8	255	255	255	248
1111 1111	1111 1111	1111 1111	1111 0000	FF	FF	FF	F0	255	255	255	240
1111 1111	1111 1111	1111 1111	1110 0000	FF	FF	FF	E0	255	255	255	224
1111 1111	1111 1111	1111 1111	1100 0000	FF	FF	FF	C0	255	255	255	192
1111 1111	1111 1111	1111 1111	1000 0000	FF	FF	FF	80	255	255	255	128
1111 1111	1111 1111	1111 1111	0000 0000	FF	FF	FF	00	255	255	255	00
1111 1111	1111 1111	1111 1110	0000 0000	FF	FF	FE	00	255	255	254	00
1111 1111	1111 1111	1111 1100	0000 0000	FF	FF	FC	00	255	255	252	00
1111 1111	1111 1111	1111 1000	0000 0000	FF	FF	F8	00	255	255	248	00
1111 1111	1111 1111	1111 0000	0000 0000	FF	FF	F0	00	255	255	240	00
1111 1111	1111 1111	1110 0000	0000 0000	FF	FF	E0	00	255	255	224	00
1111 1111	1111 1111	1100 0000	0000 0000	FF	FF	C0	00	255	255	192	00
1111 1111	1111 1111	1000 0000	0000 0000	FF	FF	80	00	255	255	128	00
1111 1111	1111 1111	0000 0000	0000 0000	FF	FF	00	00	255	255	00	00
1111 1111	1111 1110	0000 0000	0000 0000	FF	FE	00	00	255	254	00	00
1111 1111	1111 1100	0000 0000	0000 0000	FF	FC	00	00	255	252	00	00
1111 1111	1111 1000	0000 0000	0000 0000	FF	F8	00	00	255	248	00	00
1111 1111	1111 0000	0000 0000	0000 0000	FF	F0	00	00	255	240	00	00
1111 1111	1110 0000	0000 0000	0000 0000	FF	E0	00	00	255	224	00	00
1111 1111	1100 0000	0000 0000	0000 0000	FF	C0	00	00	255	192	00	00
1111 1111	1000 0000	0000 0000	0000 0000	FF	80	00	00	255	128	00	00
1111 1111	0000 0000	0000 0000	0000 0000	FF	00	00	00	255	00	00	00
1111 1110	0000 0000	0000 0000	0000 0000	FE	00	00	00	254	00	00	00
1111 1100	0000 0000	0000 0000	0000 0000	FC	00	00	00	252	00	00	00
1111 1000	0000 0000	0000 0000	0000 0000	F8	00	00	00	248	00	00	00
1111 0000	0000 0000	0000 0000	0000 0000	F0	00	00	00	240	00	00	00
1110 0000	0000 0000	0000 0000	0000 0000	E0	00	00	00	224	00	00	00
1100 0000	0000 0000	0000 0000	0000 0000	C0	00	00	00	192	00	00	00
1000 0000	0000 0000	0000 0000	0000 0000	80	00	00	00	128	00	00	00
0000 0000	0000 0000	0000 0000	0000 0000	00	00	00	00	00	00	00	00

seven bits in the address are the same. Thus, by using the mask 254.0.0.0 (11111110.00000000.00000000.00000000), all addresses between 194.0.0.0 and 195.255.255.255 can be identified by a single entry in the routing table.

Once the point in the network is reached, the remainder of the address space can be used for hierarchical routing. For example, a mask of 255.255.240.0 could be used to group networks together. This concept, if carried out on all IP addresses (and not just class C addresses), could reduce an Internet routing table from about 10,000 to 200 entries.

Additional information on CIDR is available in RFCs 1518, 1519, 1466, and 1447.

IPv6 and Address Resolution

Addresses resolution and neighbor discovery in IPv6 is not defined in the ARP operations. Rather, it is defined in the ICMP operations known as router solicitation, router advertisement, neighbor solicitation, and neighbor advertisement (see Chapter 6 for a description of these operations).

Summary

Networks need various types and levels of naming and addressing to unambiguously identify user and control traffic. The TCP/IP protocol suite provides a full array of these names and addresses, as well as several protocols for mapping between physical and network addresses.

The IP address format has become a worldwide standard for network/host identification. The subnet address space and the subnet masking operations considerably reduce the overhead associated with IP address maintenance.

4

The Domain Name System

This chapter continues the discussion on naming and addressing, concentrating on naming and internet name servers. You should be familiar with the material in Chapters 2 and 3 before reading this chapter.

The Internet Protocol (IP) address structure, which consists of 32 bits, is somewhat awkward to use. So, instead of using the IP address, most organizations use acronyms and meaningful terms to identify numeric addresses. This practice presents an interesting problem if a network user has adopted acronyms as an address but must internetwork with a network that uses numeric IP addresses. How can the non-IP identifier be mapped to an IP address?

You might think that users should conform and use the numeric IP addresses. But you cannot expect end users to remember all the values on these addresses, much less to key in these addresses at the workstation. The solution instead is to devise a naming scheme wherein end users can employ friendly, easy-to-remember names to identify sending and receiving entities. To implement this idea, procedures must first be established to provide both a framework for establishing user-friendly names and conventions for mapping the names to IP addresses.

In the Internet, the SRI Network Information Center originally organized and managed these names. It maintained a file called HOST.TXT, which listed the names of networks, gateways, and hosts and their corresponding addresses. The original structure of *flat-name* spaces worked well enough in the early days of the Internet. Flat names were a form of names consisting merely of characters identifying an object without any further meaning or structure. The SRI Network Information Center administered name spaces and assigned them to new objects identified in the Internet.

Domain Name System (DNS) Architecture

As the Internet grew, administering HOST.TXT became a big job. In recognition of this problem, the Internet administrators decided in 1983 to develop a system called the *domain name system* (DNS).

Similar to many addressing schemes (such as the ISO and ITU-T standards), DNS uses a hierarchical scheme for establishing names. Think of the hierarchies as being an organizational chart in a company. The CEO rests at the top of the tree hierarchy, with subordinates stacked in branches below. Another example of hierarchical naming is the telephone system, with country telephone codes at the top of the tree. Below country codes in the tree are area codes, then local exchange codes, and finally, at the bottom of the hierarchy, a local telephone subscriber number.

One attractive aspect of hierarchical naming is that it allows naming administrators to manage their own names at the lower levels of the hierarchy (a naming domain) and use upper-level names only if they need to operate outside their internal operations and networks. This approach permits a high-level authority to assign the responsibility for administering a subdomain name space to a lower level in a *hierarchical name space*. Even though authority for naming passes from a higher level, these designated "agents" are permitted to cross the hierarchy to send information to each other regarding names. Partitioning can therefore be done in any manner deemed appropriate by an upper-level hierarchy, and the name-space division can be small enough so the whole operation is manageable.

The concept of DNS is shown in Figure 4.1. It is organized around a root and tree structure. A *root* is the highest entry and is also called a *parent* to the lower levels of the tree. The *tree* consists of branches, which connect nodes. Each label of a node in the tree at the same node level must be completely unambiguous and distinct. That is, the

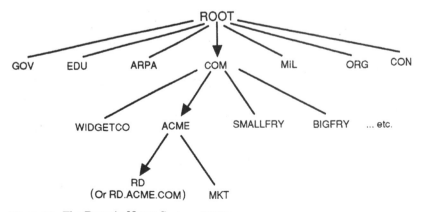

Figure 4.1   The Domain Name System (DNS).

label must be a relative distinguished name (distinguishable relative to that node level).

Hierarchical naming is established by tracing down through the tree, selecting the names attached to each label, and concatenating these labels together to form a distinguished name—distinguishable at *all* levels in the tree. For example, the first node level under the root of the tree contains several names. I will use COM as an example. Proceeding down the tree to the next level, several other names are listed, including ACME. Below ACME is RD, which is the lowest-level node in the tree. RD is called a *leaf* node because it has no dependent nodes (nodes underneath it). The concatenated name is shown at the bottom of the figure as RD.ACME.COM.

You might wonder about the notation in this example. The tree shows the hierarchy pursuing the route down to the bottom of the leaf, but the actual name is written with the local label first and the top-most domain label last. This approach is different from the practice of other standards, and it does take some adjustment if you have been using other naming conventions.

Domain names are not intended to define addresses. As you will see shortly, these services are performed by name servers and name resolvers.

Internet names are no longer designated just for hosts. For example, an information class titled *mail exchange* (MX information) is available that allows an organization to transmit mail not just to individual workstations or computers, but to any machine designed as a mail server. In addition, using a domain name allows an MX machine to have domain names without being attached to the Internet. Organizations need only direct their mail to a mail server.

Figure 4.2 shows the typical operation of a name server. If an individual wants to establish a connection (or send a message) to UBlack@RD.ACME.COM, that individual enters the name of the person to whom he or she wants to establish a connection and the person's enterprise (the domain name) into the workstation. To ascertain the network address of this name, a query is sent to a name server (or the query is matched against a table stored in the workstation). The response to the query contains the address for the name; in this hypothetical example, the address is 128.4.3.6. This address is placed into a datagram, which is then sent to a router. The router uses this address to determine where the datagram is to be routed. The datagram is then routed to a next node, identified as 128.22.3.8 in this example.

Domain Names

Each domain is identified by an unambiguous *domain name*. Because of the hierarchical nature of the DNS, a domain can be a subdomain

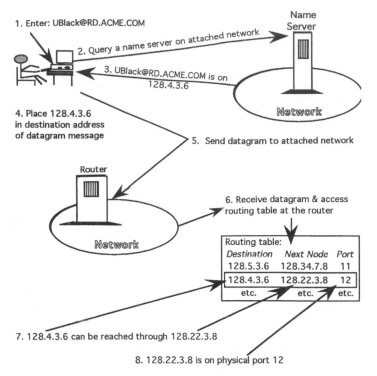

Figure 4.2   Typical Operation with a Name Server.

of another domain. Subdomains are achieved by the naming structure, which allows encapsulation of naming relationships. In the example in Figure 4.1, the domain RD.ACME is a subdomain of RD.ACME.COM.

The DNS provides two ways of viewing a name. One is called an *absolute name*, which consists of the complete name in the DNS. In the example in Figure 4.1, the absolute name is RD.ACME.COM. In contrast, a *relative name* consists of only a part of the name within a complete entry in the DNS. In Figure 4.1, RD would be a relative name. Absolute and relative names are quite similar to the OSI model's description of a distinguished name (DN) and a relative distinguished name (RDN), respectively.

Top-Level Domains

Presently, the DNS contains seven top-level domain names. They are shown in Figure 4.1 and are as follows:

GOV. Any government body

EDU. An educational institution

ARPA. ARPANET-Internet host identification

COM. Any commercial enterprise

MIL. Military organizations

ORG. Any other organization not identified by previous descriptors

CON. Countries using the ISO standard for naming their countries (ISO 3166)

The DNS is organized into domains. At the top of a domain is the root domain. Each domain is a subtree of the full Internet domain and the domain name space. In Figure 4.3, a domain is identified as *us* (the United States). Within the us domain are 50 nodes, each representing a state. In this example, four states are identified under us, and the two-letter abbreviations are the same as those used by the

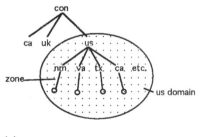

(a)

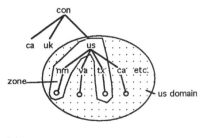

(b)

Figure 4.3 Domains and Zones.

U.S. Postal Service. Of course, a city can reside under a state node, and another node, such as an organization or host name, can reside under a city node.

To simplify the management of a domain, it can be divided into smaller parts, called *zones*. The second illustration in this figure shows that the New Mexico and Texas nodes comprise a zone, perhaps for name sharing for immigration-control purposes.

Name servers are responsible for storing information relevant to a zone. The name server responsible for a zone is known as the *authoritative* name server. A name server can have authority for one or more zones.

Figure 4.4 shows an example of how name resolvers and name servers interact. The *resolver* is a client to its name server. It forms a query for imm.santafe.nm.us and presents this name to its local name server. This resolver is called a *stub resolver* because it does nothing more than form a query and await an answer from the name server.

Also, in this example, the local name server sends and receives requests and answers to other name servers. Each name server queried sends back an error message, with a referral to another name server that is closer to the sought name. The authoritative name server finally returns the address to the local name server.

As of this writing, the Internet operates with seven root name servers and, given the size of the Internet, they are quite busy. It is

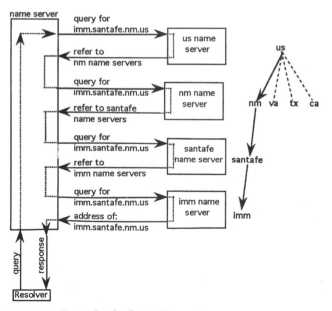

Figure 4.4 Example of a Query Operation.

not unusual for these name servers to receive from five to seven queries a second.

Domain Name Resolution and Mapping Names to Addresses

To map user-friendly names to IP addresses, an Internet user must work with the concepts of domain name resolution. Request for comments (RFC) 1035 defines the procedures for these operations.

Fortunately, the user's task is quite simple in resolving these names. The user need only provide a set of arguments to a local agent (name resolver), which retrieves information based on a domain name or sends the request to the name server. The user has a few other minor tasks, including forming the proper query to the name resolver and providing certain requirements for how the operation is performed. Figure 4.5 shows the operations for domain name resolution.

The user sees the domain tree as a single name (a single information space). Conversely, the resolver assumes the task of resolving the name or sending the name to independent cooperative systems (the name servers) for name/address resolution. As the figure shows, the name server services a request from the name resolver. Thus, the resolver acts as a service provider to the user program. In turn, the resolver acts as a user to the name server.

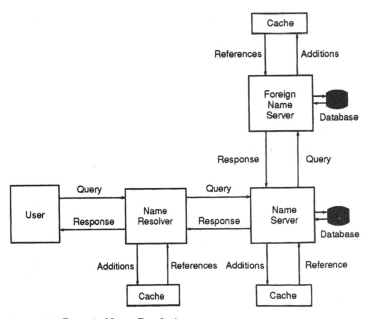

Figure 4.5   Domain Name Resolution.

Name servers can store some of the same information stored in name resolvers for efficiency and backup. Regardless of how the information is stored at the name server, the name resolver must know the name of at least one name server in order to begin the query. The query is passed to the name server from the resolver. The server, in turn, provides a response or makes a referral to yet another name server. With this approach, the resolver can learn more about the identities of other name servers and the information they hold.

Determining which name servers are to participate in the operation is based on the naming hierarchy tree shown in Figure 4.1. Each leaf entry of this tree could correspond to a name server. A server at a subdomain (leaf entry) knows which servers are under its domain and can choose the appropriate server to answer a query.

Figure 4.5 shows another component attached to the resolver, called the *name cache*. Upon receiving a user query, the resolver checks this local storage to see if the answer is available locally. If so, the answer is returned to the client in the form of a response. If the answer is not available in the name cache, the name resolver must then determine the best name servers to provide the response.

The name cache is usually incomplete, but it does provide the most frequently queried information to speed the process of name resolution. The information in the name cache is eventually erased through the use of timers.

Name Server Operations

The name server services the user's query with either recursive or nonrecursive operations. For *nonrecursive* operations, the response of the name server to a query is one of the following:

- An answer
- An identification of an error
- A referral to another server

The resolver must reissue a query to specific name servers. In contrast, a local name server can contact other servers by way of *recursive* operations. In effect, this offloads the task from the user host and requires the name server to return the queried IP address to the client. If the name server does not return the IP address, it must send a negative response. The name server is not allowed to return a referral. The effect of the nonrecursive and recursive operations ensures that the user knows at least one server is at the address. It also ensures that a name server knows the IP address of at least one other name server.

The server is responsible for maintaining a portion of a subtree of a domain space, called a *zone*: a contiguous section of the domain space. Typically, a separate database exists for each zone. The name server is required to check periodically to ensure that its zone is correct and, if not, update the zone correctly. A zone can be updated only by the proper authority. The name server uses a *zone transfer protocol* to allow more than one name server to store data about a zone. If a name server for a domain name fails for any reason, redundant copies of the naming and addressing information are available at other name servers.

A name server is classified as either *primary* or *secondary*. As suggested by these terms, the function of the primary name server can be duplicated in other machines, which, in turn, are called *secondary name servers*. This approach provides reliability and efficiency in servicing queries.

The query and reply messages transmitted between name servers can use either transmission control protocol (TCP) or user datagram protocol (UDP). Typically, connectionless UDP is used for ongoing queries because it provides better performance. For activities that require database updates, such as zone refresh operations, however, TCP is preferable for obtaining reliable transfer. Whatever the case, name servers can use either protocol.

As stated earlier, Internet domain servers are arranged conceptually in tree structures such as the one shown in Figure 4.1. Each leaf in this hierarchical tree represents a name server, which is responsible for a single domain or subdomain. The entries in the conceptual tree in Figure 4.1 do not represent any actual physical connections. They simply show name servers that are known by other name servers and with whom they can communicate. To participate in the DNS, an organization must agree to operate and support a domain name server.

Resource Records

You learned earlier that a domain name identifies a node. Each node contains information about its resources; if no resources are available, the node will have an empty resource. The resource information associated with both a node and name is called a *resource record* (RR). A resource record is contained in a database and defines domain zones. RRs are also used to map between domain names and network objects.

An RR is identified by its mnemonic type and numerical code. These types and their values are listed in Table 4.1 and will be explained in more detail shortly. RRs are stored in a standard format. Figure 4.6 shows the format for the top-level part of an RR. The contents of an RR record have a standard format:

TABLE 4.1   Type Values of the DNS.

Type	Value and meaning
A	1 = Host address
NS	2 = Authoritative name server
MD	3 = Mail destination (now obsolete; use MX)
MF	4 = Mail forwarder (now obsolete; use MX)
CNAME	5 = Canonical name for an alias
SOA	6 = Start of zone authority
MB	7 = Mailbox domain name
MG	8 = Mailbox member
MR	9 = Mail rename domain
NULL	10 = Null RR
WKS	11 = Well-known service
PTR	12 = Domain name pointer
HINFO	13 = Host information (experimental)
MINFO	14 = Mailbox or mail list information
MX	15 = Mail exchange
TXT	16 = Text strings
RP	17 = Responsible person (experimental)
AFSDB	18 = Authority format identifier-type services (experimental)
X.25	19 = X.25 address, X.121 (experimental)
ISDN	20 = ISDN address, E.163/E.164 (experimental)
RT	21 = Route through (experimental)
OSI NSAP	22 = OSI Network service access point address (experimental)

```
┌─────────────────────────────┐
│                             │
│       NAME (Variable)       │
│                             │
├─────────────────────────────┤
│                             │
│         TYPE (16)           │
│                             │
├─────────────────────────────┤
│                             │
│        CLASS (16)           │
│                             │
├─────────────────────────────┤
│                             │
│         TTL (32)            │
│                             │
├─────────────────────────────┤
│                             │
│       RDLENGTH (16)         │
│                             │
├─────────────────────────────┤
│                             │
│       RDTA (Variable)       │
│                             │
└─────────────────────────────┘
```

Figure 4.6 Resource Record (RR) Contents.

```
name   TTL   class   type   data
```

Some of these fields may be omitted in an RR. If the <TTL> field is blank, it defaults to a minimum time specified in another part of the database (explained later). If <class> is blank, it defaults to the last class specified in the database. The definitions of these fields are as follows:

name.   Contains the domain name (owner name) of the node for this RR. If blank, it defaults to the name of the previous RR.

TTL. The time-to-live parameter. It is optional and specifies the time (in seconds) that this RR definition is valid in the name server cache. If the value is 0, the RR should not be stored in cache (for example, if RR is volatile data). In practice, this value determines the time the resolver uses a server's data before it asks for an update.

class. Contains the values of the RR class code (where IN = the Internet and CH = chaos system). If blank, it defaults to the last class specified.

type. Contains a value to represent the RR type codes.

RD length. Considered a part of the data field, it specifies the length, in octets, of the RDATA field.

data (RDATA). Variable-length field describing the resource. The contents of RDATA vary depending on the type and class of RR. This field is examined in the next section of this chapter.

RDATA field

Figure 4.7 shows one of the more common RDATA formats, the "start of zone authority" (SOA). Only one SOA record per zone should exist.

As the figure reveals, the SOA RDATA contains seven subfields. Most of these fields are used to administer and maintain the name server. Their contents are as follows:

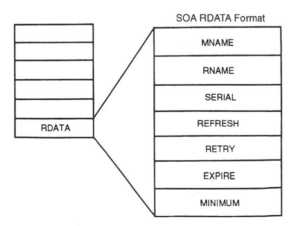

Figure 4.7 The Start of Zone Authority (SOA) Format.

MNAME.   Identifies the domain name that is the original or primary source of data for this zone.

RNAME.   Identifies a domain name to be used for the mailbox of the person responsible for this zone.

SERIAL.   Contains the version number of the original copy of the zone. Any transfers of zones must preserve this value. SERIAL is incremented when a change is made in the zone.

REFRESH.   A count (in seconds) to determine the interval for refreshing the zone.

RETRY.   A count (in seconds) that describes the interval to elapse before an unsuccessful refresh should be reattempted.

EXPIRE.   A value (in seconds) that specifies when this zone is no longer authoritative.

MINIMUM.   Contains the minimum value for the TTL field that should be exported from any RR from the subject zone. It is a lower boundary on TTL for all RRs in a zone.

Explanation of DNS Types

Figure 4.8 shows the remainder of the fields for RDATA formats. All these formats (actually, DNS types) are examined in the order they appear, from the top of the figure to the bottom. For simplicity's sake, I will not mention some of the optional entries in the formats. Refer to Table 4.1 during this discussion.

The *name server* (NS) RDATA format contains the domain name and the host name that provides the DNS service. One NS record should exist per server. Also, a name server does not have to be within the domain name. The following entry shows how the NS appears in a resource record, as well as on a hardcopy printout (machines HOSTA.RD.ACME.COM. and HOSTC.MKT.COM. provide name service for the domain RD.ACME.COM.):

```
RD.ACME.COM.NS HOSTA.RD.ACME.COM.
HOSTC.MKT.COM
```

The *MG* RDATA format contains the name of a mailbox, which is a member of a mail group specified by the name. In the figure, this value appears as MGNAME.

The *CNAME* (canonical name) RDATA format contains a domain name that is an alias (nickname) for another name (the proper, or canonical, name). CNAME allows a host to either change its name or use a shorter name, but keep its older name. For example, an alias for HOSTA.RD.ACME.COM. might be ACME.:

```
ACME. CNAME HOSTA.RD.ACME.COM.
```

The *HINFO* (host information) RDATA format contains two fields of string information. The first field identifies the CPU type, and the second field identifies the operating system running on the CPU. This data format is quite useful in obtaining hardware and software infor-

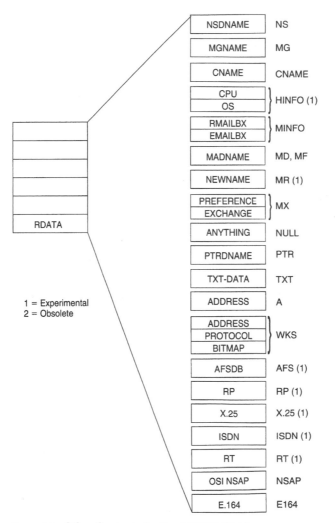

Figure 4.8 Other Contents for the RDATA Field.

mation about a host machine. For example, the HINFO for HOSTA.RD.ACME.COM. might appear as:

```
HOSTA.RD.ACME.COM. HINFO VAX-11 780 UNIX.
```

The *MINFO* (mail information) format is in the experimental stages. It contains two fields: RMAILBX and EMAILBX. RMAILBX identifies a mailbox responsible for the mailing list. It can identify the owner of the RR, which means the owner is responsible for the mail. EMAILBX identifies the mailbox that is to receive error messages.

Several type values are obsolete. These are listed in Figure 4.8 as *MD*, *MF*, and *MB* RDATA formats. Study RFC 1035 for guidance on these fields.

The *MR* RDATA format is experimental. It contains a domain name that identifies a mailbox, and it renames a specified mailbox. This record is used principally as a forwarding entry if someone has moved to a different mailbox.

The *MX* (mail exchanger) RDATA format contains two fields. The first is called a *preference* field, and its value specifies the precedence given to this RR for delivery to a host (low numbers are the highest priority). The second field is the *exchange* field, and it contains a domain name that identifies a host willing to act as a mail exchange for the owner name. The next example shows that HOSTA.RD.ACME.COM. wants its mail to be delivered to one of these machines, in the order indicated by the 10 and 20 values:

```
HOSTA.RD.ACME.COM. MX 10 HOSTC.MKT.COM.
MX 20 HOSTD.HQ.COM.
```

The *NULL* RDATA format allows anything to be placed in this field, as long as it does not exceed 65,535 octets. The *TXT* (text) RDATA field contains character strings for descriptive text.

The *PTR* (pointer) RDATA format contains a domain name that serves as a pointer to a location in the domain name space. This format is used for reverse mapping, in which Internet addresses are converted to names. So you can understand this important feature of the DNS, I must first explain the A (address) format and digress briefly to examine the IN-ADDR-ARPA domain. The *A* (address) RDATA format contains an Internet address for a name. For example, HOSTA has an internet address of 128.11.1.1; its A record is:

```
HOSTA. IN A 128.11.1.1
```

IN-ADDR-ARPA

The structure depicted in Figure 4.1 facilitates name-to-address mapping by simply tracing down the domain tree and obtaining an address. Because the index is organized around a name, however, an address-to- name mapping is not so easy.

To solve this problem, an address mapping domain name called IN-ADDR-ARPA was created. It provides a reverse mapping from address to host name using the IN-ADDR-ARPA domain. The approach is to use the host address as an index to the host's RRs. Once the RRs are located, the name can be extracted. Within the IN-ADDR-ARPA domain are subdomains for each network with the proper network address.

For example, consider that gateway 1 (GW1) needs to be located. (Gateways have the same PTR RRs as hosts and can be located solely by the network number if necessary.) Assuming that the gateway connects two networks, the A records could appear as:

```
GW1.RD.ACME.COM. IN A 128.11.1.4.
IN A 129.12.1.3.
```

In each of the networks' zones, one of these number-to-name entries is found (note that the Internet number octets are reversed for ease of use). With these entries stored in a database, the look-up for number-to-name resolution becomes a simple process using the PTR field:

```
4.1.11.128.IN-ADDR-ARPA. PTR GW1.RD.ACME.COM.
3.1.12.129.IN-ADDR-ARPA. PTR GW1.RD.ACME.COM.
```

Because gateways can be located by network number alone, each zone would have one of these number-to-name entries:

```
128.11.IN-ADDR-ARPA. PTR GW1.RD.ACME.COM.
```

```
129.12.IN-ADDR-ARPA. PTR GW1.RD.ACME.COM.
```

To continue with the other contents for the RDATA fields, the *WKS* (well-known services) RDATA format contains three fields. These fields describe services supported at a particular Internet address. The first field is a 32-bit address. The second field is called the *protocol* field and identifies an IP number. The third field is a *bitmap*. In the bitmap, each bit contains the identification of a specified protocol. For example, the first bit in this field corresponds to port 0, the second to port 1, and so on. The appropriate values for these ports and protocols can be found in RFC 1010. If the bits are set to 1, the particular protocols are supported at that host. Typically, the bits are established to identify protocols such as TCP, FTP, and SMTP. As an example of the WKS entry, HOSTA supports TCP, FTP, SMTP, and Telnet:

```
HOSTA.RD.ACME.COM. IN WKS 128.11.1.1.
TCP FTP SMTP TELNET
```

Several other experimental resource records have been added to the DNS. The *AFS* (originally called the Andrew file system) RR type maps from a domain name in the DNS to the name of an AFS database server. The record contains a host name, which must be a domain name for a host providing a service for an AFS cell database server.

The *RP* (responsible person) RR is another experimental record. It identifies the responsible person for a particular system or host. Typically, this would be a contact in the event a problem occurs at a computer. This record uses a new RR type with the mnemonic RP. An example of an RP record is as follows:

```
GW1.RD.ACME.COM. RP UDB.IEI.ACME.COM.
```

Because of the importance and prevalence of X.25-based networks and the emerging ISDN technology, the Internet has added resource records for X.25 and ISDN addresses.

The X.25 resource record is defined with the mnemonic *X25*. It allows the coding of a ITU-T X.121 address and the association of that address with a domain name. The value of this approach is that it takes only one more operation in a name-server database to relate the IP address to the domain name associated with X.121 address in the record. An example of the X.25 RR is as follows:

```
ACME.COM. X25 3110.123456789.
```

The *ISDN* RDATA format works in a similar manner to the X.25 record. It allows a relationship to be established between an ISDN address coded typically with the E.164 format. As you might guess, it is a simple step to perform an additional look-up in the file to relate an ISDN address to the IP counterpart address using the domain name (assuming these relationships were created by the network administrator). Additionally, this capability allows mapping through the name server with the domain name as the pointer to all the relationships of the addresses: X.25, ISDN, and IP. While experimental, these services hold enormous potential.

An experimental record added to the DNS by the Internet is the *RT* (route-through) record. The purpose of the RT record is to support a host that does not have its own WAN address. Its record identifies an intermediate host that can serve as the domain name for the host that does not have a WAN address. An example is ACME.COM.E164 (an ISDN number). ISO 7498.3 and X.213 (Annex A) describe a hierarchical structure for the network service access point (NSAP) address, and ISO 8348/DAD 2 (Draft Addendum 2) specifies the structure for the NSAP address. The address consists of four parts:

Initial domain part (IDP). Contains the authority format identifier (AFI) and the initial domain identifier (IDI).

Authority format identifier (AFI). Contains a two-digit value between 0 and 99. It identifies the IDI format (the authority responsible for the IDI values) and the syntax of the domain-specific part (DSP).

Initial domain identifier (IDI). Specifies the addressing domain and the network addressing authority for the DSP values. It is interpreted according to the AFI.

Domain-specific part (DSP). Contains the address determined by the network authority. It is an address below the second level of the addressing hierarchy. It can contain addresses of end-user systems on an individual subnetwork.

The NSAP RDATA record could then take the form of this type of address, with the number coded in accordance with the rules just explained. An example is ACME.COM.NSAP (an OSI NSAP number). Figure 4.9 illustrates a resource record, tying together several of the examples in the previous discussion. The top box shows the topology of two networks connected through a gateway (labeled G1). Host A is attached to network 128.11, as are workstations 1 and 2. Workstations 3 and 4 are attached to network 129.12. The Internet addresses are shown as 128.11 and 129.12 for the two networks. The local addresses are shown in the boxes next to the workstations, gateways, or hosts.

The bottom part of the figure shows the RRs for this domain. Note that this entry is written for pedagogical reasons and thus has been simplified, but it does contain the major parts of the records. The right part of the figure shows 11 notes, which describe the entries in the database. They are as follows:

Note 1. This describes the owner name as RD.ACME.COM. The IN identifies the class as the Internet. The SOA defines the type of RR record as the start of a zone authority. The right-most part of this line describes the first entry into the RDATA field for the SOA record. The name HOSTA.RD.ACME.COM. describes the first field of the SOA RDATA segment called MNAME.

Note 2. The value of 30 is in the SERIAL field.

Note 3. The value of 3600 describes (in seconds) the time allotted to REFRESH the zone. This zone is to be refreshed every 60 minutes.

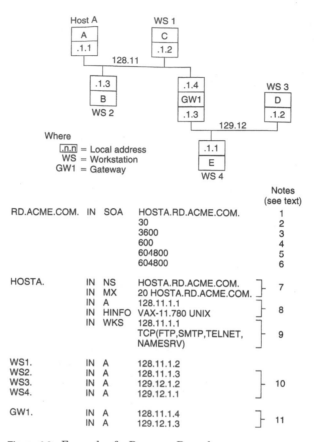

Figure 4.9   Example of a Resource Record.

Note 4.   The value of 600 describes the interval before a failed REFRESH must be reattempted. In this example, the value is 10 minutes.

Note 5.   The value of 604800 specifies an upper limit (in seconds) on the time that can elapse before the zone is no longer considered authoritative. This value translates into one week.

Note 6.   This field describes the minimum TTL value that should be exported from this zone. The value is 604800 (one week).

Note 7.   This note describes two entries in the RR file. The NS identifies the authoritative name server as HOSTA.RD.ACME.COM. and the MX identifies the host for the mail exchange support operations. The precedence field of 20 is irrelevant because only one MX is identified.

Note 8. This note shows the entry to identify HOSTA and its address of 128.11.1.1. Entry A is an example of a *glue* record. It specifies the address of the server and is used when the server for a domain is inside that same domain. The HINFO provides information about the host.

Note 9. This line depicts a WKS RDATA entry. It establishes that host A, with an Internet address of 128.11.1.1, uses TCP to support the well-known services of FTP, SMTP, TELNET, and NAMESRV.

Note 10. Four entries exist to define the Internet addresses for workstations 1, 2, 3, and 4.

Note 11. This note shows the two Internet addresses for the gateway: 128.11.1.4 and 129.12.1.3.

The structure of the DNS permits a relatively simple and easy addition of entries into the RR database. For example, assume that the networks depicted in Figure 4.9 are connected to another network. This network has its own name server for its zone. All you must do to reflect this additional interconnection is to add the entry of the name server to the local domain's name server database and reference the other network by its specific name server. The entries would use NS and A type records to indicate that the server on the other network is the authority for the newly connected network. Consequently, queries for that network would be directed to the identified name server. The new configuration is shown in Figure 4.10 along with the resulting code in the local name server database. Workstations, etc. are not shown on the new network for purposes of simplicity.

DNS Messages

Figure 4.11 shows the format of a DNS message. These messages are transferred between name servers to update the RRs. Consequently, some of the fields in the message are similar to the RR formats discussed in the previous section.

As indicated in the figure, the DNS message consists of five major sections. The *header* (which is always present) contains fields about the nature of the query and response (more about all of these fields shortly). The *question* section contains the data used to pose a query to the name server. The *answer* section contains the values of the RRs retrieved in response to the questions. The *authority* section contains RRs that point to the authoritative name server. The *additional record* section contains RRs to assist in the query; these RRs are not specifically related to the answers to the question.

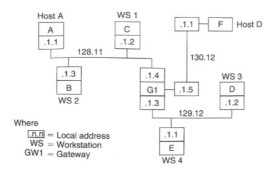

Where
- [n.n] = Local address
- WS = Workstation
- GW1 = Gateway

—Code added to name server database:

TRN.ACME.COM.	IN	NS	HOSTD.TRN.ACME.COM.
HOSTD.TRN.ACME.COM.	IN	A	130.12.1.1.
GW1.	IN	A	130.12.1.5

Figure 4.10 Adding Another Network and Server to the Database.

Header
Question
Answer
Authority
Additional

Figure 4.11 Format for the DNS Message.

Figure 4.12 shows the format of the header section. The first field is the *ID* field, which consists of 16 bits. This identifier is used with both the query and reply to match the two together. The *QR* field is a one-bit field that specifies whether this message is a query (value of 0) or a response (value of 1).

The *opcode* consists of four bits that contain the following information and values: 0 = standard query, 1 = inverse query, 2 = server status request, and 3 to 15 = reserved.

The *AA* (authoritative answer) bit is turned on (a value of 1) for a response and identifies that the responding name server is the recognized authority for the domain name being queried. The *TC* (trunca-

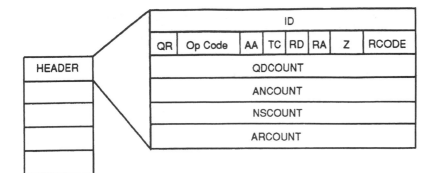

Figure 4.12 The DNS Message Header.

tion) bit is turned on to notify that this message was truncated because it was too long. The truncation depends on the length of the data unit permitted on the transmission link. The *RD* (recursion desired) bit is set to 1 to direct the name server to perform a recursive query. The *RA* (recursion available) bit is used in a response message to indicate if a recursive query capability is available in the name server. The three *Z* bits are reserved for future use.

The *rcode* consists of four bits, which are set to the following values:

0. No error occurred.

1. A format error has occurred and the name server is unable to interpret the query.

2. A problem has occurred at the name server.

3. A problem has occurred with the domain reference in the query; the server cannot find it.

4. The name server does not support this type of query.

5. The name server cannot perform the operation for administrative or policy reasons.

6–15. These values are reserved for future use.

QDCount is a 16-bit value that specifies the number of entries in the question section, *ANCount* is a 16-bit value specifying the number of RRs in the answer section, *NSCount* is a 16-bit value that specifies the number of server resource records in the authority record section, and *ARCount* is a 16-bit field that specifies the number of resource records in the additional record section. These last four fields are used by the receiver of the message to determine how to interpret the boundaries of the four fields.

Figure 4.13 shows the formats for these four sections. The *question* section contains three entries. You learned earlier that this section carries the question of the query messages. *QName* contains the domain name. The format of the field consists of a length octet followed by the appropriate number of octets. *QType* specifies the type of the query. The values in this field can contain the values of the type field discussed in the previous section (see Table 4.1). *QClass* is the last field in the question section. It specifies the class of the query. Typically, this value would be IN for the Internet.

As shown in Figure 4.13, the *answer*, *authority*, and *additional* sections of the DNS message consist of the same format. The fields for this format are as follows:

NAME.   This field identifies the domain name associated with the resource record.

TYPE.   This field contains one of the RR type codes.

CLASS.   This field specifies the data class contained in the RDATA field.

TTL.   This is the time-to-live parameter discussed in the previous section.

RDLENGTH.   This field specifies the field length.

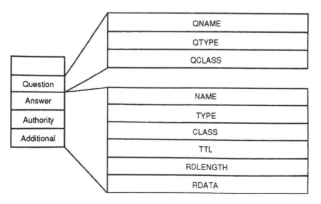

Figure 4.13   Formats for the Other Fields of the DNS Message.

RDATA. This field contains information associated with the resource. Its contents depend on the type and class of the resource record. For example, it could be an Internet address.

The *answer authority* and *additional* record sections contain a variable number of RRs. The contents and formats of these records were described earlier in conjunction with Figure 4.3.

RR Compression

It is likely that the exchange of RR messages entails duplicate domain names in succeeding occurrences of the traffic on the communications link. With this in mind, the DNS provides for message compression. The process is quite simple. Any duplicate domain name (or list of labels) is replaced with a pointer that identifies the previous occurrence of the traffic.

More Information on Names

NSLOOKUP

You might want to study RFC 1739, which contains information on NSLOOKUP. This routine is a name server program, available in many commercial and noncommercial TCP/IP software packages. You execute NSLOOKUP to examine entries in a DNS database that pertain to a particular host or domain; one common use is to determine a host system's IP address from its name or the host's name from its IP address. In addition to RFC 1739, refer to the user documentation on your specific software package.

Who is behind the name?

A routine called "whois" can be used to find out if a name is or is not being used. If the name is used, whois returns information on the entity (person, company, etc.) that owns the name and the contact information.

How to obtain a name

Contact Network Solutions (P.O. Box 17305, Baltimore, MD 21297-0525, billing at internic.net) to obtain a name.

The Berkeley Internet Name Domain (BIND)

BIND is the most widely used implementation of DNS, and is often available as part of a computer's operating system. The source code is free through anonymous FTP (ftp.uu.net) in /networking/ip/dns/bind/bind.4.8.3.tar.

Summary

The DNS provides the first international standard for name server protocols. It allows Internet users to map names to addresses and addresses to names. It also supports mailbox operations and stores host profiles about operating systems, hardware, and application architectures. Recent additions provide address and naming services for X.25 and ISDN systems. Many vendors now run DNS as part of their directory and naming services.

Chapter 5

The Internet Protocol

As discussed in Chapter 1, the Internet Protocol (IP) is a routing protocol developed by the Department of Defense. The system was implemented as part of the DARPA internetwork protocol project and is widely used throughout the world. This chapter examines IP in more detail, including its major features, its use of address and routing tables, and its relationships to other Internet, ISO, and IEEE protocols.

The last part of the chapter describes the new version of IP, which is called IP version 6, or IPv6. I will examine why the current IP (IPv4) is being revised and the rationale for the design of IPv6.

Major Features of IP

IP is quite similar to the ISO 8473 (connectionless network protocol, or CLNP), which is explained later in this chapter. Many of the ISO 8473 concepts were derived from IP.

IP is a simple connectionless service that provides no retransmisssion capabilities. It permits the exchange of traffic between two host computers without any prior call setup. (These two computers can, however, share a common connection-oriented transport protocol.) Datagrams can be lost between the two end users' stations. For example, the IP router enforces a maximum queue length size, and if this queue length is violated, the buffers will overflow. The additional datagrams are then discarded in the network. Thus, a higher-layer protocol (such as TCP) is essential to recover from these problems.

IP hides the underlying network from the end user. In this context, it creates a virtual network to the end user, allowing different types of networks to attach to an IP gateway. As a result, IP is reasonably simple to install and, because of its connectionless design, it is quite robust. But because IP is an unreliable, best-effort, datagram-type protocol, it has no reliability mechanisms. It provides no error recovery for the underlying networks and it has no flow-control mechanisms. The user data (datagrams) can be lost, duplicated, or even arrive out of order. It is not the job of IP to deal with most of these problems. As you will discover later, most of the problems are passed to the next higher layer, TCP.

IP supports fragmentation operations. The term *fragmentation* refers to an operation where a protocol data unit (PDU) is divided or segmented into smaller units. This feature can be quite useful because not all networks use the same size PDU. For example, X.25-based WANs typically employ a PDU (called a *packet* in X.25) with a data field of 128 octets. Some networks allow negotiations to a smaller or larger PDU size. The Ethernet standard limits the size of a PDU to 1500 octets. Conversely, proNET-10 stipulates a PDU of 2000 octets. Without fragmentation, a router would be tasked with trying to resolve incompatible PDU sizes between networks. IP solves the problem by establishing rules for fragmentation at the routers and reassembly at the receiving host.

IP and Networks

As shown in Figure 5.1, IP is designed to rest on top of the underlying network, as transparently as possible. This means that IP assumes little about the characteristics of the underlying network or networks. As stated earlier, from a design standpoint this tendency is quite attractive to engineers because it keeps the networks relatively independent of IP.

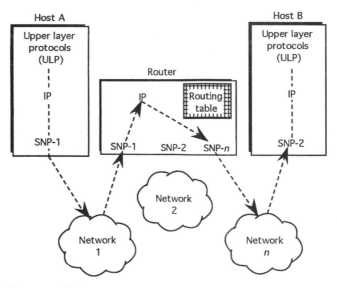

Figure 5.1 The IP/CLNP Model.

In Figure 5.1, as traffic (which consists of datagrams) is received at a router, the IP address is matched against a routing table. Based on the entries in the routing table, IP routes the datagram either to the next network or directly to the receiving host.

As you might expect, the transparency is achieved by encapsulation. The data sent by the host computer are encapsulated into an IP datagram, and the IP header identifies the address of the receiving host computer. The IP datagram and header are further encapsulated in the specific protocol of the transit network. For example, the transit network could be Frame Relay, ATM, or Ethernet.

After the transit network has delivered the traffic to an IP gateway, the router uses the destination address in the datagram header to determine where to route the traffic. Typically, it then passes the datagram to a subnetwork by invoking the network access protocol (for example, Ethernet on a LAN or X.25 on a WAN). This protocol encapsulates the datagram header and user data into the headers and trailers used by the network. This process is repeated at each router, and eventually the datagram arrives at the final destination, where it is delivered to the receiving station.

An IP router is not completely unconcerned with the access protocol of an attached network. There is nothing magic about IP; the router interface must know how to access its connected networks. Consequently, some form of communications (however limited) must occur between the router and the attached subnetworks (this is discussed in the section later in this chapter entitled *IP Service Definitions and Primitives*). The important point is that an IP module does not care about operations inside the networks.

The IP Datagram

A productive approach to analyzing IP is first to examine the fields in the IP datagram (PDU), depicted in Figure 5.2. An abbreviated description of the fields in the datagram is provided in Table 5.1.

The *version* field identifies the version of IP in use. Most protocols contain this field because some network nodes might not have the latest available release of the protocol. The current version is 4 and is referred to as IPv4 in various documents and standards.

The *header length* field contains four bits, set to a value that indicates the length of the datagram header. The length is measured in 32-bit words. Typically, a header without quality-of-service (QOS) options contains 20 octets. Therefore, the value in the length field is usually 5.

The *type of service* (TOS) field can identify several QOS functions provided for in an internet. It is quite similar to the service field that resides in the CLNP PDU. Transit delay, throughput, precedence, and reliability can be requested with this field.

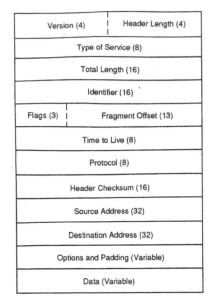

Version (4)	Header Length (4)
Type of Service (8)	
Total Length (16)	
Identifier (16)	
Flags (3)	Fragment Offset (13)
Time to Live (8)	
Protocol (8)	
Header Checksum (16)	
Source Address (32)	
Destination Address (32)	
Options and Padding (Variable)	
Data (Variable)	

(*n*) = Number of Bits in Field

Figure 5.2   IP Datagram.

TABLE 5.1   IP Protocol Data Unit.

Field	Description
Version	Identifies the version of IP
Internet header length	Specifies the length of the IP header
Type of service	Stipulates quality-of-service functions
Total length	Specifies the total length of the IP datagram, including the header
Identifier	Used with the address fields to identify the data unit uniquely (for fragmentation)
Flags	Used in fragmentation operations
Fragmentation offset	Describes where this datagram belongs within the original PDU
Time to live	Determines how many hops (nodes) the datagram can traverse
Protocol	Identifies a next-level protocol that is to receive the user data at the final destination
Header checksum	Performs an error check on the header
Source and destination addresses	Identifies the source and destination hosts and their directly attached networks
Options	Requests additional services for the IP user
Padding	Gives the datagram a 32-bit alignment
User data	Contains user data

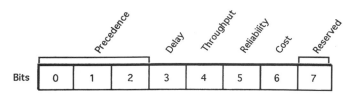

Figure 5.3 Type of Service (TOS) Field.

The TOS field is illustrated in Figure 5.3. It contains five entries consisting of eight bits. Bits 0, 1, and 2 contain a precedence value that indicates the relative importance of the datagram. The values range from 0 to 7, with 0 set to indicate a *routine precedence*. The precedence field is not used in all systems, although in some implementations the value of 7 indicates a network control datagram. The precedence field could, however, be used to implement flow control and congestion mechanisms in a network, allowing gateways and host nodes to make decisions about the order in which to discard datagrams in case of congestion.

The next three bits are used for other services. Bit 3 is the *delay bit* (D bit). When set to 1, this TOS requests a short delay through an internet. The aspect of delay is not defined in the standard, and the vendor must implement the service. The next bit is the *throughput bit* (T bit). It is set to 1 to request high throughput through an internet. Again, its specific implementation is not defined in the standard. The last bit used is the *reliability bit* (R bit), which allows a user to request high reliability for the datagram. The next two bits, 6 and 7, are not currently used.

The *cost bit* (C bit) is set to request a low-cost link (monetary cost). The last bit is not used at this time (it is reserved).

The TOS field is not used in some vendors' implementations of IP. Nonetheless, it will be used increasingly in the future as internet capabilities are increased. For example, it is used in the Open Shortest Path First (OSPF) protocol discussed in Chapter 8. Consequently, users should examine this field for future work and ascertain a vendor's use or intended support of this field.

The *total length* field specifies the total length of the IP datagram. It is measured in octets and includes the length of the header and the data. IP subtracts the header length field from the total length field to compute the size of the data field. The maximum possible length of a datagram is 65,535 octets (2 + >16 + 1 >). Routers that service IP datagrams are required to accept any datagram that supports the maximum size of a PDU of the attached networks. Additionally, all routers must accommodate datagrams of 576 octets in length.

The IP protocol uses three fields in the header to control datagram fragmentation and reassembly: *identifier*, *flags*, and *fragmentation offset.* The identifier field uniquely identifies all fragments from an original datagram. It is used with the source address at the receiving host to identify each fragment. The flags field contains bits to determine if the datagram can be fragmented. If it can be, one of the bits can be set to determine if a fragment is the last fragment of the datagram. The fragmentation offset field contains a value that specifies the relative position of the fragment to the original datagram. The value is initialized as 0 and is subsequently set to the proper number if the router fragments the data. The value is measured in units of eight octets. I will devote a special section later in this chapter to fragmentation and reassembly and the use of these three fields.

The *time-to-live* (TTL) parameter was intended (in the original IP design) to measure the time a datagram has been in an internet. It is quite similar to CLNP's lifetime field. Each router in an internet checks this field and discards it if the TTL value equals 0. A router is also required to decrement this field for each datagram it processes. In actual implementations, the TTL field is a number-of-hops value. Therefore, when a datagram proceeds through an IP node (a hop), the value in the field is decremented by a value of one. Implementations of IP might use a time counter in this field and decrement the value in one-second decrements.

The TTL field is used not only by the router to prevent endless loops, but also by the host to limit the lifetime that segments have in an internet. Be aware that if a host is acting as a router, it must treat the TTL field by the router rules. Check with the vendor to determine when a host throws away a datagram based on the TTL value. Ideally, the TTL value should be configured and its value assigned based on observing internet performance. Additionally, network management information protocols, such as the Simple Network Management Protocol (SNMP), might want to set the TTL value for diagnostic purposes. Finally, if your vendor uses a fixed value that cannot be reconfigured, make certain it allows for your internet's growth.

The *protocol* field identifies the next-layer protocol above the IP that is to receive the datagram at the final host destination. Refer back to Figure 3.9 in Chapter 3 for a review of this field. Internet standards groups have established a numbering system to identify the most widely used upper-layer protocols. Table 5.2 lists and describes some of these protocols.

The *header checksum* allows for detection of any distortions that might have occurred in the header. Checks are not performed on the user data stream. Some critics of IP have stated that the provision for error detection in the user data would allow the router at least to notify the sending host that problems have occurred. This service is indeed provided by a companion standard to IP, called the Internet Control Message Protocol (ICMP), which is discussed in Chapter 6.

TABLE 5.2   Internet Protocol Numbers (Examples)

Decimal	Key word	Protocol
0	—	Reserved
1	ICMP	Internet Control Message Protocol
2	IGMP	Internet Group Management Protocol
3	GGP	Gateway-to-Gateway Protocol
4	—	Unassigned
5	ST	Stream
6	TCP	Transmission Control Protocol
7	UCL	UCL
8	EGP	Exterior Gateway Protocol
9	IGP	Interior Gateway Protocol
10	BBN-MON	BBN-RCC Monitoring
11	NVP-II	Network Voice Protocol
12	PUP	PUP
13	ARGUS	ARGUS
14	EMCON	EMCON
15	XNET	Cross Net Debugger
16	CHAOS	Chaos
17	UDP	User Datagram Protocol
18	MUX	Multiplexing
19	DCN-MEAS	DCN Measurment Subsystems
20	HMP	Host Monitoring Protocol
21	PRM	Packet Radio Monitoring
22	XNS-IDP	XEROX NS IDP
23	TRUNK-1	Trunk-1
24	TRUNK-2	Trunk-2
25	LEAF-1	Leaf-1
26	LEAF-2	Leaf-2
27	RDP	Reliable Data Protocol
28	IRTP	Internet Reliable TP
29	ISO-TP4	ISO Transport Class 4
30	NETBLT	Bulk Data Transfer
31	MFE-NSP	MFE Network Services
32	MERIT-INP	MERIT Internodal Protocol
33	SEP	Sequential Exchange
34–60	—	Unassigned
61	—	Any host internal protocol
62	CFTP	CFTP
63	—	Any local network
64	SAT-EXPAK	SATNET and Backroom EXPAK
65	MIT-SUBN	MIT Subnet Support
66	RVD	MIT Remote Virtual Disk
67	IPPC	Internet Plur. Packet Core
68	—	Any distributed file system
69	SAT-MON	SATNET Monitoring
70	—	Unassigned
71	IPCV	Packet Core Utility
72–75	—	Unassigned
76	BRSAT-MON	Backroom SATNET Monitoring
77	—	Unassigned
78	WB-MON	Wideband Monitoring
79	WB-EXPAK	Wideband EXPAK
80–254	—	Unassigned
255	—	Reserved

Whatever one's view on the issue, the current approach keeps the checksum algorithm in IP quite simple. It does not need to operate on many octets, but it does require that a higher-level protocol at the receiving host perform an error check on the user data if the receiving host cares about its integrity.

IP carries two addresses in the datagram—the *source* and *destination* addresses—that remain the same value throughout the life of the datagram. These fields contain the Internet addresses examined in Chapter 3.

The *options* field identifies several additional services. As explained later, it is similar to the option part field of CLNP. The options field is not used in every datagram. Some implementations use this field for network management and diagnostics, and other do not use it at all.

Figure 5.4 illustrates the format of the options field. Table 5.3 contains the values currently defined in the standard. The options field length is variable because some options are of variable length. Each option contains three fields. The first field is coded as a single octet containing the option code. The option code also contains three fields, whose functions are as follows:

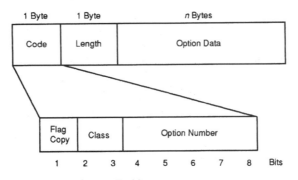

Figure 5.4 IP Option Field.

TABLE 5.3   Option Codes.

Class	Number	Length	Description
0	0	0	End of option list
0	1	0	No operation
0	2	11	Security
0	3	var	Loose source routing
0	7	var	Record route
0	8	4	Stream ID (obsolete)
0	9	var	Strict source routing
2	4	var	Internet time-stamp

- Flag Copy (one bit):

    0 = Copy option into only the first fragment of a fragmented data-gram

    1 = Copy option into all fragments of a fragmented datagram

- Class (two bits), which identifies the option class (Table 5.3):

    0 = User datagram or network control datagram

    1 = Reserved

    2 = Diagnostic purposes of debugging and measuring

    3 = Reserved

- Option Number, which identifies the option number (Table 5.3).

The next octet contains the length of the option. The third field contains the data values for the option. More detail about the option field is provided in the next section of this chapter.

The *padding* field can ensure that the datagram header aligns on an exact 32-bit boundary. Finally, the *data* field contains the user data. IP stipulates that the combination of the data field and the header cannot exceed 65,535 octets.

Major IP Services

This section reviews the major services of IP. Be aware that vendors have different products for IP and some of them might not support all the features described in this section. Indeed, some systems do not use the services provided in the options field. Later, I will explain some of the features in this field have been retained with IPv6.

Internet header check routine

When a router receives a datagram, it checks the header to determine the type of traffic it is processing. If the traffic is an internet datagram, it passes the datagram to the internet header check routine. This module then performs a number of editing and validity tests on the IP datagram header, checking for the following:

- Valid IP header length

- Proper IP version number

- Valid IP message length

- Valid IP header checksum

- Nonzero time to live field validity

If checks are performed and not passed, the datagram is discarded. If the checks are performed and passed, the internet destination address is examined to determine if the datagram is addressed to this router or destined for another router. If it is not destined for this gateway, the datagram is passed to the IP forwarding routine for further routing.

IP source routing

IP can use a mechanism called *source routing* as part of its routing algorithm. Source routing allows an upper-layer protocol (ULP) to determine how the IP routers route the datagrams. The ULP can pass a list of internet addresses to the IP module. The list contains the intermediate IP nodes to be traversed during the routing of the datagrams to the final destination. The last address on the list is the final destination of an intermediate node.

When IP receives a datagram, it uses the addresses in the source routing field to determine the next intermediate hop. As illustrated in Figure 5.5, IP uses a pointer field to learn about the next IP address. If a check of the pointer and length fields indicates that the list has been completed, the destination IP address field is used for routing. If the list is not exhausted, the IP module uses the IP address indicated by the pointer.

The IP module then replaces the value in the source routing list with its own address. It increments the pointer by one address (four bytes) for the next hop to retrieve the next IP address in the route. With this approach, the datagram follows the source route dictated by the ULP and records the route along the way.

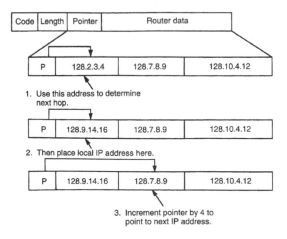

Figure 5.5 Source Routing.

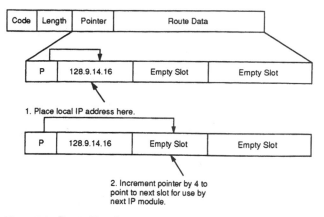

1. Place local IP address here.

2. Increment pointer by 4 to
point to next slot for use by
next IP module.

Figure 5.6   Route Routing.

Route recording

Figure 5.6 is an example of route recording. In the first step, IP uses
the pointer to locate the next address in the route data field. In this
example, it locates address 128.2.3.4 and makes a routing decision
based on the address. In the second step, it places its own address in
the route data field in the same location of the current destination
address. In the third step, it increments the pointer value to enable
the next IP module to determine the next (or final) hop in the route.

Routing operations

The IP router makes routing decisions based on the routing list. If the
destination host resides in another network, the IP router must
decide how to route to the other network. Indeed, if multiple hops are
involved in the communications process, then each router must be
traversed and the router must decide the route.

Each router maintains a routing table that contains the next node
(nn) on the way to the final destination network. In effect, the table
contains an entry for each reachable network. These tables can be
either static or dynamic, although dynamic tables are more common.
The IP module makes a routing decision on all datagrams it receives.

The routing table contains an IP address for each reachable network and the address of a neighbor router (that is, a router directly
attached to this network). The neighbor router is the shortest route to
the destination network. If no address exists for a neighbor router,

the IP router logic establishes that the router is directly connected to the network.

IP routing is usually based on a concept called *distance metric*, which is usually nothing more than the fewest hops between the router and the final destination. The router consults its routing table and attempts to match the destination network address contained in the IP header with a network entry contained in the routing table (a destination network entry). If no match is found, it discards the datagram and sends an ICMP message containing a "destination unreachable" code back to the IP source. If a match is found in the routing table, the router then uses it to determine the outgoing port.

Some implementations of TCP/IP have allowed a host to perform source route forwarding and to act as an intermediate hop through the full route. If you use a system in which a host performs source routing, the host should adhere to all the rules of a conventional router in managing source-routed datagrams. Again, I make this point to emphasize that the task of the host in any type of router function should be commensurate with the router, and the software should not be scaled down for purposes of efficiency. For example, the TTL field must be decremented by the host. The host should be able to generate the ICMP destination-unreachable messages if the source route fails or in case fragmentation cannot be performed. The host must also be able to perform the time stamp option (discussed shortly) in accordance with the proper rules of an IP router.

Loose and strict routing

IP provides two options in routing datagrams to their final destination. The first, *loose* source routing, gives the IP modules the option of using intermediate hops to reach the addresses obtained in the source list, as long as the datagram traverses the nodes listed. Conversely, *strict* source routing requires that the datagram travel through only the networks whose addresses are indicated in the source list. If the strict source route cannot be followed, the originating host IP is notified with an error message. Both loose and strict routing require that the route recording feature be implemented.

Route recording option

The route recording option operates similarly to source routing, but also uses the recording feature just discussed. Thus, any IP module that receives a datagram must add its address to a route recording list. For the route recording operation to occur, the receiving IP module uses the pointer and length fields to determine if any space is available to record the route. If the route recording list is full, the IP module simply forwards the datagram without inserting its address. If it is not full, the pointer locates the first empty full-octet slot, the address is inserted, and the IP module then increments the pointer to the next IP slot.

The time stamp option

Another option in IP is the provision for time-stamping the datagram as it traverses each IP module through an internet. This idea allows a network manager to determine not only the route of the datagram through the internet but also the time at which each IP module processed the datagram. This capability can be useful in determining the efficiency of routers, networks, and routing algorithms.

The format for the options fields for time stamp operations is shown in Figure 5.7. As with previous options, the length and pointer fields identify the proper slot in which to place an IP address *and* the time stamp that is related to this address. The pointer therefore increments itself across an IP address and the time stamp for the address. The *oflw* field is used only when an IP module cannot register a time stamp because of, for example, a lack of resources or a too-small option field. This value is incremented by each module that encounters this problem.

A four-bit flags field provides guidance to each IP module about the time stamp operations. The values of this field are as follows:

0. Only time stamps are to be recorded and stored in consecutive 32-bit words.

1. Each time stamp is to be preceded by the IP address of the relevant module.

3. IP addresses are already specified by the originator, and the router is tasked with recording the time stamp in its relevant IP address area.

The time used with the time stamp is based on milliseconds (ms) using universal time (previously called Greenwich mean time). Obviously, the use of universal time does not guarantee completely

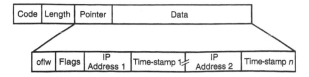

Figure 5.7   Time-Stamp Option.

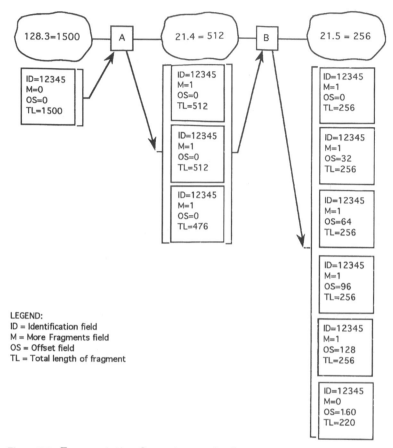

Figure 5.9 Fragmentation Operations at the Gateways.

unit into three smaller data units of 512, 512, and 476 octets. Thus, 1500 = 512 + 512 + 476. The last segment containing 476 octets is filled (padded) with zeros to equal a total size that is a multiple of 8. Therefore, this data field is 480 (480 = 476 + 4, which is an even multiple of 8).

Router A passes the data to subnetwork 21.4, which delivers it to router B. This router determines that datagram fragments are to be delivered to subnetwork 21.5. Because the router knows that this network uses a PDU size of 256 octets, it performs further fragmentation. It divides the 512-octet fragments into yet smaller data units and, using the offset values in the three incoming fragments, accordingly adjusts the offset values in the outgoing data units. Notice that the offset values are reset at router B, and their values are derived from the offset values contained in the preceding fragments.

Figure 5.10 illustrates the reassembly of the fragments, which occurs at the receiving host. The IP module sets up buffer space when the first

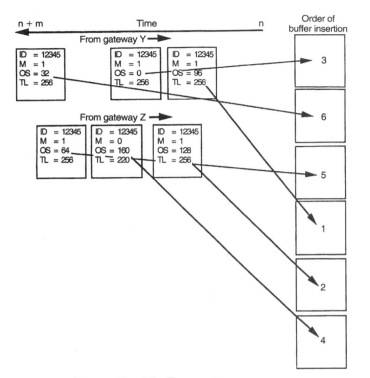

Figure 5.10 Reassembly of the Fragments.

fragment is received. A buffer is reserved for each fragment, and the fragment is placed in an area within the buffer relative to its position in the original datagram. As the fragments arrive, they are placed into the proper location in the buffer (pigeonholing). When all the fragments have been received, the IP module passes the data to the ULP in the same order that it was originally sent from the sending ULP.

For discussion purposes, assume that the datagram fragments depicted in Figure 5.9 are routed to other routers, say routers Y and Z. To continue the analysis, Figure 5.10 shows that the fragmented datagrams arrive from routers Y and Z in the order depicted by the "time arrow," with the earliest arrival at time n and the latest time of arrival being $n + m$. The fragments therefore arrive in the following order (using the offset values in the figure to identify the fragment):

First. Fragment with offset value of 96

Second. Fragment with offset value of 128

Third. Fragment with offset value of 0

Fourth. Fragment with offset value of 160

Fifth.   Fragment with offset value of 64

Sixth.   Fragment with offset value of 32

The receiving machine has a rather easy job of figuring out where the fragments are to be placed. The IP module simply multiplies the offset value by 8 to determine which slot in the buffer is to receive the fragment. For example, the first arriving fragment's relative position in the buffer is computed as $96 \times 8 = 768$, or memory address 768. (If you want to test the calculations, use position 0, not 1, as the first position.)

In Figure 5.10, the reassembling host does not know the length of the complete IP datagram until it receives the fourth fragment, which contains the $M = 0$ bit (no more fragments), the offset value, and the fragment length. Because the offset is 160 and the length is 220 octets, the host now knows that the total datagram is 1500 octets, or 160 offset values $\times$ 8 octets per value + 220 octets in final fragment.

You now see why the M bit is so important. Because the length field in the fragment does not refer to the size of the original datagram but to the size of the fragment, the only method of determining the original length (and the final fragment) is the $M = 0$ indicator.

If some fragments do not arrive or have been discarded because they exceeded the TTL parameter, IP discards the fragments of the partially reassembled datagram. In addition, upon detection of the first fragment's arrival, the receiving computer turns on a reassembly timer. This timer, which is set by the network manager, can ensure that all fragments arrive in a timely manner. If the timer times out before all fragments have arrived, the received fragments are discarded.

If fragmentation is not desired the fragment can be set flag to 1, which indicates that fragmentation must not occur. This might be desirable if fragmentation creates excessive overhead because the reassembly timer continues to discard fragments that require retransmission from higher-layer protocols. You must weigh this situation, however, against the fact that turning on the "don't fragment" flag means that datagrams will be discarded by routers if the MTU exceeds the size of the subnetwork capability.

Packet reassembly at the router.   Connectionless intermediate routers that use dynamic routing (such as IP) do not reassemble datagrams. The task is impossible because all fragments belonging to the original datagram might not be processed by the same routers. As a consequence, the router does not know how to compute the offset values for fragments it does not receive. In contrast, connection-oriented routers can perform intermediate reassembly because, by the very nature of the system, all PDUs pass through the same routers. For example, imagine in Figure 5.9 that router A is a connection-oriented router. It could reassemble the fragments for transmission over a higher-capacity subnetwork by detecting the M = 0 in the fragment, as well as the offset value of 128 and length of 476, or 1500 octets (128 offset values × 8 octets per offset + 476 octets in final fragment).

Fragments retained upon retransmission of other fragments. Several papers have expressed concern about IP discarding fragments based on the expiration of the fragmentation timer. In some instances, this discarding can create significant replicated traffic on a network. The following brief discussion, however, should shed some light on the problem. First, assume that discarded fragments are retransmitted by a higher-layer protocol (e.g., TCP). The traffic is fragmented (once again) by the originator and sent to the receiver. The retransmitted fragments contain the same values in the IP identification field as the original submission. Assuming that the receiver's software does not discard the fragments acceptable in the original transmission, one could argue that the identification field could reconstruct a complete data unit by using the fragments of the retransmissions. Of course, if a pigeonhole is full, the received duplicate fragment would be discarded. A brief analysis shows that it is not worth the effort. Filling vacant pigeonholes with retransmitted fragments is almost pure chance because some of the retransmitted fragments might undergo different fragmentation operations because the fragments were routed differently the second time. It is especially onerous if the transmitting end must determine which fragments should be transmitted and which should not. Making IP this smart also makes IP more complicated, which should be avoided. Also, be aware that the reassembly timeout is based on the remaining value of the TTL field in the IP header. This value does not work very well because the vast majority of TTL values are implemented with a hop-count metric rather than a time metric. Implementation of the reassembly timeout should therefore be based on an actual clock.

Before leaving the subject of the options within IP, let us reexamine the flag copy feature (shown in Figure 5.4). A network administrator should determine if the flag copy can be used for certain options. For example, is it useful for all fragments to have the route-recording option? After all, if these fragments move through different routes in an internet, the receiver might have difficulty determining a single list of routes. On the other hand, such a feature still does not preclude examining the routes to determine the efficiency of the internet routers and IP modules. For purposes of simplicity, however, it might make sense (and the IP standard so requires) to stipulate that a route recording option is used in only one of the fragments of a fragmented datagram.

Next, consider when the option should be copied into all fragments. One situation that comes to mind is source routing. If the user wants source routing to be applied to a datagram, it is logical to assume the user wants it applied to all fragments of a fragmented datagram.

IP Address and Routing Tables

IP uses routing and address tables to send data through an internet. Routing tables store routes within them, and address tables store the individual addresses of entities within a network. Both types of tables are discussed in the following subsections.

Address tables

The Internet Activities Board (IAB) has published the definition for the IP address table in RFC 1213. I will use this RFC as an example of an address table; actual implementations vary. This table is depicted in Figure 5.11; it consists of five columns and anywhere from one to n rows. Each row pertains to an IP address at an entity (a host, router, etc.). More than one row entry can exist if the machine has more than one IP address. The contents of this table are as follows:

Entry address.   Contains the IP address for this entry's interface.

Entry ifIndex.   Contains the interface number (port number) pertaining to this entity's connection to a subnetwork.

Entry net mask.   Column contains the subnet mask associated with the IP address in the entry address column.

	Entry Address	Entry IfIndex	Entry Net Mask	Broadcast Address	Maximum Size of Datagram
Address Entry 1					
Address Entry 2					
Address Entry n					

Figure 5.11   IP Address Table.

Broadcast address. Contains a value for the least-significant bit in the IP broadcast address. It is used for sending datagrams on the local interface and is associated with the IP address of this row.

Maximum size of datagram. Columns represents the maximum size of a datagram that can be processed by this IP module.

Routing tables

Until 1990, an IP routing table was designed based on an individual vendor's perception of the need for the entries in the table. With the publication of the Internet Management Information Base (MIB), a more formal definition of the IP routing table is now available. Figure 5.12 shows the IP routing table as defined in the MIB standard, which was published as RFC 1213. But as with the address table, actual implementations might vary.

Each row of the IP routing table contains an entry for each route that is known to the IP module storing this table. The columns represent the information available on each route. A brief description of each column follows:

- The *destination* entry contains the IP address of the destination for this route. If this column is coded as 0.0.0.0, the route is considered a default route.

- The *ifIndex* entry stands for the interface index. It identifies the local interface (more commonly known as a physical port) through which the next hop in the route can be reached.

- The next five columns are labeled *metric*. The metric entries contain information about the cost metric used for determining the route. With most systems, the cost metric is the number of hops to

	Destination	IfIndex	Metric 1	Metric 5	Next Hop	Route Type	Routing Protocol	Route Age	Routing Mask	Route Information
Route 1										
Route 2										
Route 3										
Route *n*										

Figure 5.12 One Possibility for IP Routing Table.

Datagram address.	10101100 - 00010001 - 00000101 - 00001000			
Mask.	11111111 - 11111111 - 11111111 - 11100000			
Result.	172	17	20	4
Table address.	10101100 - 00010001 - 00000101 - 00001000			
Mask.	11111111 - 11111111 - 11111111 - 11100000			
Result.	172	17	5	0

This process continues until the table has been examined. Eventually, a match is made if a valid entry exists. The following is a summary of the operations.[1]

1. Apply the mask to the destination IP address in the IP datagram header and the destination IP address in the route table.
2. Determine the longest matches by which IP addresses have the most specific route mask.
3. If the TOS field is used, find the closest match to the TOS field in the IP datagram header.
4. Select the best remaining entry in the route table that has the best route to the destination IP address.

IP Service Definitions and Primitives

IP uses two primitives to define the services it provides to the adjacent ULP. The transmitting ULP uses the SEND primitive to request the services of IP. In turn, IP uses the DELIVER primitive to notify the destination ULP of the arrival of data. The interface of IP with the upper layer is quite simple because IP is designed to operate with diverse ULPs.

IP/ULP primitives

IP's service definitions (implemented with primitives) are somewhat abstract, which allows them to be tailored to the specific host operating system. For example, the SEND and RECV services on a UNIX-based system can be implemented with UNIX system library calls (see Chapter 13).

---

[1]For more about IP addressing and address resolution, I recommend *TCP/IP Addressing*, by Buck Graham, AP Professional Press, 1997.

The relationship of IP and the ULP is shown in Figure 5.13, which depicts host A sending data to host B. The arrows are reversed if host B sends data to host A. The parameters associated with the primitives inform the ULP and IP about the operation requested from the ULP (SEND) and performed by IP (RECV).

The SEND parameters are also used to create the IP header. Consequently, they correlate closely to the IP header fields of a transmitted datagram, shown in Figure 5.2. Likewise, the parameters in the RECV primitive correlate closely to the parameters of the received datagram. The SEND primitive contains the following information:

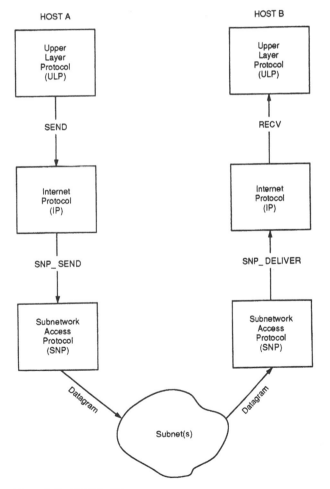

Figure 5.13 IP Primitives.

Source address.   IP address of the host sending the data

Destination address.   IP address of host to receive the data

Protocol.   Name of the recipient ULP (e.g., TCP or UDP)

TOS indicators.   Relative transmission quality associated with unit of data: precedence, reliability, delay, and throughput

Identifier.   Optional, for fragmentation control

"Don't fragment" indicator.   Yes or no

Time to live.   In number of hops

Data length.   Length of data being transmitted (0 if no data)

Buffer pointer.   Pointer to the datagram

Option data.   Options requested by a ULP (security, loose or strict source routing, record routing, stream identification, or time stamp)

Data.   Present when data length is greater than 0

Result.   Result of this SEND request; either (1) datagram sent or (2) error in arguments or network error

The RECV primitive contains the following information:

Source address.   IP address of sending host

Destination address.   IP address of recipient host

Protocol.   Name of recipient ULP as supplied by the sending ULP (e.g., TCP or UDP)

TOS indicators.   Relative transmission quality associated with unit of data: precedence, reliability, delay, and throughput

Data length.   Length of received data

Buffer pointer.   Pointer to the datagram

Option data.   Options requested by source ULP (security, loose or strict source routing, record routing, stream identification, or time stamp)

Data. Present when data length is greater than 0

Result. Result of this RECV request

IP/SNP primitives

The primitives between IP and the subnetwork access protocol (SNAP) are similar to the IP/ULP primitives. As shown in Figure 5.13, two primitives are invoked for the IP/SNP operations. The SNP_SEND primitive is used by IP to invoke a service of the SNP; the SND_DELIVER is used by SNP to deliver a datagram to the IP module. The SNPSEND primitive contains the following information:

Local destination address. Subnetwork address of the destination

TOS indicators. Relative transmission quality associated with unit of data: precedence, reliability, delay, and throughput

Datagram The SNP_DELIVER primitive contains the datagram and error indicators (the latter is optional and not defined in the standard).

Other IP/SNP service definitions

Many IP modules rest on top of IEEE LANs and interface with IEEE 802.2 (logical link control, or LLC). Figure 3.5 in Chapter 3 explains the method by which LLC and IP use the LSAP header extension to coordinate their operations. As of this writing, no RFC exists to explain the relationship of IEEE 802.2 LLC primitives and IP. The next section provides this explanation.

Network layer/LLC primitives

The IP/SNP primitives explained in the previous section are not designed for the LLC interface. If an implementation uses only the LLC connectionless data transfer service, the interface is simple. A brief explanation of this service follows (see Figure 5.14).

Two primitives are used for connectionless data transfer. They are passed between LLC and its upper-layer protocol (which could be IP or some other module):

DL-UNITDATA.request. Source address, destination address, data, priority

DL-UNITDATA.indication. Source address, destination address, data, priority

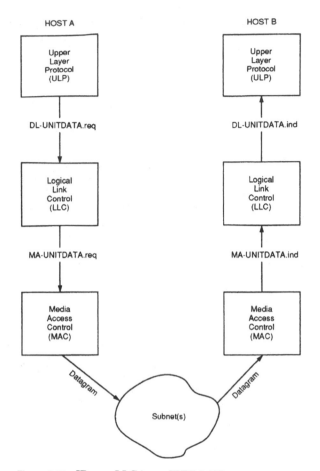

Figure 5.14   IP over LLC in an IEEE LAN.

The request primitive is passed from the network layer to LLC to request that a link service data unit (LSDU) be sent to a remote link service access point. The address parameters are equivalent to a combination of the LLC SAP and MAC addresses. The priority field is passed to the media access control (MAC) and implemented (except for 802.3, which has no priority mechanism). The indication primitive is passed from LLC to the network layer to indicate the arrival of an LSDU from a remote entity.

A comparison of Figures 5.13 and 5.14 reveals close similarities between IP/SNP and ULP/LLC operations, but differences do exist in the parameters associated with the IP/SNP and ULP/LLC primitives.

If IP is placed on top of LLC, a convergence protocol must be implemented to map the SNP_SEND primitive and its parameters to the DL-UNITDATA.request and its parameters. The protocol must also map the SNP_DELIVER primitive and its parameters to the LLC DL-UNITDATA.indication and its parameters. The address fields present no major problem if RFC 1042 is followed (see Chapter 2, *Extension of LSAP Header*). A potential problem, however, is in deciding how to handle the TOS parameters. Perhaps the best approach is to ignore them at the LLC and MAC levels, as they are mostly irrelevant for use in a high-capacity LAN.

Multicasting

The Internet network layer supports multicasting. The concept is quite similar to LAN multicasting, in which a single PDU (in this case an IP datagram) is sent to more than one host. The set of hosts forms a *multicast* group.

IP multicasting allows hosts to operate on one or multiple physical networks. A host might belong to more than one multicast group or a permanent multicast group (a *well-known* group), or it can dynamically enter and leave groups as the need dictates. Also, a host does not have to be a member of the multicast group to send data to the group.

Multicasting is accomplished through the use of the IP class D address, discussed in Chapter 3. The first four bits of the 32-bit address field are set to 1110; the next 28 bits identify the specific multicast group. Because of the structure of the address space, the classes of A, B, and C addresses are meaningless with multicasting.

The permissible ranges for multicast addresses are from 224.0.0.0 through 239.255.255.255. The Internet does not allow the address space of 224.0.0.0 to be used, and the address space of 224.0.0.1 is reserved for an *all-hosts* group. An all-hosts group identifies all hosts and routers, participating in an internet IP multicast operation.

Figure 5.15 shows an example of how IP multicasting operates. Router 1 (R1) receives an IP datagram from another part of an internet. The destination IP address is a multicast address (a source address is not allowed to contain multicast values, for obvious reasons). The router is responsible for interpreting the multicast address and forwarding it to the proper hosts (for which it has authority) and to other participating multicast routers (R2). In this example, hosts A, C, and E are members of the same multicast group. R2 and host F are also members.

One approach to sending this traffic to the proper host on a LAN is to map the IP multicast address to an Ethernet multicast address. The mapping is quite simple and proceeds as follows: The low-order 23 bits of the IP address are mapped into the low-order 23 bits of the Ethernet multicast address. This approach is not perfect because a one-to-one relationship does not exist between the 28 bits of the IP address and the 23 bits of the Ethernet address. It is a reasonable

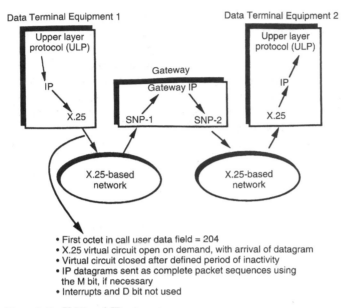

Data Terminal Equipment 1   Data Terminal Equipment 2

• First octet in call user data field = 204
• X.25 virtual circuit open on demand, with arrival of datagram
• Virtual circuit closed after defined period of inactivity
• IP datagrams sent as complete packet sequences using
  the M bit, if necessary
• Interrupts and D bit not used

Figure 5.17 X.25 and IP.

The X.25 packet switch must react to datagrams on demand and create a virtual circuit when a datagram arrives. RFC 877 does not define the details of how IP addresses are mapped to corresponding X.25 data terminal equipment (DTE) addresses, nor does it define how long the virtual circuit remains open if no activity occurs from IP. The standard requires that the first octet in the X.25 call user data field be coded to decimal 204 (binary 11001100). This value identifies the IP.

IP datagrams are sent as complete packet sequences and, if necessary, the M bit is used to ensure that if the IP datagram is fragmented, it can be reassembled properly at the other end. Either user can close the virtual circuit at any time. Upper-layer protocols such as TCP, SNA path control, and UDP are not affected by this implementation scheme.

IP, Frame Relay, and ATM

A common practice is to use Frame Relay and ATM networks to route IP datagrams between hosts. These operations are becoming commonplace and are discussed in more detail in Chapter 14.

Other Thoughts on IP

You might be surprised at the brevity of this discussion of IP. I am not shirking my responsibility in the analysis; rather, I am merely reflecting the fact that IP does not contain a great number of functions. Indeed, one of the attractive aspects of IP is its simplicity and efficiency. You might surmise, however, that the protocols that support IP (such as TCP) and the addressing resolution and naming service protocols, discussed in earlier chapters, provide for a complex and rich internetworking environment.

Earlier chapters stated that IP is one of the most widely used routing protocols in the world. Today, hundreds of products are available in the marketplace that use the IP architecture. Nonetheless, the use of IPv4 will diminish as users and vendors move to another version of IP (IPv6) in order to overcome the limitations of the IP address space (this protocol is discussed shortly).

Classless Interdomain Routing (CIDR)

Chapter 3 stated that the internet IP address organization was changed in 1993. With this change, the concept of a class for an IP address is dropped, hence the term *classless routing*. Routing is conducted on a variable-length part of the IP address. In addition, IP numbers are to be assigned on the basis of topology to make CIDR concepts more effective. The change means that IP addresses must now be assigned based on where the IP user is connected into the Internet. The end result of CIDR will be to extend the length of time that the current IP address can be used. It also places more restrictions on the assignment of class B addresses and will increase the use of class C addresses. One final point is noteworthy. Blocks of class C addresses are released (delegated) to Internet service providers (ISPs), and it is the user's task to obtain an IP number from the appropriate service provider. For more information, read RFC 1466 and RFC 1481.

Connectionless-Mode Network Service (ISO 8473)

ISO 8473 is a specification that describes the architecture for connectionless-mode network service, also called the connectionless network protocol (CLNP). It is quite similar to IP in the functions it performs, but it is not compatible with IP.

ISO 8473 is designed to operate with the hosts attached to public and private networks and the routers that service hosts and networks. The protocol does not involve itself with the particular characteristics of underlying subnetworks. Like IP, the basic idea is to demand little in the way of services from the subnetworks, except to transport the PDU.

The protocol communicates by exchanging internetwork PDUs (IPDUs) in a connectionless (datagram) fashion. Each IPDU is treated independently and does not depend on the state of the network for any particular establishment connection time (because no connection exists in a connectionless network). Routing decisions are made independently by each forwarding internetworking node. It is also possible for the source user to determine the routing by placing the routing information in the IPDU source routing field.

The ISO 8473 connectionless-mode network service is provided by two primitives: N-UNITDATA.request and N-UNITDATA.indication. These two primitives are quite similar to the primitives used by the IP. Note that the protocol uses no connection and clear primitives, which is a rather obvious indication of its connectionless attributes. The two primitives each contain four parameters:

- NS-source-address
- NS-destination-address
- NS-quality-of-service
- NS-userdata

The ISO 8473 PDU

A brief description of the fields of the 8473 PDU is provided in Table 5.5. As you review this material, you will see the similarity to the IP datagram. Figure 5.18 shows the format of the data unit. The following sections discuss how the fields are used in 8473 operations.

Quality-of-service functions

An underlying subnetwork can provide several quality-of-service (QOS) functions. The services are negotiated when the primitives are exchanged between layers. Of course, the primitive parameters must be based on *a priori* knowledge of the availability of the services within the subnetwork. It does little good to ask for a QOS feature if the subnetwork does not provide it. Be aware that the values of QOS apply to both ends of the network connection (NC), even though the NC spans several subnetworks that offer different services.

For QOS choices, ISO 8473 uses the following QOS functions, described in ISO 8348:

Transit delay.   Establishes the elapsed time between a data request and the corresponding data indication. This QOS feature applies only to successful PDU transfers. The delay is specified by a desired value, up to the maximum acceptable value. All values assume a PDU of 128 octets. User-initiated flow control is not measured in these values.

TABLE 5.5   Functions of Fields in the ISO 8473 PDU.

Protocol identifier	Identifies the protocol as ISO 8473
Length indicator	Describes the length of the header.
Version/protocol	Identifies the version of ISO 8473.
Lifetime	Represents the lifetime of the PDU. It is coded in units of 500 ms.
Segmentation permitted	Indicates if segmentation is permitted. The originator of the PDU determines this value, and it cannot be changed by any other entity.
More segments	Indicates if more user data is forthcoming. It is used when segmentation takes place. When the bit equals 0, it indicates that the last octet of the data in this PDU is the last octet of the user data stream (the network service data unit, NSDU).
Error report	Indicates that an error report is to be generated back to the originator if a data PDU is discarded.
Type code	Describes the PDU as a data PDU or an error PDU.
PDU segment length	Specifies the length of the PDU (header and data). If no segmentation occurs, the value of this field is identical to the value of the total length field.
Checksum	Calculated on the entire PDU header. A value of 0 in this field indicates that the header is to be ignored. A PDU is discarded if the checksum fails.
Destination and source addresses and address lengths	Because the source and destination addresses are variable in length, the length fields are used to describe their length The actual addresses are network service access points (NSAPs).
Data unit identifier	Identifies an initial PDU to reassemble a segmented data unit correctly.
Segmentation offset	If the original PDU is segmented, this field specifies the relative position of this segment in relation to the initial PDU.
Total PDU length	Contains the entire length of the original PDU which includes both the header and data. It is not changed for the lifetime of the PDU.
Options	Optional parameters are placed in this part of the PDU such as route recording, quality-of-service parameters, priorities, buffer congestion indication, padding characters, and designation of security levels.
Data	Contains the user data

Residual error rate (RER). Ratio of total incorrect, lost, or duplicated PDUs to total PDUs transferred:

$$RER = \frac{N(e) + N(1) - N(x)}{N}$$

where RER = residual error rate, $N(e)$ = PDUs in error, $N(1)$ = lost PDUs, $N(x)$ = duplicate PDUs, and N = number of PDUs.

Cost determinants. Defines the maximum acceptable cost for a network service. It can be stated in relative or absolute terms. Final actions on this parameter are left to the specific network provider.

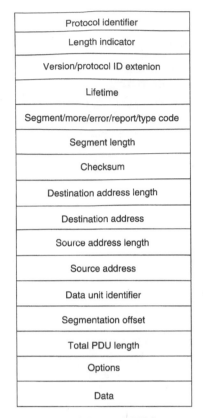

| Protocol identifier |
| Length indicator |
| Version/protocol ID extenion |
| Lifetime |
| Segment/more/error/report/type code |
| Segment length |
| Checksum |
| Destination address length |
| Destination address |
| Source address length |
| Source address |
| Data unit identifier |
| Segmentation offset |
| Total PDU length |
| Options |
| Data |

Figure 5.18   ISO 8473 PDU format.

Priority.   Determines preferential service in the subnetwork. Outgoing transmission queues and buffers are managed based on the priority values contained in the PDU header options field.

Protection against unauthorized access.   Directs the subnetwork to prevent unauthorized access to user data.

Protocol functions

ISO 8473 includes several optional and required protocol functions. Each function provides a specialized service to the network user. In a sense, the ISO 8473 protocol functions are similar to the QOS features, except that they are performed as an integral part of the protocol.

Traffic management between subnetworks

This section illustrates how a connectionless-mode internetwork protocol transfers data between subnetworks. While different vendors use various techniques to provide connectionless service, many use the concepts described herein.

When the protocol receives the NS-source-address and NS-destination-address parameters in the N-UNITDATA.request primitive from an upper layer, it uses them to build a source address and destination address in the header of the PDU. The NS- source-address and NS-quality-of-service parameters are used to determine which optional functions are to be selected for the network user. At this time, a data unit identifier is assigned to identify this request from other requests. This identifier remains unique for the lifetime of the initial PDU and any segmented PDUs in the networks. Subsequent or derived PDUs are considered to correspond to the initial PDU if they have the same source address, destination address, and data unit identifier. At first glance, this rule might appear to be connection-oriented, but it applies only to PDUs created as a result of segmentation.

The PDU is then forwarded through the subnetworks. Each hop examines the destination address to determine if the PDU has reached its destination. If the destination address equals a network service access point (NSAP) served by the network entity, it has reached its destination. Otherwise, it must be forwarded to the next node.

When the PDU reaches its destination, the receiver removes the protocol control information (PCI) from the PDU. It also uses the addresses in the header to generate the NS-source-address and NS-destination-address parameters of the UNITDATA indication primitive. It preserves the data field of the PDU until all segments (if any) have been received. The options field of the PDU header is used to invoke any QOS parameters at the receiving end.

Unlike connection-oriented networks, an ISO 8473 connectionless-mode network is more flexible in terminating service to a user. For example, if a new network connection request is received that has a higher priority than an ongoing data transfer, the network can release the lower-priority transfer. Moreover, users can establish priorities for data transfers. Network connections with a higher priority have their requests serviced first, then the remaining resources of the network attempt to satisfy the lower-priority network connections.

User data is given a specific *lifetime* in the network(s). This mechanism is useful for several reasons. First, it prevents lost or misdirected data from accumulating and consuming network resources. Second, it gives the transmitting entity some control over the disposition of aged data units. Third, it greatly simplifies congestion control,

First, of course, is the limited IP address space. Various estimates have been made about when the 32-bit space will be used up. Regardless of the exact time, it will indeed become exhausted. Second, a number of operations in IPv4 are inefficient and are not used due to their overhead. Third, much as been learned about data networks since the inception of IPv4, and many IPv6 features take advantage of this knowledge.

The design philosophy behind IPv6

IPv6 is designed to overcome the limitations of IPv4. As I mentioned earlier, the major design philosophy behind IPv6 is to extend the IP address base and, at the same time, to make the protocol simpler to use and more efficient in its operations. Clearly, its intent is to migrate from a data-specific protocol to a multiservice protocol. However, it was emphasized throughout the design process that IPv4 had been quite successful and most of the characteristics were being retained. Additionally, IPv6 is designed to be complementary to other related protocols that have been developed or are in development at the writing of this book. These protocols concern themselves with the support of voice, video, data, or other traffic through an internet.

Before analyzing the IPv6 datagram, I need to describe the rationale for the very large address space of 128 bits. Many proposals pertaining to the size of the address space were placed before the Internet Engineering Task Force. These deliberations began in 1992, with the final completion of the specification in 1995. In essence, the IPv6 designers held fast to the notion that the Internet should be able to connect anyone on earth who wants to connect through it. Since IPv6 is positioned for the future, various estimates were made as to how many people would be on the planet in the next century. The study projected growth to 2020. In addition, with the proliferation of computers into many people's lives, it was essential that the IP address space accommodate the probability of one person using multiple computers. Some studies hypothesize that in the future perhaps one person could use as many as 100 computers. This might seem far-fetched, but remember that computers are inculcating themselves into almost every facet of our lives. Computers run in our watches and even in our automobiles. LANs run underneath our automobile hood, and all these components need addresses in order to function properly. At any rate, the value of 2^{128} was believed to be sufficient for long-term growth in order to accommodate approximately 10 billion people (projections to the year 2020), with each person accessing at least 100 computers.

The IPv6 address

As stated earlier, the IPv6 address is 128 bits. The convention for writing the address is as four-bit integers, with each integer represented by a hexadecimal (hex) digit. The address is clustered as eight 16-bit integers (four hex digits), separated by colons. For example:

```
68DA:8909:3A22:FECA:68DA:8909:3A22:FECA
```

It is unlikely that initial implementations will use all 128 bits; some of them will be set to 0, as shown here:

```
68DA:0000:0000:0000:68DA:8909:3A22:FECA
```

You can shorten this notation by substituting four 0s in the hex 16-bit cluster, as follows:

```
68DA:0:0:0:68DA:8909:3A22:FECA
```

In addition, if more than one consecutive hex cluster of 16 bits is null, they can be replaced by two colons:

```
68DA::68DA:8909:3A22:FECA
```

In order to determine how many hex clusters have been substituted by the colons, you must examine how many hex clusters are in the notation and then simply fill in the 0000 sets to equal eight 16-bit integers. Consider the following:

```
68DA::8909:3A22:FECA = 68DA:0:0:0:0:8909:3A22:FECA
```

Since four 16-bit integers are present, the double colon represents four null sets. This convention restricts the double colon to being used in an address only once. That is, the address 0:0:0:FECA:68DA:0:0:0 can be coded as ::FECA:68DA:0:0:0 or 0:0:0:FECA:68DA::, but not ::0:FECA:68DA::.

Since the IPv4 address notation is in decimal (dot) form, IPv6 allows an IPv4 address to have the following notation:

```
::47.192.4.5
```

Hierarchical addresses

The point was made earlier in this chapter that hierarchical addresses are preferable to flat addresses, and IPv6 stipulates just such a hierarchical address format. The format of the address is coded with a prefix and contains the following five hierarchical subfields (listed in order):

Prefix (010).   Provider-based addresses

Registry ID.   Registry in charge of allocating addresses (the Internet NIC in the U.S.)

Provider ID.   Internet service provider (ISP)

Subnetwork ID.   Subscriber ID, which is obtained from the ISP

Subnetwork ID.   Subnetwork of the subscriber

Interface ID.   Host address on the subnetwork

Special addresses

Several special addresses are provided in IPv6 (which includes the standard prefix of 010). The coding rules for these addresses are provided in Table 5.6.

An unspecified address consists of all 0s, can be coded in a source address, and is used in situations where a station has not been config-

TABLE 5.6   Special Addresses.

Use	Special Prefix
0000 0000	Reserved
0000 0001	Unassigned
0000 001	ISO/ITU-T NSAP addresses
0000 010	IPX addresses
0000 011	Unassigned
0000 1	Unassigned
0000 10	Unassigned
0001	Unassigned
001	Unassigned
010	Provider-based unicast addresses
011	Unassigned
100	Geographic-based unicast addresses
101	Unassigned
110	Unassigned
1110	Unassigned
1111 0	Unassigned
1111 10	Unassigned
1111 110	Unassigned
1111 1110 0	Unassigned
1111 1110 10	Link local addresses
1111 1110 11	Site local addresses
1111 1111	Multicast addresses

ured with an address. A loopback address is 0:0:0:0:0:0:0:0:1, which allows a node to send a datagram to itself (for example, when the source and destination application reside in the same node).

OSI network service access points (NSAPs) and Novell IPX addresses are supported in IPv6 due to their wide use in other systems.

The site local address prefix is used if an organization wants to set up its own private addresses in its internet and cannot be employed in the Internet. Additionally, a node can be given a link local address is it has not been assigned a link local address or a provider-based address.

Like IPv4, IPv6 also supports unicasting and multicasting, and IPv6 adds additional functionality to multicasting. For example, the multicast address contains a field to limit the scope of the multicast operation to a local site, local link, global, etc.

The IPv6 datagram

Figure 5.19 illustrates the IPv6 datagram. This section describes each field in the datagram, and the next section compares the IPv6 fields with the fields in the IPv4 datagram.

The header consists of a 64-bit control field followed by a 128-bit source address and a 128-bit destination address. This initial 64 bits are:

- Version field, 4 bits
- Priority field, 4 bits
- Flow label field, 24 bits
- Payload length, 16 bits

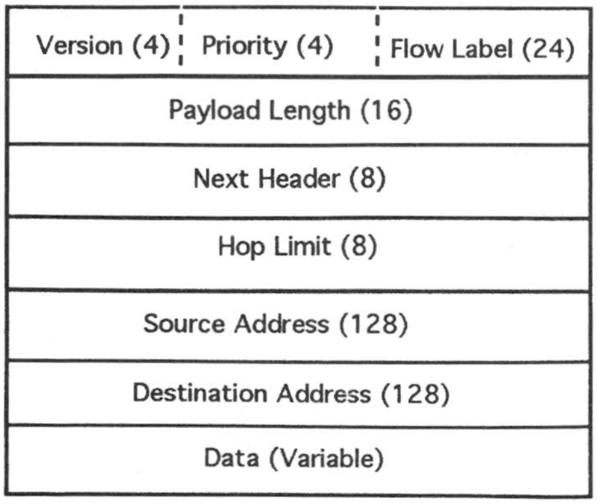

Figure 5.19 The IPv6 Datagram.

- Next header type, 8 bits
- Hop limit, 8 bits

The *version* field identifies the version of the protocol. For this implementation, the code is 6 (in decimal) or 0110 (in binary) for the 4-bit field.[1]

The *priority* field is new. It can be coded to indicate 16 possible values and is intended to play a role similar to the precedence field of IPv4. It is anticipated that the IPv6 priority field will support different types of traffic, from synchronous real-time video to asynchronous data.

The *flow label* field is also new in contrast to IPv4. Like the priority field, it is also designed to handle different types of traffic, such as voice, video, and data.

It is important to understand that IPv6 does not define the exact usage of the priority and flow label fields. Their use will be defined further in subsequent RFCs; in many instances, their use will be dictated by individual implementations.

The *payload length* field identifies the length of the payload. Since its length is 16 bits, the payload size is limited to 64 kilobytes. However, the protocol does support larger packets by using the next header field.

The *next header* field represents one of the major changes from IPv4. It replaces the options field and, for default implementations, identifies the next header to be TCP or UDP. This simply means that the first part of the payload is carrying TCP or UDP traffic. Other headers can be placed in the payload, however; they are called *extension headers* and they reside between the IP header and the TCP or UDP header and payload. This approach simplifies the processing of a packet at a node. Since the basic header is now a fixed length, the processing is simplified significantly.

Finally, the *hop limit* field is simply a reflection of how many hops the datagram is permitted to traverse during its stay in an internet. This implementation is specific to the needs of the application.

Comparison of IPv6 and IPv4

This section compares the headers of IPv4 and IPv6, which will allow another level of detail about IPv6. I will start with the IPv4 header fields and explain their fate in IPv6.

- The version field identifier is retained, with the value of 6.

---

[1]Also, IPv6 now has an EtherType identifier which is 86DD (in Hex) in contrast to IPv4's EtherType field of 800 (in Hex).

- The IPv4 header length field is eliminated, and the IPV4 total length field is replaced by the IPv6 payload length. This latter field defines the contents of only the data (and not the header) field.

- The IPv4 type-of-service (TOS) field is eliminated in IPv6, and parts of its contents (and functions) are placed in the IPv6 priority and flow label fields.

- The identification, flags, and fragment offset fields in IPv4 are removed and similar functions are placed in an optional header extension.

- The IP protocol field is removed and its function is retained in yet another extension header.

- The IPv4 time-to-live (TTL) field is renamed the hop limit field in IPv6. With the revision, however, the field's name is now accurate, because IPv6 uses it as a count of the number of hops the IP datagram has traversed.

- The header checksum is eliminated in IPv6. This removal reflects the fact that the vast majority of communication systems in operation today perform error checks at lower layers. This means that the encapsulated IP datagram is inherently checked for errors.

- The options field in IPv4 is not used much. It is awkward to implement, and in some cases leads to considerable overhead in processing its contents because the field requires the execution of special routines in the IP software. It is replaced with IPv6 header extensions, discussed in the next section.

IPv6 extension headers

The approach in IPv6 is to use extension headers, with each extension header stipulating what is in effect an option. As shown in Figure 5.20, the next header field describes a header that is inserted between the internet header and the actual user payload. Indeed, there might be more than one header inserted here, with the fields coded to identify each successive header. In effect, a header is identified by its header type, which also carries a header type of the next header in the chain (if any exists). The IPv6 RFC describes six extension headers:

- Fragment header
- Hop-by-hop options header
- Authentication header
- Routing header
- Encrypted security payload header
- Destination options header

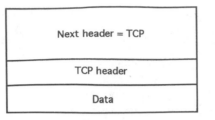

(a) No extenstions, TCP header follows.

```
┌─────────────────────────────────┐
│                                 │
│     Next header = Routing       │
│                                 │
├─────────────────────────────────┤
│                                 │
│       Routing header            │
│     & Next Header = TCP         │
│                                 │
├─────────────────────────────────┤
│                                 │
│         TCP header              │
├─────────────────────────────────┤
│           Data                  │
└─────────────────────────────────┘
```

(b) One extensison header, then TCP follows.

Figure 5.20   Header Extension Example.

Fragment header.   IPv4 permitted the fragmentation of large PDUs into smaller datagrams. This operation is quite powerful and useful, but it leads to extraordinary overhead in an internet. Consequently, IPv6 nodes will not fragment large PDUs. In effect, the system reacts as if the IPv4 "don't fragment" bit is turned on. IPv6 does permit the PDUs to be fragmented before they are sent into the network, however. In addition, the fragments can be sent independently through an internet and arrive at different times and in different sequences at the receiver. The fragmentation operations of IPv6 are quite similar to IPv4, discussed earlier in this chapter.

Hop-by-hop options header.   You will learn that the destination option header is used at the final destination, but intermediate nodes (hops) might need to exercise some operations to process the datagram (functions such as ongoing debugging and network management operations come to mind). Therefore, the hop-by-hop options extension header is used for this purpose. The contents of the hop-by-hop options header must be defined based on the individual implementation, but one service is defined in the current IPv4 RFC: the jumbo payload option. This option permits large PDUs whose length exceeds what is encoded in the 16-bit length field to be sent. When this option is implemented, the IPv6 length field is set to all 0s. The processing node must then use a field in the hop-by-hop options to understand how to process the PDU.

Authentication header. This header is described in Chapter 12.

Routing header. The routing header is quite similar in IPv6 to the source routing option in the options field of IPv4. Like its predecessor, the IPv6 routing header carries a list of intermediate IP addresses through which the datagram must be relayed. In IPv4, the option field stipulated either strict or loose source routing; IPv6 has a more efficient method of using source routing. The IPv6 node examines the routing header only if it knows that one of its own addresses is in the destination IP field of the header. Otherwise, it simply ignores the header extension. This will certainly result in less overhead in processing the source routing feature.

Encrypted security payload header. This header is described in Chapter 12.

Destination options header. In many systems, it is desirable to relay information transparently through an internet to be used only by the receiving end station. The IPv6 destination options header provides for this service. Interestingly, it contains an options field within the header, which is acted upon by the end-user application. If the options field is not recognized by the destination, then this feature provides for the ability to generate an ICMP report, which stipulates the problem that occurred by receiving an unrecognized options.

Summary

The IP is a widely used routing protocol. It is implemented on both LANs and WANs, and is designed to operate in a connectionless mode. It does, however, support a number of quality service options called type of service (TOS). IP remains transparent to the underlying network, so it can be placed on a variety of networks. IP does not perform route discovery. Instead, it uses routing tables created by route discovery protocols.

IPv6 is now an approved RFC. It retains the attractive aspects of IPv4, discards the unattractive features, and expands the IPv4 address space from 32 to 128 bits.

6

The Internet Control Message Protocol

The Internet Protocol has no error-reporting or error-correcting mechanisms. It relies on a module called the Internet Control Message Protocol (ICMP) to report errors in the processing of a datagram and to provide for administrative and status messages. This chapter examines the major features of ICMP and provides guidance on its effective use.

ICMP resides in either a host computer or a gateway as a companion to IP (see Figure 1.7 in Chapter 1). As illustrated in Figure 6.1, ICMP is used between hosts or gateways when datagrams cannot be delivered, when a gateway directs traffic on shorter routes, or when a gateway does not have sufficient buffering capacity to hold and forward datagrams.

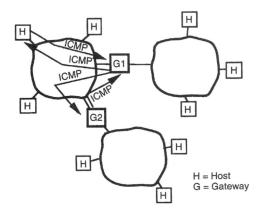

Figure 6.1 ICMP Activities.

ICMP notifies the host if a destination is unreachable. It also transmits a time-exceeded message if the lifetime of the datagram expires. Also, ICMP performs certain editing functions to determine if the IP header is in error or otherwise unintelligible.

Certain implementations of TCP/IP have been rather relaxed in returning ICMP datagrams when an error is detected. I will discuss when ICMP error messages should be used prudently, and there are some instances when they should not be used at all. Check the product being used in your installation to ensure that ICMP datagrams are generated for errors and are generated logically. For example, there is a phenomenon in this protocol suite nicknamed the "black-hole disease," where datagrams are sent out but nothing is returned, not even ICMP errors. This facet of ICMP makes troubleshooting very difficult.

Note the following aspects of ICMP:

- ICMP is a user of IP. IP encapsulates the ICMP data unit into IP datagrams for transport across an internet.

- IP must use ICMP.

- ICMP does not make IP reliable; its function is to report errors. Therefore, even with the use of ICMP, datagrams might still be lost or delivered out of sequence. Reliability is the responsibility of a higher-layer protocol such as the transmission control protocol (TCP) or an application-layer protocol.

- ICMP reports errors on IP datagrams, but it does not report errors on ICMP data units. To do so would create a catch-22 situation, wherein infinite repetitions could occur in error reporting.

- If IP uses fragmented datagrams, ICMP reports an error only on the first fragment of the received datagram.

- ICMP is not required to report errors on datagram problems. In actual situations, however, gateways generally create ICMP error messages. Reporting is less certain with regard to a host computer generating ICMP messages; check for individual variations in the vendor's product line.

ICMP Message Format

The ICMP message format is shown in Figure 6.2. ICMP messages are carried in the user portion of the IP datagram. The protocol field in the IP header is set to 1 to signify the use of ICMP.

All ICMP messages contain three fields:

The type field.   Defines the type of message

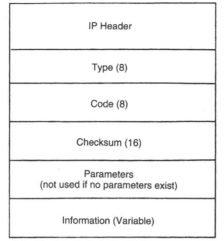

(n) = Number of bits in the field

Figure 6.2   ICMP Message Format.

The code field.   Describes the type of error or status information

A checksum field.   Computes a 16-bit one's complement on the ICMP message.

The ICMP error- and status-reporting message also carries the internet header and the first 64 bits of the user data field. These bits are useful for troubleshooting and problem analysis.

ICMP Error- and Status-Reporting Procedures

The error-reporting and status-reporting services reported by ICMP are as follows (and then explained in the following subsections):

- Time exceeded on datagram lifetime
- Parameter unintelligible
- Destination unreachable
- Source quench for flow control
- Echo and echo reply
- Redirect
- Time stamp and time stamp reply
- Information request or information reply
- Address mask request and reply
- Router advertisement

TABLE 6.1   ICMP Type Codes.

Type Code Value	Type of ICMP Message
0	Echo reply
3	Destination unreachable
4	Source quench
5	Redirect
8	Echo request
9	Router adjustment
10	Router solicitation
11	Time exceeded
12	Parameter unintelligible
13	Time-stamp request
14	Time-stamp reply
15	Information request
16	Information reply
17	Address mask request
18	Address mask reply

As stated earlier, the type code identifies the type of message and the format of the ICMP protocol data unit. This field is coded as shown in Table 6.1.

Time exceeded

This service is executed by a gateway when the time-to-live field in the IP datagram expires (its value becomes zero) and the gateway has discarded the datagram. This service is also invoked if a timer expires during the reassembly of a fragmented datagram.

The ICMP message consists of the IP header and 64 bits of the original data in the first fragments (if fragmentation is used) of the datagram. The ICMP code field is set to 0 if the time-to-live value has been exceeded in transit, or 1 if the fragment assembly time has been exceeded. Code 0 can be generated by the gateway, and code 1 by the host.

Parameter unintelligible

The destination host or gateway can invoke this service if it encounters problems processing any part of an IP header. Typically, this occurs if a field is unintelligible and the host or gateway cannot process the datagram.

The ICMP message contains a pointer field whose value points to the byte that created the problem in the original datagram header. The ICMP data unit also carries the IP header and the first 64 bits of the problem datagram. The code field is set to 0 if the pointer is used. A code field set to 1 indicates a problem with the IP service options.

Destination unreachable

This service is used by a gateway or the destination host and is invoked if a gateway encounters problems reaching the destination network specified in the IP destination address. This service can also be used by a destination host if an identified higher-level protocol is not available on the host or if a specified port is not available (inactive).

The ICMP message contains the IP header and the first 64 bits of the problem datagram. The code field of the ICMP header is coded as follows:

1. Host unreachable

2. Protocol unreachable

3. Port unreachable

4. Fragmentation needed, but do not fragment flag set

5. Source route failed

6. Destination network unknown

7. Destination host unknown

8. Source host isolated (no longer used, obsolete)

9. Destination network administratively prohibited

10. Destination host administratively prohibited

11. Network unreachable for TOS

12. Host unreachable for TOS

13. Communication administratively prohibited

14. Host precedence violation

15. Precedence cutoff in effect

Source quench

This service is a simple form of flow and congestion control and is used if the machine has insufficient buffer space for queuing incoming datagrams. If the datagram is discarded, the gateway can send this message to the host that originated the datagram. It performs the same function as the receive not ready (RNR) signal in many other protocols. The destination host can use the source quench message service if datagrams are arriving too fast to process.

In actual operation, this service notifies the transmitting host to reduce the number of datagrams being transmitted to the destination host. Therefore, it acts as a flow control entity for an internet node.

A gateway has the option of sending a source quench message for every datagram it discards. Upon receiving this message, the source host should reduce the datagram traffic. ICMP has no message to reinstate transmission; flow control is reinitiated when the transmitting host no longer receives any source quench messages. Typically, the host can increase traffic (perhaps gradually) until running at full-transmit rate or until it receives another source quench message.

It is prudent to issue a flow-control signal before a machine's capacity is exceeded. Consequently, the source quench message can also be issued when the machine's capacity is being approached. If this approach is used, the datagram that initiates the flow-control message can be delivered.

This ICMP data unit contains the relevant type value of 4. The code field is set to 0 and, as with other ICMP error messages, the internet header and the 64 bits of the problem datagram reside within the unit.

Echo request and reply

Echo request and reply is a valuable tool to determine the state of an internet. It can be sent to any IP address, such as a gateway, which must return a reply to the originator. In this manner, a network administrator can find out about the state of network resources because a reply is sent only in response to a request. If a problem exists, a reply is not returned.

Echo service can also determine if another host is active and available in the network. To initiate the service, a host sends the ICMP data unit with the address of the destination host and the IP address field. If the queried host is indeed active, it returns an echo reply to the querying host.

This service is named PING in some systems. It uses the ICMP echo and echo reply, but embellishes the basic operation with additional features, including the ability to specify the interval between requests and the number of times to send the request. For example, the IBM version of PING can perform the following services:

PING LOOPBACK.   Verifies the operation of TCP/IP software

PING my-IP-address. Verifies whether the network resource can be addressed

PING a-remote-IP-address. Verifies whether the network can be accessed

PING a-remote-host-name. Verifies the operation of the name server or name resolver

The ICMP message contains two fields that follow the checksum field. The identifier field correlates the two echo messages, from the sender (request) to the receiver (reply) and from the receiver to the sender. The sequence number field is incremented when a new echo request is sent.

The ICMP message type field identifies an echo message with a 1 and an echo reply message with a 0.

Redirect

This service is invoked by a gateway and sends the ICMP message to the source host. It provides routing management information to the host by indicating that a better route is available. Typically, this message means the host should send its traffic to another gateway. Under most circumstances, the gateway generates a redirect message if its routing table indicates that the next hop, either the host or gateway, is on the same network as the network contained in the source address of the IP header.

You might wonder why a host would not know an optimum route to a destination. In many installations, the host IP tables are created initially with very little routing information in order to simplify system generation at the host for the TCP/IP software and supporting tables. In the simplest form, a host routing table might begin with only an entry to one gateway. The table is then updated as gateways discover paths through an internet. Consequently, a host might not know a route, and a redirect message can be sent from the gateway to the host to inform the host of a better choice. The redirect message is not sent if the IP datagram is using the source route option, even if a better route to the final destination exits. The code field is datafilled to convey the following information:

0. Redirect datagrams for the network

1. Redirect datagrams for the host

2. Redirect datagrams for the type of service and network

A router advertises routes by sending a router advertisement message onto all of its interfaces that are capable of multicasting or broadcasting. This message contains addresses of which the router is aware, the time that they are considered valid, the address of the router that sent the message, and the preference default router address (if other routers are on the same network). This message is sent in a periodic manner, typically between 450 and 600 seconds.

The host advertises by sending a router solicitation message. For this operation, the host is not advertising routes, but informing the routers on the network about the host's address. Typically, the host sends the solicitation message during a bootstrap operation.

For more information about this operation, refer to RFC 1256.

Other Thoughts on ICMP

Some implementations of ICMP have resulted in the proliferation of unnecessary status or error messages. The key to using protocols as flexible as those in the TCP/IP suite is to accept almost anything and send out almost nothing. Some ICMP messages that should not be sent are broadcast and multicast addresses messages. Sending error messages for this type of traffic has a tendency to create broadcast storms on a network. As stated before, ICMP should not report on itself.

Additionally, ICMP messages should be sent cautiously on user datagram protocol (UDPs) traffic. Although I have not yet discussed UDPs, keep in mind that sending error messages relating to unidentified UDP ports could create significant problems with the ICMP destination unreachable report. This problem can occur in computers that have not established a client for the destination port identifier in the UDP segment.

IPv6 and ICMP

Since ICMP uses IP addresses, it too must be revised to operate with IPv6. It was decided by the task force that since IP had to be changed, they would make it more efficient and remove unused or little-used functions. The IPv4 Internet Group Membership Protocol (IGMP) was incorporated into ICMP. Of course, the revised ICMP is no longer compatible with the old ICMP.

The IPv6 ICMP messages have the same general format as IPv4 ICMP messages; they include a type field, code field, checksum, and variable-length data part. The IPv6 ICMP also defines ICMP type messages that are similar to IPv4. There are currently 14 different types defined:

1   Destination unreachable

2   Packet too big

3   Time exceeded

4   Parameter problem

128   Echo request

129   Echo reply

130   Group membership query

131   Group membership report

132   Group membership termination

133   Router solicitation

134   Router advertisement

135   Neighbor solicitation

136   Neighbor advertisement

137   Redirect

Summary

ICMP is used by an internet to provide error, status, and administrative messages between gateways and hosts. The protocol relies on IP to deliver its messages, although ICMP reports on the IP operations. ICMP is often used as a diagnostic tool because of its echo, time stamp, parameter unintelligible, and destination unreachable features. It must be implemented as part of the IP operations.

establish and manage sessions (logical associations) between its local users and these users' remote communicating partners. Thus, TCP (and the computer's operating system) must constantly be aware of the user's ongoing activities to support the user's data transfer through the internet.

TCP Overview

As depicted in Figure 1.7 of Chapter 1 and Figure 7.1 here, TCP resides in the transport layer of the conventional seven-layer model. TCP is situated above IP and below the upper layer(s). Figure 7.1 also illustrates that TCP is not loaded into the router to support user data transfer. It resides in the host computer or in a machine tasked with the end-to-end integrity of transferring user data. If TCP runs in the router, it does so to support activities such as network management and terminal sessions with the router.[1]

Figure 7.1 also shows that TCP is designed to run over the IP. Because IP provides no sequencing or traffic acknowledgment and is connectionless, the tasks of reliability, flow control, sequencing application session, opens, and closes are given to TCP. Although TCP and IP are tied together so closely that they are used in the same context

---

[1]There are exceptions to this rule, especially in IBM Token Ring networks, where the router uses TCP to account for user traffic.

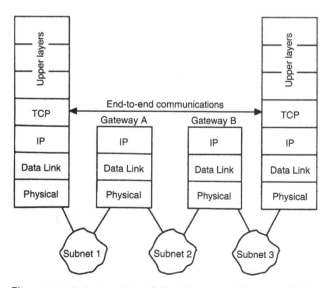

Figure 7.1 Relationship of the Transport Layer to Other Layers.

(TCP/IP), TCP can also support other protocols. For example, another connectionless protocol, such as the ISO 8473 connectionless network protocol (CLNP), could operate with TCP, with certain adjustments to the interface between the modules.

Application protocols, such as the File Transfer Protocol (FTP) and the Simple Mail Transfer Protocol (SMTP), rely on the services of TCP. Many of the TCP functions (such as flow control, reliability, and sequencing) could be handled within an application program. It makes little sense, however, to code these functions into each application. Moreover, applications programmers are usually not versed in error-detection and flow-control operations. The preferred approach is to develop generalized software that provides community functions that are applicable to a wide range of applications, and then invoke these programs from the application software. This approach allows the application programmer to concentrate on solving the application problem and thus isolates the programmer from the nuances and problems of network control.

Major Features of TCP

TCP provides the following services to the upper layers:

- Connection-oriented data management
- Reliable data transfer
- Stream-oriented data transfer
- Push functions
- Resequencing
- Flow control (sliding windows)
- Multiplexing
- Full-duplex transmission
- Precedence and security
- Graceful close

TCP is a *connection-oriented protocol*. This term refers to the fact that TCP maintains status and state information about each user data stream flowing into and out of the TCP module. TCP also is responsible for the end-to-end transfer of data across one network or multiple networks to a receiving user application (or the next upper-layer protocol). Referring back to Figure 7.1, TCP ensures that the data are transmitted and received between two hosts across three networks (subnet 1, subnet 2, and subnet 3) via sequence numbers and positive acknowledgments.

Although mapping ports to higher-layer processes can be handled as an internal matter in a host, the Internet publishes numbers for frequently used higher-level processes. Table 7.1 lists some commonly used port numbers, along with their names and descriptions.

Although TCP establishes specific numbers for frequently used ports, the numbers and values above 1024 are available for private use. These values have the low-order 8 bits set to zero and are available to any organization to use as it chooses. The numbers 0 through 1023 are always reserved and should be avoided.

Examples of port assignments and port bindings

Figure 7.2 shows how port numbers are assigned and managed between two host computers. In event 1, host A sends a TCP segment to host C. This segment is a request for a TCP connection to communicate with a higher-level process. In this instance, it is the well-known port 25, which is the assigned number for the SMTP. The destination port value is fixed at 25. The source port identifier, however, is a local matter. A host computer can choose any number convenient to its internal operations. In this example, a source of port 3000 is chosen for the first connection. The second connection, noted by the

TABLE 7.1 Common Internet Port Numbers (Not Exhaustive)

Number	Name	Description
5	RJD	Remote job entry
7	ECHO	Echo
11	USERS	Active Users
13	DAYTIME	Daytime
20	FTP-DATA	File transfer (data)
21	FTP	File transfer (control)
23	TELNET	TELNET
25	SMTP	Simple mail transfer
37	TIME	Time
42	NAMESERV	Host name server
43	NICKNAME	Who is
53	DOMAIN	Domain name server
67	BOOTPS	Bootstrap protocol server
68	BOOTPC	Bootstrap protocol client
69	TFTP Trivial file transfer	
79	FINGER	Finger
101	HOSTNAME	NIC host name server
102	ISO-TSAP	ISO TSAP
103	X400	X400
104	X400SND	X400. SND
105	CSNET-NS	CSNET mailbox name server
109	POP2	Post office protocol 2
111	RPC	SUN RPC portmap
137	NETBIOS-NS	NETBIOS name service
138	NETBIOS-DG	NETBIOS datagram service
139	NETBIOS-SS	NETBIOS session service

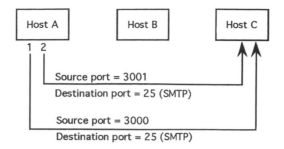

Figure 7.2 Establishing Sessions with a Destination Port.

numeral 2, is also destined for host C to use SMTP. Consequently, the destination port of 25 remains the same. The source port identifier is different; in this instance it is set to 3001. The use of two different numbers for the access prevents any confusion between the two sessions in hosts A and C.

Figure 7.3 shows how the two segments establish the connections in Figure 7.2. Hosts A and C typically store the information about TCP connections in *port tables*. Notice the inverse relationship of these tables in relation to the source destination. In the host A port table, the sources are 3000 and 3001, and the destination is 25 for both connections. Conversely, in the host C port table, both sources are 25, and the destinations are 3000 and 3001. Thus, the TCP modules reverse the source and destination port numbers to communicate.

Murphy's Law is alive and well, even with TCP. It is possible for another host to send a connection request to host C, with the source port and destination port equal to the same values. It certainly would not be unusual for the destination port to be the same value because well-known ports are frequently accessed. In this case, a destination port of 25 would identify the SMTP. Because source port identifiers are a local matter, you can see in Figure 7.4 that host B has chosen its source port to be 3000.

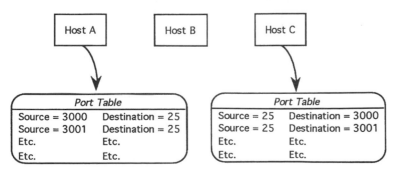

Figure 7.3 Binding with Port Numbers.

Without an additional identifier, the first connection between hosts A and C and the connection between hosts B and C are in conflict because they use the same source and destination port numbers. In this cases, host C can easily discern the difference by using the IP addresses in the IP header of these datagrams. So the source port numbers can be duplicates, while the internet address distinguishes between the sessions.

In addition to IP addresses and port numbers, many systems further identify a socket with a "protocol family" value. For example, IP is one protocol family and DECnet is another. The manner in which protocol families are identified is dependent upon the vendor and the operating system.

Using sockets to support multiplexing

Because port numbers can be used by more than one end-point connection, users can simultaneously share a port resource. That is, multiple users can simultaneously be multiplexed across one port. In Figure 7.4, three users are sharing port 25 (UDP also supports port multiplexing, as explained later).

Passive and Active Opens

Two forms of establishing a connection are permitted with TCP ports: passive open and active open. The *passive open* mode allows the ULP (for example, a server) to tell the TCP and host operating system to wait for the arrival of connection requests from the remote system (for example, a client process) rather than issue an *active open*. Upon receiving this request, the host operating system assigns an identifier to this end. You could use this feature to accommodate communications from remote users and avoid the delay of an active open.

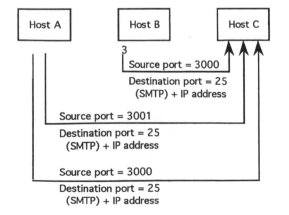

Figure 7.4 Distinguishing between Port Identifiers.

The application process requesting the passive open can accept a connection request from any user (given a profile that matches requirements). If any call can be accepted (without profile matching), the foreign socket number is set to all zeros. Unspecified foreign sockets are allowed only on passive opens.

The second form of connection establishment, the active open, is used when ULP designates a specific socket through which a connection is to be established. Typically, an active open is issued to a passive open port to establish a connection.

TCP supports a scenario in which two active opens are issued to each other at the same time. TCP then makes the connection. This feature allows applications to issue an open at any time without concern that another application has issued an open.

TCP provides conventions on how active and passive opens can be used together. First, an active open identifies a specific socket and, as options, its precedence and security levels. TCP grants an open if the remote socket has a matching passive open or if it has issued a matching active open. Certain implementations of TCP define two types of passive opens:

Fully specified passive open.   The destination address in the active and passive open are the same. Therefore, the local passive open operation has fully specified the foreign socket. The security parameter in the active open is within the range of the security parameter in the passive open.

There are exceptions to this rule, especially in IBM Token Ring networks.

Unspecified passive open.   Addresses need not match, but the security parameters should be within an acceptable range. Alternatively, no security parameters are checked at all.

An example of a TCP process that requires little or no authentication during an open is anonymous FTP. This service is offered by a number of organizations through the Internet. It requires the user to identify itself to the FTP server with a password such as "guest."

The Transmission Control Block

Because TCP must remember several things about each connection, it stores information in a *transmission control block* (TCB). Among the entries stored in the TCB are the following:

- Local and remote socket numbers
- Pointers to the send and receive buffers
- Pointers to the retransmit queue

- Security and precedence values for the connection

- Current segment

The TCB also contains several variables associated with the send and receive sequence numbers. These variables are described in Table 7.2, and the next section examines how they are used.

TCP Window and Flow-Control Mechanisms

Using the entries in Table 7.2, we will examine how TCP/IP provides flow-control mechanisms between two connection end points. To begin, let us examine Figure 7.5. The boxes labeled A and B depict two TCP modules. Module A is transmitting two units of data, or two bytes, to module B (although it is unusual to send just two octets, this example keeps matters simple). These segments are labeled SEQ = 1 and SEQ = 2. You can see the effect of this transfer by examining the send variables in the box at the bottom part of the picture. The SND UNA variable identifies the bytes not yet acknowledged (byte 2). Also, as indicated by the arrows below this variable name, the values less than this range have been sent and acknowledged (byte 0). Numbers greater than the range (bytes 1 and 2) have been sent but not acknowledged. SND NXT identifies the sequence number of the next octet of data to be sent (byte 3). The window limit indicator is the largest number that can be sent before the window is closed. The send window value is derived from the value in the TCP window segment field. At the box at the bottom of Figure 7.5, the window limit is computed as SND UNA + SND WND. This value is 5 because SND UNA = 2 and SND WND = 3.

TABLE 7.2   Send and Receive Variables

Variable name	Purpose
	Send sequence variables
SND.UNA	Send unacknowledged
SND.NXT	Send next
SND.WND	Send window
SND.UP	Sequence number of last octet of urgent data
SND.WL1	Sequence number used for last window update
SND.WL2	ACK number used for last window update
SND.PUSH	Sequence number of last octet of pushed data
ISS	Initial send sequence number
	Receive sequence variables
RCV.NXT	Sequence number of next octet to be received
RCV.WND	Number of octets that can be received
RCV.UP	Sequence number of last octet of received urgent data
RCV.IRS	Initial receive sequence number

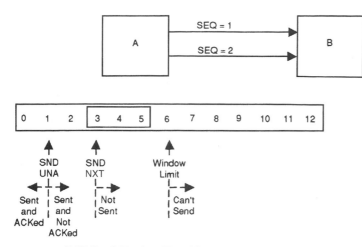

Figure 7.5   TCP Send Window Variables.

Because A has transmitted units 1 and 2, its remaining send window is three units. That is, A can transmit units 3, 4, and 5, but not unit 6. This window is indicated in the figure by the boxed area.

TCP is somewhat unusual compared to other protocols in that it does not use just the acknowledgment number for window control. As just stated, it has a separate number carried in the TCP segment that increases or decreases the sending computer's send window. This concept is illustrated in Figure 7.6, where B returns a segment to A. The segment contains, among other fields, an acknowledgment field of 3 and a send window field of 6. The acknowledgment field simply acknowledges previous traffic. Used alone, it does not increase, decrease, open, or close A's window. Window management is the job of the send window field. Its value of 6 states that A can send octets based on this value of 6 plus the acknowledgment value. Hereafter, the window limit = ACK + SND WND. As depicted in the bottom part of this figure, the window is 9 (3 + 6). The window is thus expanded as indicated by the boxed area in this figure.

The size of the window could have been reduced by computer B. The send window field permits the window to be expanded or contracted as necessary to manage buffer space and processing. This approach is more flexible than using the acknowledgment field for both traffic acknowledgment and window control operations. (Be aware that window shrinkage can seriously affect traffic flow. At best, it complicates matters.)

TCP is allowed to send an urgent data segment even if its transmit window is closed. This segment contains a bit (the urgent bit) set to 1 if urgent data need to be transmitted. This bit will be explained in more detail shortly.

I once sat in a meeting with two of my clients (who were writing code for a proprietary transport layer). We were discussing sliding windows, rejects, selective rejects, and inclusive ACKs for a 512-byte PDU. These two individuals got into a rather heated debate on whether the inclusive ACK number should be 512 or 513. I told them the answer depended on whether the number 0 was used as part of the *initial sequence (ISS)* number. Consider the following (for a 10-byte PDU, for simplicity). First, using an ISS of 0,

	ISS									
Sequence No.	0	1	2	3	4	5	6	7	8	9
	↓	↓	↓	↓	↓	↓	↓	↓	↓	↓
Bytes Sent	1	2	3	4	5	6	7	8	9	10

Therefore, an inclusive ACK = 10, NAK = 0. (This protocol used NAKs.)

Next, using an ISS number of 1,

	ISS									
Sequence No.	1	2	3	4	5	6	7	8	9	10
	↓	↓	↓	↓	↓	↓	↓	↓	↓	↓
Bytes Sent	1	2	3	4	5	6	7	8	9	10

Therefore, an inclusive ACK = 11, NAK = 1.

So, for Fig. 7.7, if TCP A were sending 10 bytes in a segment with an ISS number of 3,

	ISS									
Sequence No.	3	4	5	6	7	8	9	10	11	12
	↓	↓	↓	↓	↓	↓	↓	↓	↓	↓
Bytes Sent	1	2	3	4	5	6	7	8	9	10

The inclusive ACK = 13 and NAK would be 3 (although remember that TCP does not know how to NAK.) Because this example sends 300 octets in a segment, the ACK value of 303 is the proper value.

This discussion might seem somewhat trivial, but these simple misunderstandings can cause problems and result in software bugs in the communications system.

Box 7.1   Sequence Numbering and ACKs.

Event 6.   TCP B successfully receives the segment number 603, which was transmitted in event 5. TCP B then sends back a segment with ACK 303 because it is still expecting segment number 303.

Event 7.   Eventually, TCP A times out and resends the segments for which it has not yet received an acknowledgment. In this example, it must resend the segments beginning with numbers 303 and 603. The idea depicted in event 7 has its advantages and disadvantages. It makes the protocol quite simple, because TCP simply goes back to the last unacknowledged segment number and retransmits all succeeding segments. On the other hand, it likely retransmits segments not in error, such as the segment beginning with number 603, which had arrived error-free at TCP B. Nonetheless, TCP operates in this fashion for the sake of simplicity even at the risk of degraded throughput.

Event 8. All traffic is accounted for after TCP B receives and error-checks segments 303 and 603, and returns an ACK value equal to 903.

Estimating Timers for Time-Outs and Retransmissions

This section describes the approach taken by TCP to estimate a value for the time-out and retransmission. I will begin with earlier approaches and conclude with recent changes to the TCP retransmission algorithm. Choosing a value for the retransmission timer is deceptively complex, because of the following reasons:

- There is a delay in receiving acknowledgments from the receiving host varies in an internet.

- Segments sent from the transmitter can be lost in an internet, which obviously invalidates any round-trip delay estimate for a spurious acknowledgment.

- Acknowledgments from the receiver can be lost, which further invalidates the round-trip delay estimate.

Because of these problems, TCP does not use a fixed retransmission timer. Rather, it uses an adaptive retransmission timer derived from an analysis of the delay encountered in receiving acknowledgments from remote hosts.

In Figure 7.8, the round-trip time (RTT) is derived from adding the send delay (SD), the processing time (PT) at the remote host, and the receive delay (RD). If the delay were not variable, this simple calculation would suffice for determining a retransmission timer. Because delay in an internet is often highly variable, however, other factors must be considered.

The approach taken with earlier versions of TCP was to analyze each round-trip sample and develop an average RTT for the delay. This simple formula for RTT is a weighted value based on the following:

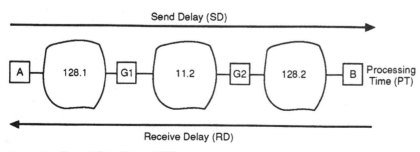

Figure 7.8   Round-Trip Time (RTT).

$$SRTT = (\alpha \times OSRTT) + ([1 - \alpha] \times NRTT)$$

where SRTT = the smoothed round-trip time, α = the smoothing factor (ranging near 1 for accommodating the changes that last for a short period), OSRTT = the old smoothed RTT (near 0 to respond to delays quickly), and NRTT = the new RTT sample. The next step in computing the timer is to apply a weighting factor to RTT as follows:

$$VT = \beta \times SRTT$$

where VT = the value for a time-out and β = a constant weighting factor that must be greater than RTT. Some implementations varied this formula, as follows:

$$VT = \min (Ubound, \max [Lbound, \{\beta \times SRTT\}])$$

where Ubound = an upper bound on the time-out and Lbound = the lower bound on the time-out.

This method of calculating the variable for the timeout did not work well because of the variable delay and loss of acknowledgments in an internet. Ideally, the timeout timer should be quite close to RTT. Due to the variable nature of RTT, however, the time-out timer expired too quickly in many instances and resulted in unnecessary segments being reintroduced into the internet. On the other hand, using a small value for the time-out allows segment loss to be handled more quickly.

One solution to the problem was provided by Phil Karn, and is known as *Karn's algorithm*. The approach is twofold: TCP does not modify its estimate for any retransmitted segments, and the time-out is increased each time the timer expires and initiates a retransmission. You might recognize that this approach is quite similar to the Ethernet back-off algorithm, except that Ethernet uses an exponential back-off because of increased traffic collisions on the network.

The Karn formula is NVT = MF $\times$ VT, where NVT = new value for time-out and MF = a multiplication factor (usually a value of 2 or a table of values).

The approach is to recalculate the RTT on a segment that was not retransmitted. It works well enough except in an internet with large RTT variations.

RFC 1122 concedes that the original TCP approach to time-out and retransmission is inadequate. With new systems, *Van Jacobsen's* slow-start approach is used: Upon a time-out, TCP shuts its window to one. Upon receiving an ACK, it opens its window to half the size the window was before the time-out occurred.

The newest TCP implementations take advantage of Poisson distribution and network usage factors regarding RTT. Additional computations take into account varying delay as a function of network usage.

These learning timers, while very valuable, can have a negative effect on an application's performance and throughput. In essence, the operation makes TCP "courteous" because it backs off when network congestion is high; "noncourteous" protocols (such as UDP) have no back-off operation and can continue to transmit. Under high-traffic conditions, courteous protocols do not send much traffic, but noncourteous protocols do.

TCP and User Interfaces

TCP works with the service definition/primitive concept to interface with an upper-layer user. The interface is achieved with the commands and messages summarized in Table 7.3. Be aware that primitives are abstract and their actual implementation is dependent on a host's operating system. Furthermore, RFC 793 defines those interfaces in generally; vendor implementations vary. (Chapter 13 provides more information on this topic.) Figure 7.9 shows the relationship of the ULP, TCP, and IP.

The service definitions between TCP and its lower layer are not specified in the TCP standard. It is assumed in the TCP operations that TCP and the lower layer can pass information to each other asynchronously. TCP expects the lower layer to specify this interface. (The OSI model follows the same practice.) This lower-layer interface is defined in the IP specification (see Chapter 6) if IP rests below TCP.

Segments

The PDUs exchanged between two TCP modules are called *segments*. Figure 7.10 illustrates the format for a segment. Each field is examined in this section.

The segment is divided into two parts, the *header* and the *data*. As depicted in Figure 7.10, the data part follows the header. The first two fields of the segment are the *source port* and *destination port*. These 16-bit fields identify the upper-layer application programs using the TCP connection.

The next field is the *sequence number*. This field contains the sequence number of the first octet in the user data field. Its value specifies the position of the transmitting module's byte stream. Within the segment, the first user data octet in the segment is specified.

The sequence number is also used during a connection management operation. If a connection-request segment is used between two TCP entities, the sequence number specifies the *initial send sequence* (ISS) number to be used to subsequently number the user data.

The *acknowledgment number* is set to a value that acknowledges data previously received. The value in this field contains the value of the sequence number of the next expected byte from the transmitter.

TABLE 7.3   Typical TCP User Interface

Command	Parameters
\multicolumn{2}{c}{Service request primitives (ULP to TCP)}	
UNSPECIFIED-PASSIVE	Local port, ULP timeout (1),* timeout action (1), precedence (1)
OPEN	Security (1), options (1) → local connection name
FULL-PASSIVE-OPEN	Local port, destination socket, ULP timeout (1), timeout action (1), precedence (1), security (1), options (1)
ACTIVE-OPEN	Local port, foreign socket, ULP timeout (1), ULP timeout action (1), precedence (1), security (1), options (1)
ACTIVE-OPEN WITH DATA	Source ports, destination address, ULP timeout (1), ULP timeout action (1), precedence (1), security (1), data, data length, push flag, urgent flag (1)
SEND	Local connection name, buffer address, byte count, push flag, urgent flat, ULP timeout (1), ULP timeout action (1)
RECEIVE	Local connection name, buffer address, byte count, urgent flag, push flag
ALLOCATE	Local connection name, data length
CLOSE	Local connection name
ABORT	Local connection name
STATUS	Local connection name
\multicolumn{2}{c}{Service response primitives (TCP to ULP)}	
OPEN-ID	Local connection name, foreign socket, destination address
OPEN-FAILURE	Local connection name
OPEN-SUCCESS	Local connection name
DELIVER	Local connection name, buffer address, byte count, urgent flag
CLOSING	Local connection name
TERMINATE	Local connection name, description
STATUS RESPONSE	Local connection name, source port and address, foreign port, connection state, receive and send window, amount-waiting-ACK and -receipt, urgent mode, timeout, timeout action
ERROR	Local connection name, error description

* A notation of (1) means parameters are optional.

Because this number is set to the next expected octet, it provides an inclusive acknowledgment capability; it acknowledges all octets up to and including this number minus 1.

The *data offset* field specifies the number of 32-bit aligned words that constitute the TCP header. This field determines where the data field begins. As you might expect, the *reserved* field is reserved. It consists of six bits that must be set to zero. They are reserved for future use.

The next six fields are called *flags*. They are labeled as control bits by TCP, and they specify certain services and operations to be used

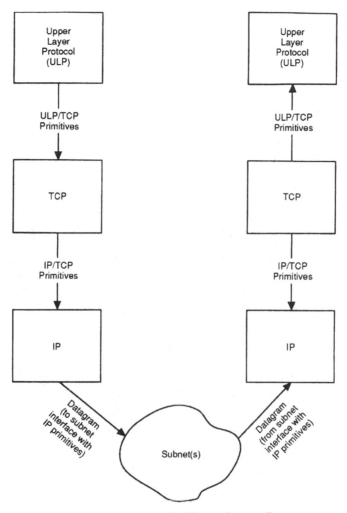

Figure 7.9 Relationships of the Upper Layer, Transmission Control, and Internet Protocols.

during the session. Some of the bits determine how to interpret other fields in the header. These six flags convey the following information:

URG. Whether the urgent pointer field is significant

ACK. If the acknowledgment field is significant

PSH. That the module is to exercise the push function

RST. That the connection is to be reset

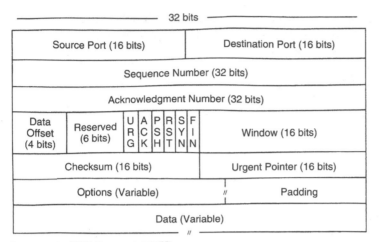

Figure 7.10   TCP Segment (PDU).

SYN. That the sequence numbers are to be synchronized; it is used as a flag with the connection-establishment segments to indicate that handshaking operations are to take place.

FIN. That the sender has no more data to send; it is comparable to the end-of-transmission (EOT) signal in other protocols.

The next field is labeled *window*. Its value indicates how many bytes the receiver is willing to accept (2 = 65535 bytes). The value is established based on the value in the acknowledgment field (acknowledgment number). The value in the window field window is added to the value of the acknowledgment number field.

The *checksum* field performs a 16-bit one's complement of the one's complement sum of all the 16-bit words in the segment, including the header and text. The purpose of the checksum calculation is to determine if the segment has arrived error-free from the transmitter. It uses a pseudo-header as UDP (which is explained in the UDP section).

The next field in the segment is labeled the *urgent pointer*. This field is used only if the URG flag is set. The purpose of the urgent pointer is to signify the data byte in which urgent data is located. Urgent data is also called *out-of-band* data. TCP does not dictate what happens for urgent data; it is implementation-specific. TCP signifies only where the urgent data are located. The urgent data comprise the first byte in the stream; the pointer also indicates where the urgent data ends. The receiver must immediately inform the application using TCP that urgent data have arrived. Urgent data could be control signals such as interrupts, checkpoints, or terminal control characters.

The *options* field was conceived to provide for future enhancements to TCP. It is constructed in a manner similar to that of the IP datagrams option field, in that each option specification consists of a single byte containing an option number, a field containing the length of the option, and the option values themselves. The option field is quite limited in its use. Currently, only three options are defined for the TCP standard:

0. End-of-option list

1. No operation

2. Maximum segment size

Other options have been added to TCP. For option 3, a window scale factor is available; for option 8, a timestamp is available. These options can be studied in more detail in RFC 1323.

Finally, the *padding* field is used to ensure that the TCP header is filled to an even multiple of 32 bits. After that, as the figure illustrates, user data follows.

Effect of segment size (length) on performance.

Because TCP is designed to support variable-length segments, the options field can be used by the receiver to inform the transmitter of the maximum buffer size that can be accommodated. In this manner, a limit is placed on the size (length) of the segment to be transmitted to the receiver. Otherwise, segments can vary in length up to the maximum length. If this is the case, the length of the segments could affect the length of the frames on the network because the segments are encapsulated into the frames.

Frame length is an important aspect of network performance, and it can affect bridges and gateways. Imagine that two variable-length frame sets are sent across an Ethernet network. One set of frames contains 1500 bytes; the other set contains 64 bytes each. Large frames provide better throughput on a local area network (LAN), because the number of user bytes per overhead segment and Ethernet frame header is a greater ratio than the smaller 64-octet frame. Moreover, a point that is often overlooked is the *interframe gap*, which is the time between frames when no transmission occurs. TCP cannot directly affect the interframe gap; it is determined by lower-layer protocols. However, the effect of using a larger frame gives a bridge or gateway more time to examine and make decisions on the frame than if a smaller frame is arriving with the same interframe gap as the large frame. Indeed, you need to carefully examine how TCP segments data and the speed at which these segments are sent to a lower layer because the ability of a bridge to forward traffic and filter irrelevant traffic is a function of both the frame length and interframe gap.

This is not to say that TCP is solely responsible for these operations. As mentioned earlier, some of the activities are determined by the lower LAN layers. Nonetheless, the situation warrants examination to tune the upper layers to the LAN protocol layers. Some Internet service providers will notify users of the maximum segment size that is permitted as part of the log-on process.

The TCP Connection Management Operations

TCP is a state-driven protocol. As such, its operations must conform to many rules on how and when specific segments are exchanged between the TCP entities. These rules are described in a state transition diagram. A general depiction of the TCP connection management operations is illustrated in Figure 7.11. I will use this figure to explain several features of TCP.

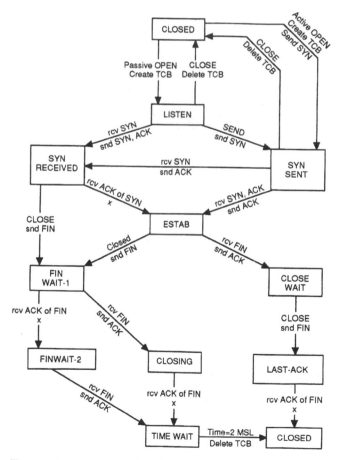

Figure 7.11 TCP Connection Management State Diagram.

The TCP operations of open, data transfer, and close are explained in the following sections. Before explaining these TCP operations, however, I first need to define the terms *type* and *instance* in regard to a communications protocol.

Type describes an object. In this example, TCP is an object. *Instance* describes the manifestation of an object. Therefore, each time TCP is invoked, it manifests itself. Because many user processes can use TCP simultaneously, each user session invokes the TCP logic, and each invocation is an instance of type TCP. In more pragmatic terms, each user invocation of TCP represents executing some of TCP's services to support a session. Each instance of TCP requires that TCP maintain information about the event. These pieces of information are kept in the TCB about *each* user session.

TCP open

Figure 7.12 illustrates the major operations between two TCP entities establishing a connection. TCP user A has sent an active-open primitive to TCP. The remote user has sent a passive open to its TCP provider. These operations are listed as events 2 and 1, respectively, although either event could have occurred first.

Invoking an active open requires TCP A to prepare a segment with the SYN bit set to 1. The segment is sent to TCP B and is depicted in the figure as 3 and coded as SYN SEQ 100. In this example, sequence (SEQ) number 100 is used as the ISS number, although any number could be chosen within the rules discussed earlier (the most common approach is to set the value to 0). The SYN coding simply means the SYN bit is set to the value of 1.

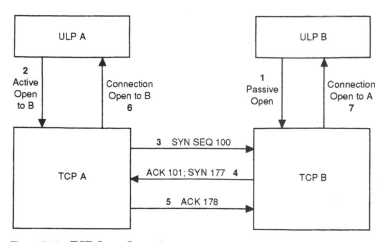

Figure 7.12   TCP Open Operations.

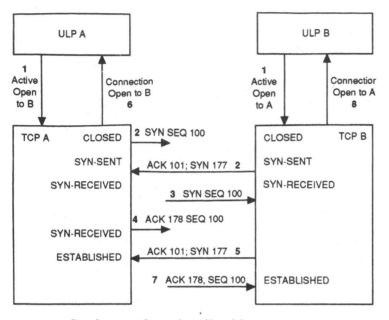

Figure 7.14 Simultaneous Opens from Closed States.

Event 3.   The SYN segment from TCP A finally arrives at TCP B. The results of the SYN segments in event 2 move the two TCP modules from CLOSED to SYN-SENT to SYN-RECEIVED.

Events 4 and 5.   Both TCP modules issue an ACK segment, which, as you learned earlier, acknowledges the SYN segments. TCP B's segment in event 5 arrives before TCP A's segment in event 4. This somewhat asynchronous aspect of TCP simply results from the variable delay in an internet. The delay varies in both directions.

Event 6.   Upon receipt of the ACK at TCP A (in event 5), TCP A sends a connection open signal to its ULP.

Event 7.   The ACK segment from TCP A finally arrives at TCP B.

Event 8.   To complete the connection, TCP B sends a connection open to its ULP.
Notice the effect of the arrival of the ACKs in events 5 and 7 when the ULPs are issued the open primitives in events 6 and 8.

Receiving a call at a receiving module in which a TCP does not exist results in an error condition if the operating system has not generated some control information indicating that the user does have access to the connection identified in the open call.

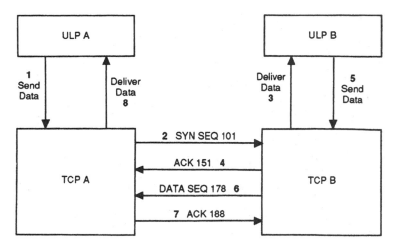

Figure 7.15   TCP Data Transfer Operations.

TCP data transfer

Figure 7.15 shows the TCP entities after they have successfully achieved a connection. In event 1, ULP A sends data down to TCP A for transmission with a SEND primitive. Assuming 50 bytes are to be sent, TCP A encapsulates this data into a segment and sends the segment to TCP B with sequence number of 101, as depicted in event 2. Remember that this sequence number identifies the first byte of the user data stream.

At the remote TCP, data is delivered to the user (ULP B) in event 3, and TCP B acknowledges the data with a segment acknowledgment number of 151, depicted in event 4. The acknowledgment number of 151 acknowledges inclusively the 50 bytes transmitted in the event 2 segment.

Next, the user connected to TCP B sends data in event 5. This data is encapsulated into a segment and transmitted as event 6 in the diagram. The initial sequence number from TCP B was 177, so TCP begins its sequencing with 178. In this example, it transmits 10 octets.

TCP A acknowledges TCP B's 10 segments in event 7 by returning a segment with the acknowledgment number 188. In event 8, this data is delivered to TCP user A. Remember that the data transfer operations pertaining to retransmission and time-outs were discussed in an earlier section (refer back to Figure 7.6).

TCP close

Figure 7.16 shows a close operation. Event 1 illustrates that TCP user A wants to close its operations with its upper peer layer protocol

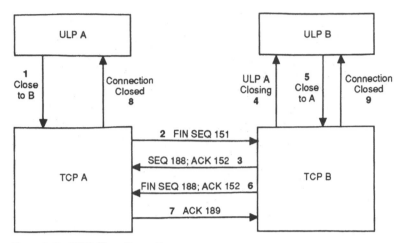

Figure 7.16 TCP Close Operations.

at TCP B. The effect of this primitive (CLOSE) is shown in event 2, where TCP A sends a segment with the FIN bit set to 1. The sequence number of 151 is a continuation of the operation of Figure 7.15. This is the next sequence number the TCP module is required to send.

The effect of this segment is shown as event 3 from TCP B. TCP B acknowledges TCP A's FIN SEQ 151. Its segment has SEQ = 188 and ACK = 152. Next, it issues a closing primitive to its user, which is depicted as event 4.

In this example, the user application acknowledges and grants the close as event 5. It might choose to do this, depending on the state of its operations. For simplicity, however, assume that the event depicted in 5 does occur. This primitive is mapped to event 6, which is the final segment issued by TCP B. Notice that in event 6, the FIN flag is set to 1, SEQ to 188, and ACK to 152. Finally, TCP A acknowledges this final segment with event 7 as ACK = 189. The effect of all these operations is shown in events 8 and 9, where connection closed signals are sent to the user applications.

To complete this analysis of TCP connection management, Figure 7.17 shows the close operations in relation to the relevant part of the state diagram. Again, as with an earlier example of the open operations, the top part of the figure is a scaled-down version of Figure 7.16 in which only the segment transmissions are shown. The effect of these operations is depicted with the state notations located inside each box and the outlined numbers and figures shown on the state diagram in the bottom part of the figure.

Figure 7.18 shows a typical open and close from the perspective of a client (say, a user application) and a server (FTP, DNS, etc.). The less typical operations have been deleted from the figure to simplify the example. Also, state transitions (symbolized with arrows) beginning

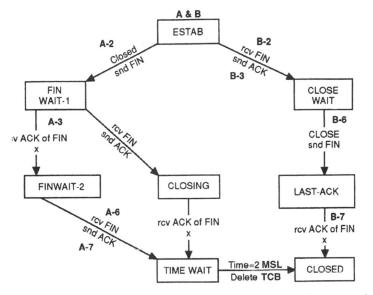

Figure 7.17 Relationship of Close Operations, Segment Exchanges, and State Transitions.

with the initial A show the operations of the user application, and the operations beginning with the initial S show the operations of the server.

TCP connection table

The Internet MIB requires the use of a TCP connection table. The table contains information about each existing TCP connection. As depicted in Figure 7.19, the table consists of five columns and a row for each connection. The columns are as follows:

Connection State.   Describes the state of each TCP connection (for example, closed, listen, fin Wait 1, and closing)

Local Address.   Contains the local IP address for each TCP connection (in a listen state, this value must be 0.0.0.0)

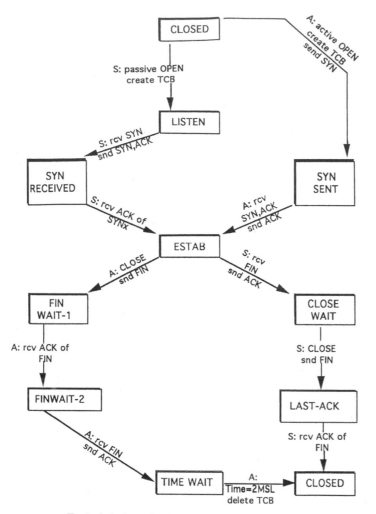

Figure 7.18 Typical Actions for an Open and Close:Client Application (A) and Server (S).

Local Port. Contains the local port number for each TCP connection

Remote Address. Contains the remote IP address for each TCP connection

Remote Port. Contains the remote port number for each TCP connection

TCP with Bulk and Interactive Traffic

Even though many organizations send about the same amount of bulk and interactive traffic in relation to the number of segments

	Connection State	Local Address	Local Port	Remote Address	Remote Port
Connection 1					
Connection 2					
Connection 3					
Connection n					

Figure 7.19 TCP Connection Table.

transmitted, Figure 7.20 shows that the ratio of bytes sent varies greatly. Several studies have revealed that about 90 percent of the bytes sent in a system consist of bulk data traffic, such as FTP and database down loads, and about 10 percent of the traffic is interactive data, such as Rlogin and Telnet.

In addition, interactive traffic is sent in very small units. For some applications, such as Rlogin, only one byte is sent in a segment. Obviously, this type of operation translates into considerable overhead, since this one byte is wrapped inside the TCP, IP, and link layer headers and trailers.

The methods of flow control and acknowledgment differ between bulk and interactive traffic. For bulk data applications, the common practice is to set up a buffer at the receiver that is large enough to accommodate enough traffic for continuous transfer of data from the application. Then the receiver periodically sends a acknowledgment (ACK) of this traffic to the sender. For interactive traffic, some applications require that the receiver echo back the character (byte) that was sent. This echo goes back to the application. In addition, if the application is running on top of TCP, an ACK is sent back to TCP. Some implementations hold back the ACK for a brief time and attempt to piggyback the ACK onto an echo segment in order to reduce the amount of traffic sent onto the network.

TCP and IP Header Compression

Several organizations and individuals have expressed concern about the overhead contained in TCP and IP headers. This overhead reduces throughput on the communications link and can also lead to degraded

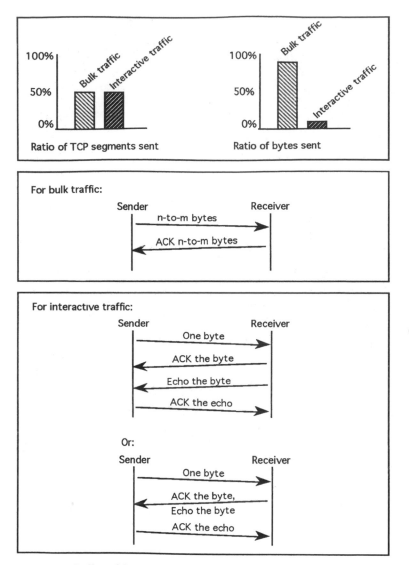

Figure 7.20   Bulk and Interactive Traffic.

response time. For example, if a terminal user enters data on a device that uses echo procedures, a one-byte character can result in 40 bytes of TCP/IP header and one byte of data being sent across the channel and echoed back to the receiver. Moreover, when small transactions are sent on nonecho devices,, the overhead still remains high.

The ratio of overhead to user data might not be a serious concern on some communications links such as high-speed LAN media and optical fiber. However, for the vast majority of end-user devices (which are saddled with the relatively slow 20-kbps EIA-232, V.24/V.28 interface), the overhead can consume precious bandwidth.

In view of this situation, a number of studies have been conducted that focused on reducing the overhead by compressing certain fields in the TCP/IP header (see Figure 7.21). One study was released as RFC 1144 and another one was released as RFC 914.

The basic approach is to transmit only the fields in the headers that change during the TCP/IP connection. Through the use of a preestablished connection identifier that is carried (although not shown in this figure), the fields shaded in the figure can be eliminated. And if, during the connection establishment, this connection identifier is associated with the source and destination addresses and the source and destination ports, then these fields can also be eliminated.

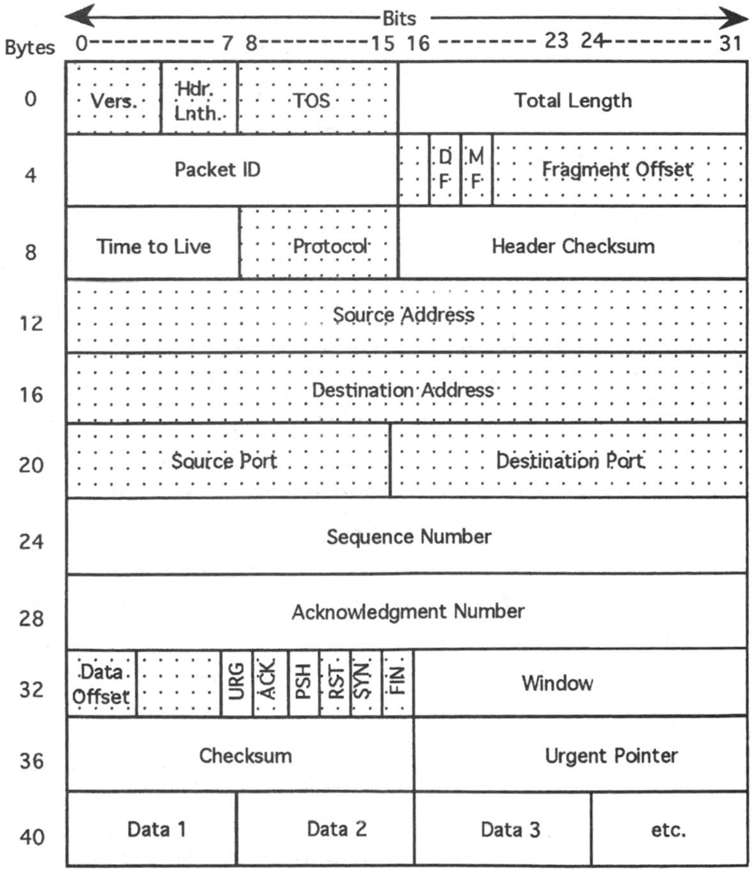

Note: Dotted fields are subject to compression.

Figure 7.21   1 Compression Possibilities in the TCP/IP Headers.

There are other fields that can be compressed. For example, the total length field could be eliminated if the data link control was designed to derive the length field (most modern-day data link protocols are so designed).

Potential Wraparound Problems

A number of studies have been conducted to evaluate potential problems related to the limited sequence number field in the TCP header. The TCP sequence number is 32 bits, which appears at first glance to be a huge number space. But TCP is a stream-oriented protocol and sequences on individual bytes are not blocks of traffic such as packets and PDUs.

The problem revolves around using a sequence number more than once during a connection. This problem has not been addressed in the past because transmission systems were relatively slow and did not "push" much traffic through internets at a very fast rate. However, with the increasing use of fiber optics and the approaching new digital hierarchy (supporting multigigabit ranges), traffic can be transmitted so quickly that the sequence number space is wrapped around and reused.

Why does this present a problem? It is conceivable that at a very high data rate, the TCP/IP sequence will be exhausted and reused. Due to the variable nature of data transmissions with adaptive routing, a TCP segment could be delayed in an internet and could then be received at the receiving TCP entity as either an old duplicate or in place of the new TCP data unit that was recently introduced into the network. In either case, data corruption would occur because the protocol is not designed to handle transmission speeds that result in duplicate wrap-around sequence numbers. In addition, if a TCP port is disconnected and later opened, it is possible that a segment from the terminated connection could be accepted by the new connection.

A study contained in RFC 1185 shows the value of a wraparound counter (a sequence number) based on the transmission of protocol data units through different types of networks and transmission media (see Table 7.4). Obviously, reusing sequence numbers is not a problem with lower-speed networks such as 56-kbps ARPANETs, nor is it a problem with technology such as DW1 and Ethernet. The concern emerges with the use of high-speed links based on optical fiber. For example, in an FDDI LAN, the sequence number space will be exhausted in 170 seconds.

Of course, you could argue that while exhausting the sequence number in 17 seconds on a gigabit network could result in duplicate sequence numbers arriving and other problems, each socket connection operates with a separate sequence number. Therefore, is it rea-

TABLE 7.4   Thresholds for Wrap-Around

Network Type	Speed	Sequence Number Wraparound
ARPANET	56 Kbps	~3.6 days
DS1	1.5 Mbps	~3 hours
Ethernet	10 Mbps	~ 30 minutes
DS3	45 Mbps	380 seconds
FDDI	100 Mbps	170 seconds
Gigabit	1 Gbps	17 seconds

SOURCE: RFC 1185

sonable to assume that one socket on an end-user device will monopolize the bandwidth? The answer is yes. In emerging applications that require gigabit rates with video, color, bit-mapped graphics, and variable-speed video, it is quite possible, with RISC and parallel processors, that a gigabit network or gigabit line capacity could be consumed by one TCP connection.

Moreover, the manner in which the TCP sequence number is incremented can affect the outcome of a study such as the one conducted in this example. For example, several systems increment the sequence number variable every half second by 64,000, which would result in a wrap-around every 9.5 hours.

Other Considerations in Using TCP

As explained earlier in this chapter, the TCP stream data are acknowledged by the receiver on a byte basis (not on a PDU). The acknowledgment number, returned by the receiver, refers to the highest byte in the data stream that has been received. The sending TCP software keeps a copy of the data until it has been acknowledged. Once acknowledged, it turns off a retransmission timer and deletes the segment copy from a retransmission queue. If necessary, it will retransmit lost or errored data.

As mentioned previously in the book, the term associated with this technique is *inclusive acknowledgment*. It works well on systems that deliver data in sequential order, but the underlying IP might deliver data out of order or discard data altogether. In such an event, TCP has no way to notify the sender that it has received certain or no segments of a transmission. It can relay only the value of the contiguous, accumulated bytes. Consequently, the sending TCP software might time-out and resend data segments that have already been successfully received.

A *push* function is available to force TCP to send data immediately. This function ensures that traffic is delivered in order to avoid deadlock at the other end. The stream concept does not deal with structured data streams, and it cannot delineate between records in a file transfer. Therefore, the applications must have some means of identifying the logical records before they begin their communications.

Also mentioned earlier in the book, TCP has a function similar to the OSI TP4 credit scheme, called the *window advertisement* field. A value is returned to the sending TCP in this field to inform it of the number of bytes of additional data the receiver is prepared to receive. If the sender receives a larger value in the window advertisement field, it can change the transmit window accordingly. It is not advisable to shrink the window advertisement past previously acceptable positions in the data stream unless it is accompanied by a complementary acknowledgment. That is, the window size can change as it slides forward.

Finally, TCP has the potential for providing considerable information to network managers (for example, if TCP is sending excessive retransmissions, it might provide a clue to problems in the network, such as dead gateways or timers that are not functioning properly). The positive acknowledgments can also be used to determine how well certain components in an internet are functioning.

User Datagram Protocol (UDP)

Previous chapters have discussed the concepts of a connectionless protocol. You might recall that the connectionless protocol provides no reliability or flow-control mechanisms. It also has no error-recovery procedures. UDP is classified as a connectionless protocol, although the operating system must maintain information about each UDP socket that is active. Perhaps a better description of UDP is that it is connection-oriented, but does not employ the extensive state management operations normally used in connection-oriented protocols. It is sometimes used in place of TCP in situations where the full services of TCP are not needed. For example, the Trivial File Transfer Protocol (TFTP) and Remote Procedure Call (RPC) use UDP.

UDP serves as a simple application interface to IP. Since it has no reliability, flow-control, or error-recovery measures, it serves principally as a multiplexer/demultiplexer for receiving and sending IP traffic. Figure 7.22 illustrates how UDP accepts datagrams from IP.

UDP makes use of the port concept to direct datagrams to the proper upper-layer applications. UDP datagrams contains a destination port number and a source port number. The destination number is used by the UDP module to deliver traffic to the proper recipient.

Format of the UDP message

Perhaps the best way to explain this protocol is to examine the message and the fields residing in the message. As Figure 7.23 illustrates, the format is quite simple and contains the following fields:

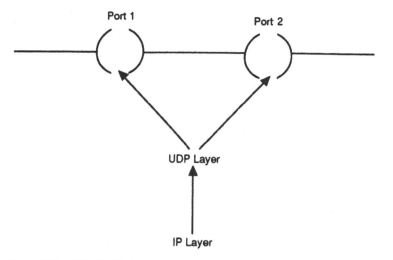

Figure 7.22   UDP Multiplexing.

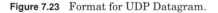

Figure 7.23   Format for UDP Datagram.

Source port   This value identifies the port of the sending application process. The field is optional. If it is not used, a value of 0 is inserted in this field.

Destination port.   This value identifies the receiving process on the destination host machine.

Length.   This value indicates the length of the user datagram, including the header and the data. This value implies that the minimum length is eight octets.

Checksum.   This optional value is the 16-bit one's complement of the one's complement sum of the pseudo-IP header, the UDP header, and the data. It also performs a checksum on any padding (if it was necessary to make the message contain a multiple of two octets).

The pseudo-header (also used in TCP) ensures that the UDP data unit has arrived at the proper destination address. Therefore, the pseudo-header includes the IP addresses and is included as part of the checksum calculation. The final destination performs a complementary checksum on the pseudo-header (and, of course, the remainder of the UDP data unit) to verify that (a) the traffic is not altered and (b) it reached the correct destination address.

There is not a lot more to be said about UDP. It is the minimal level of service used in many transaction-based application systems. It is, however, quite useful if the full services of TCP are not needed.

IPv6 and TCP/UDP

The implementation of IPv6 will also affect the TCP and UDP operations. The impact is not significant, but the following changes will be necessary. First, since TCP and UDP use IP addresses, the operating system that interworks these programs in IP must be modified. Second, the error checking performed by TCP and UDP entails the use of a pseudo-header, which is the IP header. The idea is to include the IP source and destination address and checksum in order to detect delivery problems. Obviously, these upper-layer checksums must be altered to account for the new IPv6 address base.

Since error checking with the checksum is deleted in IPv6, the TCP/UDP checksums become even more important; they are mandatory in both TCP and UDP operations.

Summary

TCP provides a simple set of services for the ULPs of internets. TCP has relatively few features, but the features are designed to provide end-to-end reliability, graceful closes, unambiguous connections, handshakes, and several quality-of-service operations. The internet transport layer also provides a connectionless operation called the UDP. This is a minimal level of service, principally to use the source and destination ports for multiplexing. With UDP, the user application is typically tasked with performing most of the end-to-end reliability operations that would normally be done by TCP.

8

Route Discovery Protocols

Because the TCP/IP protocol suite is based on the concept of internetworking, routers play a very important role in TCP/IP-based networks. Indeed, the IP protocol is designed around the concept of internetworking host computers with gateways and routers. This chapter is devoted to the various types of route discovery protocols used in internets. The last part of the chapter discusses several newer techniques used in internetworking and router operations. You should be familiar with routers, bridges, and gateways, described in Chapter 2, prior to reading this chapter. In this discussion, I will use the terms *gateway* and *router* interchangeably. More concise definitions are available in Chapters 2 and 3. Remember as you read this chapter that IP is not a route discovery protocol. It uses routing tables that are created as a result of the operation of the protocols explained in this chapter.

Terms and Concepts

A computer acting as a switch can join together individual networks. As discussed in Chapters 2 and 7, the switch operations are programmed to route the traffic to the proper network by examining a destination address in the datagram and matching the address with entries in a routing table. Those entries should indicate the best route to the next network or next gateway.

Although the individual networks can be administered by local authorities, it is common practice for a group of networks to be administered as a whole system. From the perspective of an internet, this group of networks is called an *autonomous system* and is administered by a single *authority*. Examples of autonomous systems are networks located on sites such as college campuses, hospital complexes, and military installations. Networks located at these sites are connected together by a gateway. Because the gateways operate within an autonomous system, they often choose their own mechanisms for routing data.

Routing data between autonomous systems is usually controlled by a single (global) administrative authority. Thus, the local administrative authorities must agree on how they provide information (advertise) to each other on the reachability of the host computers inside the autonomous systems. The advertising responsibility can be given to one or a number of gateways.

The autonomous systems are identified by autonomous system numbers. How this is accomplished is up to the administrators, but the idea is to use different numbers to distinguish different autonomous systems. Such a numbering scheme is helpful if a network manager does not want to route traffic through an autonomous system. Even if the network is connected to the manager's network, the network might be administered by a competitor, or might not have adequate or proper security services. By using routing protocols and numbers that identify autonomous systems, gateways can determine how to reach each other and exchange routing information.

Distance vector and link state metric protocols

Route discovery operations are classified as either distance vector or link state metric protocols. The distance vector protocol determines a best route to a destination based on the distance (the fewest number of hops) to a vector (a destination end point usually identified by an address). The link state metric protocol uses a value assigned to each communications link attached to each router either in an internet or within a subnet or area in an internet. This value can represent delay, line speed, or anything the network administrator wants. The route is determined by examining these values and deciding which output link from a node represents the best route. In both operations, the best path is the smallest value computed by summing the hop count or total link state values from the source to the destination for all possible routes. For large networks, do not attempt to calculate this best path by hand. Although the formula is simple, it requires too many iterations.

Routing based on the fewest hops (distance vector)

The majority of systems route traffic based on the idea that it is best to transmit datagrams through the fewest number of networks and nodes (hops). In the past, network designers believed that this approach led to the most efficient route through an internet and, perhaps more to the point, it was easy to implement. The value of a fewest-hops approach can be debated, but I will confine myself to discussing how the approach works rather than its relative merits. Later in this chapter, the newer routing techniques are examined in considerable detail.

Figure 8.1 is an example of how a fewest-hops routing directory (table) can be employed. This figure actually shows a topological database, but it serves the purposes of this discussion. The next section explains a condensed version of the topological database, which can be used as the routing directory or table.

The routing directory contains values that represent the number of intermediate gateways (hops) between the originator of the traffic (for example, the source at node A) and the receiver (for example, the destination at node G). For simplicity, any intervening networks are not shown in this figure. The datagrams are routed to the adjacent gateway closest to the final destination. A datagram at node A destined

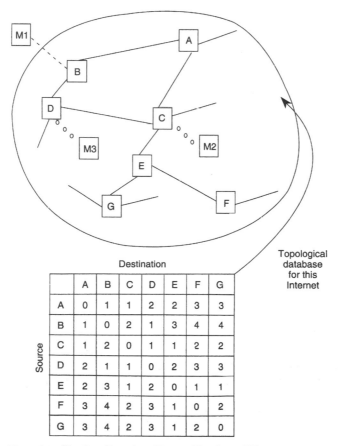

Topological database for this Internet

Destination

	A	B	C	D	E	F	G
A	0	1	1	2	2	3	3
B	1	0	2	1	3	4	4
C	1	2	0	1	1	2	2
D	2	1	1	0	2	3	3
E	2	3	1	2	0	1	1
F	3	4	2	3	1	0	2
G	3	4	2	3	1	2	0

Source

Figure 8.1   Routing Based on Fewest Number of Hops.

transported from A to J. The numbers on the links between the gateways reflect traffic conditions between the two gateways connected to the link. The larger numbers are weighted to indicate more delay. Each node communicates with its neighbor nodes (those directly connected to it) by exchanging status messages. If the information in the message indicates that the status of the neighbor has changed, the routing table must be changed. This new information is broadcast to all other nodes and used to update their routing tables.

In Figure 8.2b, the dashed lines show that the datagrams follow the path A → C → D → E → G → I → J. The total time-weighted value for the end-to-end path is 15, which represents the path that has the shortest overall delay between A and J.

The datagrams from A might take different paths and traverse different nodes en route to J. If link, node, or network conditions change, as in Figure 8.2c, the end-to-end path could also change (on the E–F, F–H, G–H, H–J, and I–J links). In this example, the datagrams now follow the path A → C → D → E → F → H → J. Take care when designing and implementing adaptive routing schemes in order to prevent the datagrams from oscillating in an internet. If the routing tables are updated too frequently because of unstable network performance, datagrams might take circuitous routes and perhaps never reach their final destination. It is easy to understand the value of the time-to-live parameter of the IP datagram in this situation. Oscillating datagrams are eventually discarded and then retransmitted later by the TCP module at the originating host computer.

Core and noncore gateways

Internet gateways have been classified as being *core* or *noncore*. The terms are not used as much today, however, as they were in the past. Core gateways are administered by a single authority; noncore gateways are outside the control of the single administrative authority and are controlled by individual groups.

When ARPANET was first implemented, it consisted of a single backbone network. As it evolved and grew, ARPANET provided attached gateways to local Internet networks. The *gateway-to-gateway protocol* (GGP), was used for these core gateways to inform each other about their attached local networks. Traffic passing between two local networks passed through two gateways, and each core gateway had complete routing information on the other.

Because these gateways had complete routing information, they did not need the default route described in Chapter 3. Things changed, however, as the Internet grew. Backbone networks were added to the original backbone, and local networks were attached to other local area networks (LANs). The same growth also occurred on many private internets. The concept of a gateway holding the complete routing information of an internet thus became too unwieldy.

Exterior and interior gateways

To solve this problem, gateways were given responsibilities for only part of an internet. In this manner, a gateway did not need to know about all the other gateways, but relied on neighbor gateways and gateways in other autonomous systems to reveal their routing information. Indeed, if the gateways had insufficient knowledge to make a routing decision, they simply chose a default route. This change resulted in two other terms: *exterior gateways* and *interior gateways*. An exterior gateway supports the exchange of routing information between different autonomous systems; interior gateways belong to the same autonomous system.

From these definitions are derived two other definitions. An *exterior neighbor* is a gateway that exchanges routing information between two autonomous systems. An *interior neighbor* exchanges information within the same autonomous system. Figure 8.3 shows the relationship between external and internal gateway protocols. A set of packet-switched networks is labeled as autonomous system 1 and is connected to another set of packet-switched networks, labeled autonomous system 2. Gateway 1 (G1) and gateway 2 (G2) use an *external gateway protocol* (EGP) to exchange data and control information. The two internets use their own *internal gateway protocols* (IGP) for route management inside each autonomous system. It is not unusual for a gateway to support two (or more) route discovery protocols, depending on where the traffic is destined. These gateways use an IGP within their autonomous systems and an EGP between each autonomous system.

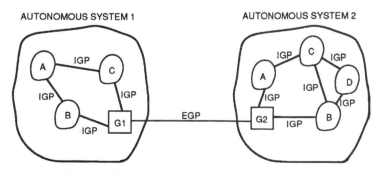

Figure 8.3 External Gateway Protocols and Internal Gateway Protocols.

Border routers and boundary routers

The terms described thus far would seem to cover all bases (or at least all nodes), but not quite. It is now accepted that an autonomous system might need to be further divided to achieve efficient and manageable routing tables and protocols. Therefore, an autonomous system can be divided into *areas*.

Areas can contain one to n subnets that exchange information through an IGP. In turn, areas have a designated *border gateway* that exchanges information with other border gateways. Finally, designated *boundary gateways* exchange information between autonomous systems.

If some of these terms seem similar to other terms described earlier, then you are following this narrative quite well because some of the terms *are* redundant. For example, an EGP gateway is the same as a border router. So why did the Internet authorities expand the vocabulary? The terms *border* and *boundary router* were added to the Internet vocabulary with the publication of the open-shortest-path-first (OSPF) standard, which is described later in this chapter.

How autonomous systems or areas exchange information

Figure 8.4 is a slight alteration of Figure 8.1, showing internetworking concepts in more detail. For simplicity, the networks between the gateways are not included in this figure. Be aware that the example is a generic example of route discovery. Later in this chapter, I will examine the specific rules for each internet gateway protocol. Nodes C and X are designated as gateways for autonomous systems 1 and 2, respectively. The term *autonomous systems* also applies to areas. In Figure 8.4a, gateway C's routing table (shown in the box) is sent to gateway X, which uses it to update its routing table containing reachability information pertaining to nodes A, B, C, D, E, F, and G. Gateway X is not concerned with how this information was obtained by gateway C. The internal operations of Gateway C remain transparent to gateway X.

To expand this discussion, assume that nodes F and K also exchange routing information. An autonomous system is not restricted to one core gateway, but an area usually designates only one router for each area. Now assume (as in Figure 8.4b) that the link or network connection is lost between E and F. Gateway C discovers this problem through its IGP and typically enters a value symbolizing infinity in its routing table entry for F (16, 255, or whatever the protocol stipulates to represent infinity). An "F = 16, through C" message is sent to gateway X, as shown by the arrow from C to X in Figure 8.4b.

Gateway X, however, likely knows of a better route. Because F and K have exchanged routing information, the IGP exchange between X

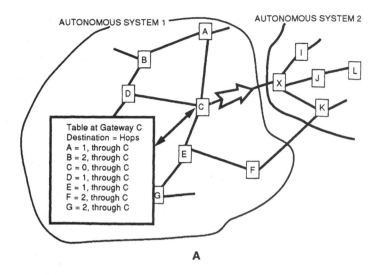

A

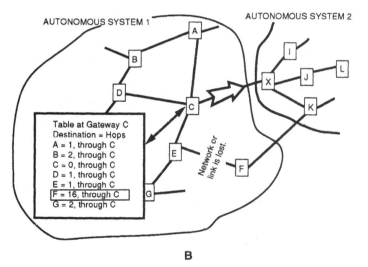

B

Figure 8.4 (a) Interactions of Autonomous Systems or Areas, (b) Losing a Network Connection, and (c) Receiving Routing Information from Gateway X.

and K reveals that a path better than 16 exists to F. X stores in its routing table that this path is through K. It also sends an EGP message to core gateway C that F can be reached through X with a cost metric of 3. Because 3 is less than 16, gateway C updates its routing table accordingly, as shown in Figure 8.4c. This process is known as *repairing partitions*. This term is not used much in internet networks, but is common in OSI-based networks.

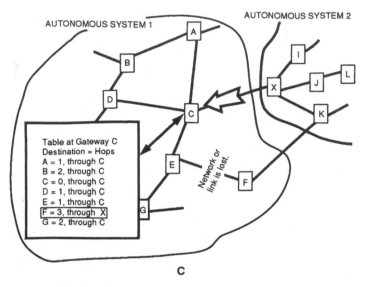

Table at Gateway C
Destination = Hops
A = 1, through C
B = 2, through C
C = 0, through C
D = 1, through C
E = 1, through C
F = 3, through X
G = 2, through C

Figure 8.4 Continued

In summary, routing tables are changed at gateways when an arriving message indicates that:

- A new network has been found
- A better path to a network has been found
- A former "better" path must be degraded

In an actual internetworking situation, a network might not be allowed to repair its partition with another network. While the routers might be capable, a network administrator (say, of network A) might not want a foreign network's traffic to flow through network A. Moreover, the software might not be designed to support this operation.

Who participates in exchanging routing information and executing routing logic?

As stated in previous chapters, both hosts and gateways can execute routing logic, and it is possible for a host to fulfill both functions. I have also said that when using a host computer as a gateway, you must consider the issues of delay, throughput, and efficiency. Typically, the host in an internet does not have as much knowledge as the gateway has about the network. The host usually routes traffic through the IP routing algorithm and default values in the routing tables; in general, it routes traffic to gateways. These gateways, thus, have a more thorough knowledge of the network and perform more elaborate routing functions.

Internet protocols are based on using partial routing tables at some gateways and full routing tables at others. This approach represents a compromise between, at one extreme, loading full routing tables in all machines and, at the other extreme, using schemes without directories. The practice of using full routing tables could be unduly burdensome for a number of reasons. First, all machines do not need to know the locations of all other machines. Second, excessive memory could be consumed to store complete routing information in large tables. Third, searching tables to extract the routing information could consume considerable CPU processing time. In any event, you need to consider these factors very carefully before making a decision to load the tasks onto an applications processor or a specialized switching processor.

The practical approach is to use a relatively small number of gateways that maintain complete routing tables for the networks, with the outlying gateways keeping only partial information (the host might have even more limited routing tables). With this approach, the managers of outlying networks need not concern themselves with the onerous task of maintaining large tables of routing information. They need be concerned only with their specific networks.

In summary, the principal advantages to partial routing tables are storage saving, CPU cycle saving, and the ability of outlying network managers to manage their routing operations in a relatively simple fashion without affecting other networks.

Clarifying terms

Before I examine specific gateway protocols, I should first define several terms introduced earlier in this chapter:

Gateway-to-gateway protocol (GGP). Provides routing information between core gateways

External gateway protocol (EGP). Provides routing information between autonomous systems

Internal gateway protocol (IGP). Provides routing information within an autonomous system and perhaps within an area.

Remember that some people use these three terms generically to describe a concept. This practice is acceptable, as long as it is understood how the terms are used.

GGP and EGP also identify two specific internet gateway standards. They are older protocols and have been removed from most systems, so they are not described in this book. IGP does not identify a specific standard, but rather a concept and a family of interior gateway protocols.

Now that we have analyzed the general concepts of gateways, we can move on to the specific gateway protocols. I will introduce BGP first, and continue with IDRP. I will then examine IGPs, notably the routing information protocol (RIP), and the OSPF specifications.

The Border Gateway Protocol

The border gateway protocol (BGP) is an interautonomous system protocol (also known as an interdomain protocol) and a relatively new addition to the family of route discovery protocols. It has been used since 1989, but not extensively until recently. BGP is published in RFC 1267.

BGP has a number of significant advantages over EGP. First, it can operate with networks that have looped topologies, using algorithms that prune the loops out. Second, BGP does not have the "count to infinity" problem found in many route discovery protocols because it advertises all autonomous systems (transit machines) on the path to a destination address. Third, as a result of this full advertising, a node that receives more than one possible path (in advertisements) to a destination can, without ambiguity, choose the best path. In addition, BGP does not care what type of intra-autonomous route discovery protocol is used, nor if multiple inter-autonomous protocols are employed.

BGP is designed to run with a reliable transport layer protocol, such as TCP. An implementor of BGP need not be concerned about reliable receipt of traffic, segmentation, etc. because these potential problems are handled by the transport layer.

BGP operations

BGP systems initially exchange routing information by sending an entire BGP routing table. Thereafter, only updates are exchanged. As with most routing exchange protocols, BGP uses keep-alive messages to ensure that a connection is up.

The key aspect to BGP is the idea of *path attributes*, which are contained in the update messages, along with network addresses of the advertised networks. The following are definitions of several major attributes:

ORIGIN.   Defines the origin of the path information, and describes the origin as an IGP, EGP, or an origin of some other means

AS_PATH.   Lists the autonomous systems (ASs) that must be traversed to reach the advertised networks

NEXT_HOP.   Contains the IP address of the border router that is to be used as the next hop to reach the networks listed in an update message

UNREACHABLE.   Notifies the speaker that a previously advertised route has become unreachable.

A BGP machine that sends BGP messages is called a *BGP speaker*. When a BGP speaker receives a new route advertisement from a BGP peer over an external BGP link (from another autonomous system), it advertises this route to all other BGP speakers in the autonomous system if the route is better than other known routes to the advertised network or if no acceptable routes are known. Unreachable routes are also advertised. This information is contained in the UPDATE message, and the path attributes are part of this message.

A BGP speaker must generate an update message to all peers when it selects a new route. Be aware that RFC 1267 does not define the rules for how alternative routes are selected and compared.

BGP messages

Figure 8.5 shows the header of the BGP message. The marker field is used for authentication or to detect a loss of synchronization between BGP peer nodes. Its contents are application-dependent. The length field indicates the length of the entire message in octets, including the header. The type field indicates the type of message: open, update, notification, or keep-alive.

The open message establishes a relationship with a peer BGP entity. Its contents are shown in Figure 8.5b. The version number field contains the value of the current version of BGP (currently 3). The my autonomous number field contains the autonomous number of the sender of the message. Hold time indicates the maximum time expected between the receipt of successive keep-alive, update, or notification messages. The BGP identifier is an IP address of one of the sender interfaces; the value remains the same for all messages from all interfaces. The authentication code identifies the type of authentication procedure used to authenticate the sender, the meaning of the next field (authentication data), and the algorithm for computing the marker fields. Its contents are application-dependent.

The update message is used to exchange routing information between BGP peers. Its contents are shown in Figure 8.5c. The length field indicates the length of the path attributes field. The path attributes field contains a number of bits to indicate if the information is optional or required, partial or full, and other values. It also contains an attribute value that indicates the internet network numbers

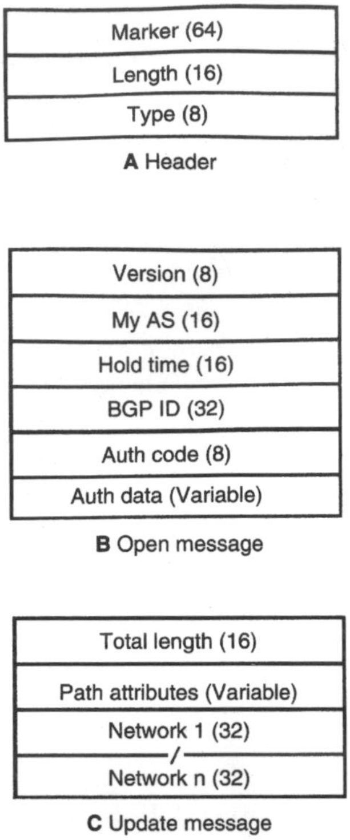

```
+---------------------------+
|       Marker (64)         |
+---------------------------+
|       Length (16)         |
+---------------------------+
|        Type (8)           |
+---------------------------+
```

A Header

```
+---------------------------+
|       Version (8)         |
+---------------------------+
|        My AS (16)         |
+---------------------------+
|       Hold time (16)      |
+---------------------------+
|        BGP ID (32)        |
+---------------------------+
|       Auth code (8)       |
+---------------------------+
|     Auth data (Variable)  |
+---------------------------+
```

B Open message

```
+---------------------------+
|      Total length (16)    |
+---------------------------+
|  Path attributes (Variable)|
+---------------------------+
|      Network 1 (32)       |
+------------/--------------+
|      Network n (32)       |
+---------------------------+
```

C Update message

Figure 8.5 BGP Messages.

advertised in the message. The keep-alive and notification messages are not shown here. Their purpose is to ensure that BGP peers are up and running and to exchange diagnostic messages.

Interior Gateway Protocols

I stated earlier in this chapter that the term *interior gateway protocol* (IGP) is both a generic term that refers to a concept, as well as a specific system. Unfortunately, the Internet has no clear IGP "leader" because of the somewhat unsystematic way IGPs were developed and promulgated. In fairness, I should state that network administrators prefer different IGP approaches because of different internal network management requirements. Nonetheless, as this book's subject is TCP/IP and internet protocols, my focus in the next several sections is three internet-related IGPs: RIP, hello, and gated. Then I will examine OSPF, which is a better IGP.

Even though BGP is an improvement over the older GGP and EGP systems, it suffers from several deficiencies. BGP operates only with IP and not CLNP, IPX, or other layer-three routing protocols. A more serious problem is that it supports only one route to a destination IP address. This handicap limits its applicability to large, complex networks that need multiple choices with varying performance criteria. Also, BGP does not advertise routes very efficiently, nor does it aggregate and converge routing information very well.

Interdomain Routing Protocols (IDRP)

IDRP is a recent addition to the route advertising protocol family. It is built on many of the concepts discussed for the border gateway protocol (BGP). For example, it distributes routing information with path vector values and is able to aggregate routes. It is an improvement of BGP because it allows the identification of more autonomous systems; unlike BGP, IDRP allows the control of routing information to nonadjacent domains. Perhaps the most serious problem that BGP exhibits, which is solved with IDRP, is that BGP provides only one route to a destination. This is a serious shortcoming and is corrected in IDRP.

Another feature of IDRP operation is called a *routing domain confederation* (RDC). This allows a further hierarchical entity in the network, which allows a specific domain to belong to more than one routing domain confederation.

Domains are identified with a *routing domain identifier* (RDI), which can be coded with OSI X.213 network addresses. In turn, each RDC is assigned a routing domain confederation identifier (RDCI). While IDRP defines the rules for the use of these addresses, it does not stipulate how they are assigned or managed.

Like BGP, IDRP uses link attributes such as throughput, delay, security. IDRP does not place any restrictions on the metrics, but leaves it to the network layer protocol, such as IP or CLNP, to provide the combinations. This flexibility makes IDRP particularly attractive for operations in more complex networks in which more than one layer-three routing protocol is employed.

IDRP is also similar to BGP in that it operates with three major types of functions: acquiring neighbors, determining the reachability to neighbors, and exchanging route advertising with neighbors.

IDRP has its own "layer-four reliability" mechanism, where it doesn't need to operate with TCP. The most common practice is for IDRP to operate over CLNP and RIP.

Routing Information Protocol

The RIP system was developed based on research at the Xerox Palo Alto Research Center (PARC) and Xerox's PUP and XNS routing protocols. Interestingly, RIP's wide use was due to its implementation at the University of California at Berkeley (UCB) in a number of LANs. UCB also distributed RIP with its UNIX system. Note that RIP is not standardized across vendor product lines, and most vendors offer value-added extensions to the protocol. This section describes the RIP version published in RFC 1058.

Because RIP was designed for LANs, it is based on a broadcast technology; a gateway periodically broadcasts its routing table to its neighbors. The broadcast aspect of RIP has brought forth complaints about its efficiency.

RIP is classified as a distance-vector algorithm routing protocol. RIP routing decisions are based on the number of intermediate hops to the final destination. Early descriptions of this type of protocol were provided by L. R. Ford and D. R. Fulkerson (*Flows in Networks* published by Princeton University Press, Princeton, NJ, 1962). RIP is thus sometimes called a Ford-Fulkerson algorithm or a Bellman-Ford algorithm because R. E. Bellman devised the routing equation (*Dynamic Programming* by Princeton University Press, Princeton, NJ, 1957).

RIP advertises only network addresses and distances (number of hops). It is similar to GGP in that it uses a hop count to compute the route cost, but it uses a maximum value of 16 to indicate that a network is unreachable. GGP uses a value of 255 to designate a network unreachable. Also, RIP needs information on all networks within the autonomous system. Similar to GGP, it exchanges information only with neighbors. Machines that participate in RIP operations are either active or passive devices. Active machines (usually gateways) advertise routes to other machines; passive machines (usually host computers) do not advertise routes, but receive messages and update their routing tables.

The hop count is a metric for the cost of the route. Other metrics can be used, such as delay, security, and bandwidth, but most implementations use a simple hop count. RIP also uses UDP and UDP port 520 is used by the RIP machines to send and receive RIP messages. Each machine that uses RIP must have a routing table. The table contains an entry for each destination serviced by the machine. Each entry in the table must contain at least the following information:

- The destination IP address
- A metric (between 1 and 15) of the cost (number of hops) to reach the destination
- The IP address of the next gateway in the path to the destination
- Indicators to determine if the route has changed recently
- Timers associated with the route

RIP timers

Two timers are associated with each route: a *time-out timer* and a *garbage collection timer*. The time-out timer is set each time a route is initialized or updated. If 180 seconds elapse before an update is received or if the update contains a distance metric of 16, the route is considered obsolete. The route is not removed, however, until the garbage collection timer has also expired. This timer is set for another 120 seconds, and after it expires the route is removed from the routing table. The route continues to be included in all update messages until the garbage collection timer expires.

Another timer is used to send updates (called *responses in RIP*) to neighboring machines. Every 30 seconds, these messages are broadcast by active gateways. They contain pairs of values; one value of the pair is an IP address and the other is the hop count to that address from the source of the message. The original versions of RIP broadcast their entire routing table every 30 seconds, regardless of whether the table had changed—a rather obvious deficiency that has been corrected in newer versions.

Example of RIP operations

Figure 8.6 is an example of RIP operations. Gateways G5 and G6 report a (D,V) of (1,5) in regard to network 5, meaning they can reach network 5 with a metric cost of 1. This message is relayed to G3, which updates its routing table entry to network 5 with a cost of 2. G3 then sends a message to G1 and G2, which store a cost of 3 to network 5. In turn, G1 and G2 advertise a (D,V) of (3,5) to other gateways, and so on.

Like most route discovery protocols, RIP is based on trust: the router receiving an advertisement trusts that it is accurate, and uses it to make routing decisions. Thus, in Figure 8.6, when G4 receives the message from G2 that G2 is three hops away form network 5, G5 must take the position of, "If you are three hops away from network 5, then I must be four hops away, and I can reach network 5 through you."

G5's routing table regarding network 5 would appear as shown in Table 8.1. The Destination column is the address of the destination network, as shown by G5 (in TCP/IP based networks, an IP address). Next Hop is the address of the node that is to receive the traffic next. An entry is 0 in this column means that no next hop occurs. The Metric column states how many hops are between this machine and the destination network. The Direct or Remote column is either D (directly attached) or R (a remote network, not directly attached). The Local or RIP column is either L (the network was discovered because it is local) or R (the network was discovered through RIP messages).

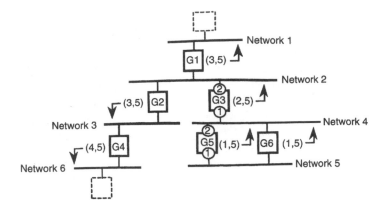

Where: (D,V) = (D) distance to (V) vector (IP address)

ⓝ = physical port (interface) number

Figure 8.6   Examples of RIP Operations.

TABLE 8.1   G5 Routing Table

Destination	Next Hop	Metric	Direct or remote	Local or RIP	Interface
Network 5	0	1	D	L	1

The Interface column identifies the physical port on G5 at which the discovery was made. Because all gateways receive advertisements from each other, reachability to all networks can be computed. As another example, Table 8.2 is the routing table as viewed by G3.

RIP requires that a route, once learned, cannot change until a (D,V) is received that represents a better route to the vector. If a gateway receives a message of the same metric distance to a network (as G3 did by receiving messages from G5 and G6), then the gateway uses the first arriving message.

TABLE 8.2   G3 Routing Table

Destination	Next Hop	Metric	Direct or Remote	Local or RIP	Interface
Network 1	G1	2	R	R	2
Network 2	0	1	D	L	2
Network 3	G2	2	R	R	2
Network 4	0	1	D	L	1
Network 5	G5	2	R	R	1
Network 6	G2	3	R	R	2

RIP problems

In retrospect, the internet authorities would most likely have opted for a route advertising protocol other than RIP. Indeed, changes have been made to the original version to correct some rather serious deficiencies. One of these problems, called *counting to infinity*, is shown in Figure 8.6. Gateway 5 has lost its connection to network 5. When this event occurs, it sends an RIP message through network 4 to gateway 3 with a (D,V) of (16,5), signifying that it has an infinite distance (16) to network 5.

As noted in event 1, however, gateway 3 understands that it has a metric distance of 2 to gateway 5. Because this value is better than (16,5), it maintains its routing table entry and advertises the value back to G5. G5, upon receiving the message that network 5 can be reached through G3 with a metric of 2, changes its update table as indicated in event 3 with (D,V) = (3,5): two hops through gateway 3 plus one more hop from gateway 5, for a total of three hops. This message is related back to G3, and you can see in event 4 that it changes the routing table to (D,V) = (4,5) because it believes that to get to network 5 through G5 it must add one more hop to the value of 3 (which occurred in event 3). Thus, the two gateways increment their metric distance each time an RIP message is exchanged between them. Moreover, they continue to send the datagram back and forth until the IP time-to-live value expires. The values are eventually incremented to the RIP infinity value of 16.

To make matters worse, the 30-second rule means it might take a long time for the network to converge (complete the advertisements and build the revised routing tables). For the worst case, seven minutes are required, which includes propagation delays and processing time. An average of $3\frac{1}{2}$ minutes expires before the internet converges.

Recent RIP implementations handle this problem with a technique called the *split horizon* update. This approach requires a gateway to remember the neighbor from which the route was received. The gateway is not allowed to send updates to a neighbor about a route it learned from that neighbor. A variation on this is the *split horizon with poisoned reverse*, which allows the routes to be included in the updates, but their metrics are set to infinity (a value of 16).

Another approach, used in conjunction with the poisoned reverse technique, is called a *triggered update*. This technique requires a gateway to send an immediate RIP message when it receives messages indicating a problem. The gateway is not allowed to wait for the next ongoing broadcast. In other words, the approach requires that bad news about a connection or another aspect of the network be propagated as quickly as possible.

These techniques ameliorate the routing exchange problems inher-

```
0          7 8        15 16                    31
┌─────────────┬────────────┬──────────────────────┐
│  Command    │  Version   │      All zeros        │
├─────────────┴────────────┼──────────────────────┤
│     Address family       │      All zeros        │
├──────────────────────────┴──────────────────────┤
│                  IP address                      │
├──────────────────────────────────────────────────┤
│                  All zeros                       │
├──────────────────────────────────────────────────┤
│                  All zeros                       │
├──────────────────────────────────────────────────┤
│                   metric                         │
├──────────────────────────────────────────────────┤
│           repeat of previous 20 bytes            │
└──────────────────────────────────────────────────┘
```

(a) RIP-1

```
0          7 8        15 16                    31
┌─────────────┬────────────┬──────────────────────┐
│  Command    │  Version   │    Routing domain     │
├─────────────┴────────────┼──────────────────────┤
│     Address family       │      Route tag        │
├──────────────────────────┴──────────────────────┤
│                  IP address                      │
├──────────────────────────────────────────────────┤
│                  Subnet mask                     │
├──────────────────────────────────────────────────┤
│               Next hop IP address                │
├──────────────────────────────────────────────────┤
│                   metric                         │
├──────────────────────────────────────────────────┤
│           repeat of previous 20 bytes            │
└──────────────────────────────────────────────────┘
```

(b) RIP-2

Figure 8.8   Routing Information Protocol (RIP) Messages.

Subnet mask.   This is associated with the IP address in the message.

Next hop IP address.   If this field is 0, it indicates that datagrams should be sent to the address that is sending the RIP message. Otherwise, it contains an IP address, which indicates where the datagrams should be sent.

RIP vs. OSPF

Due to the technical deficiencies and lack of standardization in RIP, the Internet Engineering Task Force developed the OSPF protocol. It eliminates the routing loops and dead-ends described earlier in this chapter. The OSPF protocol does not broadcast its entire table to other routers. Rather, it sends information only about its own links to each router. Each receiving router must acknowledge this traffic to the transmitting router. After receiving the information, each router builds appropriate entries in its own routing table. OSPF is described in detail later in this chapter.

RIP and IPX

Novell's RIP, known as IPX, was derived from RIP. These two protocols are more similar than they are different. Both are based on distance vectors, but IPX is proprietary and does not adhere to the Internet RIP RFC. RIP IPX also has a number-of-ticks field, which can be used as a measure of delay. IPX advertises every 60 seconds and has a useful mechanism for allowing a router to gracefully close and go offline by informing other routers of this event.

The Hello Protocol

In the past, the Hello protocol was widely used throughout TCP/IP-based systems. I mention it here for a historical perspective. Digital Equipment Corporation's old LSI/11 minicomputer uses Hello in its "fuzzball" software. It differs rather significantly from RIP, principally because the delay is based on time rather than hop counts. A gateway protocol advertising delay requires that the gateways have network clocks that are reasonably accurate in their alignment with each other. Hello thus periodically provides messages for clock synchronization. In addition to carrying routing information, a Hello message also contains a time stamp for use in checking time-related events.

The Hello message format

The Hello message format is shown in Figure 8.9. The checksum field checks for errors in the message. The date field is the value of a local date of the message sender, and the time field contains the local time of the sender. The time stamp field is used by the machines to determine the round-trip delay of the message. This field is important for a protocol such as Hello, which uses delay as a metric for computing routes. The offset field is a pointer into the delay and offset entries. The hosts field specifies the number of entries that follow in the list of hosts. The delay host and offset host fields contain the delay to reach a host machine and an estimate between the difference (offset) between the sender's clock and the receiver's clock. If you want more information on Hello, refer to RFC 891.

Gated

Another "old" protocol is Gated. This internal gateway protocol has also seen considerable use. For example, IBM uses it in its UNIX implementation on some personal computers. Gated combines many

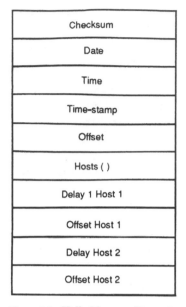

Checksum
Date
Time
Time-stamp
Offset
Hosts ( )
Delay 1 Host 1
Offset Host 1
Delay Host 2
Offset Host 2

Figure 8.9 Hello Message Format.

of the functions of RIP, Hello, and EGP. The program was developed at Cornell University and operates with UNIX. It allows network managers to establish how Gated can advertise routes to other exterior gateways. It is designed to accept either RIP or Hello messages and modify them for advertising within the Gated framework.

Summary of Distance-Vector Protocols

The major features of distance vector protocols can be summarized as follows:

- Neighbor gateways exchange routing information.
- All gateways must participate in the operations, thus creating the potential for large message exchanges.
- Gateways might not know about other gateways beyond their neighbors. They know only that their attached networks are reachable through a neighbor gateway.
- Messages are generally large and contain all routing entries.
- Neighbors periodically test each other's status.
- Distance vector protocols adjust slowly to topology changes.

Choosing the Optimum Path with a Shortest Path Algorithm

The Internet Engineering Task Force published RFC 1247, the OSPF protocol (OSPF stands for "open shortest path first"). The term is, however, inaccurate; the protocols described thus far in this chapter are designed to choose the optimum rather than the first path. OSPF is based on well-tested techniques used in the industry for a number of years. In this section, I will describe these techniques; in the next section, I will concentrate on the primary features of OSPF. (In this discussion, the term *node* is synonymous with *gateway* and *router*.)

I have already explained that data communications networks are designed to route user traffic based on a variety of criteria, generally referred to as *least-cost routing* or *link metrics*. The name does not mean that routing is based solely on obtaining the least-cost route in the literal sense, however. Other factors are often part of a network routing algorithm:

- Capacity of the links
- Delay and throughput requirements
- Number of datagrams awaiting transmission onto a link
- Load leveling through the network
- Security requirements for the link
- Type of traffic based on the type of link
- Number of intermediate links, networks, and gateways between the transmitting and receiving hosts
- Ability to reach (connect to) intermediate nodes and the final receiving host

Although networks vary in least-cost criteria, three constraints must be considered: the delay, throughput, and connectivity. If the delay is excessive or if the throughput is too little, the network will not meet the needs of the user community. The third constraint is quite obvious. Gateways and networks must be able to reach each other; otherwise, all other least-cost criteria are irrelevant.

As you have learned in this chapter, algorithms that are used to route data through an internet vary. Recently, the attention of the data communications industry has focused on two classes of routing algorithms. The first technique, called *bifurcated routing*, is designed to minimize the average network delay. The second technique, called *shortest path routing*, provides a least-cost path between a communicating pair of users and minimizes the delay to the users. Bifurcated routing is not used much, so I mention it only in passing. For further information, examine *Computer-Communication Network Design and Analysis*, by M. Schwartz (Prentice Hall, 1977).

Several shortest-path algorithms are used in the industry, most of which are based on what is called *algorithm A*. This has been used as the model for newer internet SPF protocols, and has been used for several years to establish optimum designs and network topologies.

One final point is in order before I explain algorithm A. Many vendors have been developing route-discovery protocols for over a decade based on dynamic adjustments to link conditions or the state of a neighbor node. Their research and implementations are impressive. Some of these vendors believe that their proprietary solutions are superior to standardized approaches such as OSPF. While this view has merit, it means that their proprietary solutions are "closed" and their switch (node) will not interwork with a competitor's node. This approach might be attractive to the vendor, especially if the vendor's product has a significant market share. It might also be attractive to the vendor's clients if they do not mind a sole-sourced internet. Other clients, however, prefer a multivendor operation. While this sort of operation is technically feasible, it entails a long and complex migration away from the closed solutions deeply embedded in many vendors' architectures.

Figure 8.10 is based on Figure 8.2, but applies to algorithm A using node A as the source and node J as the destination (sink). (The topology represented in this figure is for illustration, not implementation.) Algorithm A is defined generally as follows:

- Least-cost criteria weights are assigned to the paths in the network (Figure 8.10a).

- Each node is labeled (identified) with its least-cost criteria from the source along a known path. Initially no paths are known, so each node is labeled with infinity. Updates to the values once the weights are established are the same as an initialization.

- Each node is examined in relation to all nodes adjacent to it. The source node is the first node considered, and becomes the working node (Figure 8.10b). This step is actually a one-time occurrence wherein the source node is initialized with the costs of all its adjacent nodes.

- Least-cost criteria labels are assigned to each of the nodes adjacent to the working node. Labels change if a shorter path is found from this node to the source node. In OSPF, this situation would occur with sending link status messages on a broadcast basis to all other nodes.

- After the adjacent nodes are labeled (or relabeled), all other nodes in the network are examined. If one has a smaller value in its label, its label becomes permanent and it becomes the working node (see Figure 8.10c).

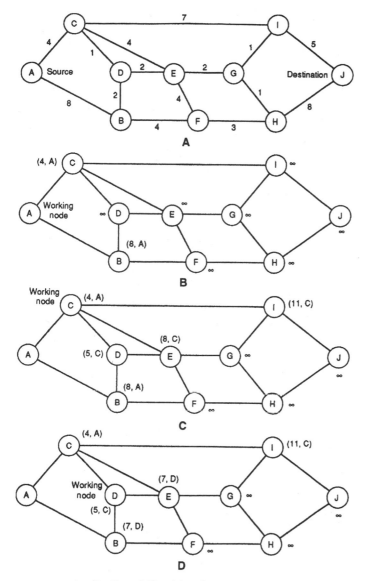

Figure 8.10 Application of Algorithm A.

- If the sum of the node's label is less than the label on an adjacent node, the adjacent node's label is changed because a shorter path has been found to the source node. In Figure 8.10d, node B is relabeled because node D is a shorter route through node C.

- Another working node is selected, and the process repeats itself until all possibilities have been searched. The final labels reveal the least-cost, end-to-end path between the source and other nodes.

These nodes are considered to be within a set N as it pertains to the source node.

The following steps illustrate the preceding discussion:

1. Let $D(v)$ = the sum of link weights on a given path.
2. Let $c(i,j)$ = the cost between node i and j.
3. Set n = (1).
4. For each node (v) not in N, set $D(v) = C(1,v)$.
5. For each step, find a node w not in N for which $D(w)$ is a minimum; add w to set N.
6. Update $D(v)$ for all nodes still not in N by $D(v) = \min [D(v), D(w) + c(w,v)]$
7. Repeat steps 4 through 6 until all nodes are in set N.

The results of the algorithm are shown in Table 8.3. The steps are successively performed until all nodes are in N. The process is performed for each node, and a routing table is created for the node's use. Each node's table is constructed in the same manner just discussed. The routing topology for node A is shown in Figure 8.11. The numbers in parentheses represent the order of selection as reflected in Table 8.3.

Let us examine the weighted paths in Figure 8.10a. You might wonder why certain paths are weighted with large or small numbers. Consider that node A could have two communication links available for transmission. The link from A to C could be a microwave land link, and the A-to-B link could be a satellite circuit. If an interactive application were being routed through node A, the satellite link would be heavily weighted to discourage its use. As another example, the user data might need a secure link, and the A-to-B link might not use encryption/decryption devices. Networks might not route traffic based on factors such as security or other QOS parameters, but rather rely on performance criteria such as minimum delay.

TABLE 8.3   Choosing the Nodes

Step	N	A(B)	A(C)	A(D)	A(E)	A(F)	A(G)	A(H)	A(I)	A(J)
Initial	{A}	8	4	.	.	.	.	.	.	.
1	{A,C}	8	(4)	5	8	.	.	.	11	.
2	{A,C,D}	7	4	(5)	7	.	.	.	11	.
3	{A,C,D,B}	7	4	5	(7)	11	.	.	11	.
4	{A,C,D,B,E}	(7)	4	5	7	11	9	.	11	.
5	{A,C,D,B,E,F}	7	4	5	7	11	(9)	14	11	.
6	{A,C,D,B,E,F,G}	7	4	5	7	11	9	(10)	10	.
7	{A,C,D,B,E,F,G,H}	7	4	5	7	11	9	10	(10)	18
8	{A,C,D,B,E,F,G,H,I}	7	4	5	7	(11)	9	10	10	15
9	{A,C,D,B,E,F,G,H,I,J}	7	4	5	7	11	9	10	10	(15)

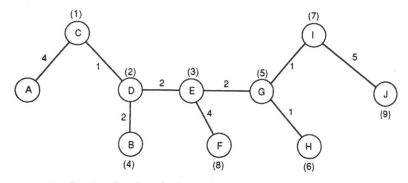

Figure 8.11 Routing Topology for Route A.

If the least-cost criteria includes factors other than link and node capacity, a separate capacity analysis is required to determine the ability of the network to handle the traffic. In this regard, the network capacity is like a chain that is no stronger than its weakest link. Likewise, a network has no more capacity than a specific combination of its lowest-capacity resources.

You might argue that network switching provides the means to route traffic around nodes and links that are either saturated or of insufficient capacity to handle the load. Nonetheless, at some point the traffic reaches an area within the network that is a bottleneck. This bottleneck limits the throughput of the entire network.

To determine why this limit exists, assume that the least-cost weights in Figure 8.10a represent the maximum link and node capacities for traffic flow in one direction. A set of nodes and links can be identified that act as the lowest common resource for network capacity. One method of obtaining this information is a *cut*, which is the removal of connections (paths) between two nodes so the two nodes are disconnected. In other words, they cannot reach each other. Network designers look for the minimum cut through a network. A minimum cut describes an area with the minimum capacity and thus a potential bottleneck. Each cut is given a capacity that is the sum of the weights of the links through the cut. The cut with the lowest sum is the minimum cut.

Open Shortest Path First Protocol

This section provides an examination of OSPF. This protocol, designed by the OSPF working group of the Internet Engineering Task Force, is an IGP: gateways and routers are all within one autonomous system. Also, as stated earlier, OSPF is a link state or SPF protocol, in contrast to most other protocols, which are based on some type of Bellman-Ford approach. The protocol, although it relies on techniques designed outside the IP environment, is tailored specifically for IP and includes capabilities such as subnet addressing and TOS routing, the latter being found in the TOS field of the IP datagram header (see Figure 5.2 in Chapter 5).

OSPF bases its routing decisions on two fields in the IP datagram: the destination IP address and the TOS. Once it decides how to route the IP datagram, the datagram is routed without additional headers; that is, no additional encapsulation occurs. This approach is different from many networks in which PDUs are encapsulated with some type of internal network header to control the routing protocol within the subnetwork.

As stated earlier in this chapter, OSPF is classified as a dynamic, adaptive protocol in that it adjusts to problems in the network and provides short convergence periods to stabilize the routing tables. It is also designed to prevent traffic looping, a capability that is quite important in mesh networks or LANs where multiple bridges are available to connect different LANs.

Note that OSPF uses the term *router* to describe the internetworking unit. Many vendors use *router* and *gateway* synonymously. In addition, the OSPF PDUs exchanged between routers and networks are called *packets*.

OSPF operations

Each router contains a routing database. The database contains information about operable interfaces at the router, as well as status information about each neighbor to a router. The database is the same for all participating routers.

The routing database information focuses on the topology of the networks, using a directed graph. Routers and networks form the vertices of the graph. Periodically, this information is broadcast (flooded) to all routers in the autonomous system (or area). An OSPF router computes the shortest path to the other routers in the autonomous system/area with regard to itself as the working node (the working node is termed the *root* in this protocol). Separate cost metrics can be computed for each TOS. If the calculations reveal that two paths are of equal value, OSPF distributes the traffic equally over these paths.

OSPF can support one or many networks. The networks can be grouped into an *area*, and the protocol allows one area to be hidden from other areas. Indeed, an area can be hidden from the full autonomous system. Because of increasing concerns about security, OSPF includes authentication procedures, and routers must go through a procedure to authenticate the traffic between them. I will go into more detail about the authentication aspects of this protocol shortly.

The directed graphs contain values between two points, either networks or gateways. The values represent the weighted shortest path value, with the router as the root. Consequently, the shortest path tree from the router to any point in an internet is determined by the router that performs the calculation. The calculation reveals the next hop to the destination in the hop-to-hop forwarding process. The topological database used in the calculation is derived from the information obtained by advertisements of the routers to their neighbors, with periodic advertisements throughout the autonomous system or area.

Thus far I have discussed how OSPF performs route discovery within the autonomous system or area only in general terms. The method to determine routing information outside the autonomous system is referred to as *external routing*. Routing information pertaining to this capability is typically derived from OSPF as well as other protocols, such as the EGP or BGP. Alternately, routing information can be established through static routes between the autonomous systems or even by default routes. This information is also distributed through the autonomous system.

Two types of external routing capabilities exist with OSPF. In type-1 external routing, the external metrics are the same as the internal OSPF link state metric. Type-2 external metrics use only the cost of the router to the external autonomous system. The type-2 method is simple and based on the assumption that routing between autonomous systems is the major cost of routing the packet (which, in some operations, is not true). This approach eliminates conversion between the internal link state metrics of OSPF and external costs (in which the autonomous system might have little influence).

The OSPF working group also adapted a very sound concept of autonomous system *areas*, in which contiguous networks and hosts can be grouped together. In this situation, each area runs its own SPF algorithm and has its own topological database that differs from other areas. The purpose of the area concept is to isolate and partition portions of the autonomous system and thus reduce the amount of information a router must maintain about the full autonomous system. Having such an area also means that the overhead information transmitted between routers to maintain OSPF routing tables is reduced.

OSPF used the term *backbone* to define the part of an autonomous system that conveys packets between areas. For example, in Figure 8.12 the routers R4 and R2 and their links serve as the backbone between the areas. The full path of a packet proceeds as follows: (1) an intra-area path to a router attached to the backbone, (2) the backbone path to the destination area router, and (3) the destination intra-area path to the destination network.

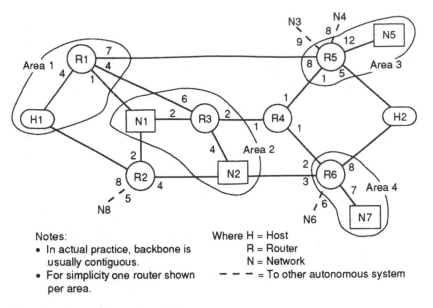

Figure 8.12   OSPF Concepts and Terms.

The resources (links and routers) of a backbone need not be contiguous. For example, R2 in Figure 8.12 has network N1 between it and backbone router R4. This configuration is permissible; the intervening networks simply become *virtual links* within the backbone when the topological database is constructed.

OSPF uses a Hello protocol for advertising state information between neighbors. Hello packets confirm agreements among routers in a common network about a network mask and certain timers (dead interval, Hello interval). In effect, the Hello protocol ensures that neighbor relationships make sense.

Classification of routers

The OSPF routers are classified according to the functions they perform:

Internal router.   All networks directly connected to this router belong to the same area; routers with only backbone interfaces are internal routers.

Border router.   Any router that is not an internal router.

Backbone router.   Any router that has an interface to the backbone.

Boundary router. A router that exchanges information with another autonomous system.

Types of advertisements

The purpose of OSPF is for routers to inform each other about internet paths via advertisements. These advertisements are sent to routers by update packets. Four types of advertisements are used:

Router link advertisement. Contains information on a router's interfaces into an area. It is used by all routers and flooded throughout an area.

Networks link advertisement. Contains a list of routers connected to a network. It is used by a broadcast network and flooded throughout an area.

Summary link advertisement. Contains information on routes outside an area. It is used by border routers and flooded to the border routers' areas (but inside the autonomous system).

Autonomous systems (AS) extended link advertisement. Contains information on routes in other autonomous systems. It is used by a boundary router and flooded through the autonomous system.

Example of the OSPF shortest path tree

This discussion expands on earlier discussions of how OSPF uses least-cost-path logic to obtain a directed graph and the pruned tree. The example is a very simple topology. RFC 1131 has an excellent and detailed example if you need more information. Figure 8.12 is based on the previous examination of algorithm A, but in this example the labels identify hosts, networks, and routers (gateways). The autonomous system consists of areas 1, 2, 3, and 4. Routers 2, 5, and 6 provide connections to other autonomous systems with the EGP or BGP software.

For this illustration, the numbers have been rearranged from the previous examples. These numbers represent costs determined by the network administrator for each output port at each router. In this example, a lower-cost value determines a better route. Two numbers might be shown for a link in which two routers are directly connected. The numbers reflect the cost at each router's output port. For example, a connection between routers R3 and R4 indicates that the cost of moving traffic from R3 to R4 is 2 and the cost from R4 to R3 is 1. This cost can vary because of different traffic loads and queue sizes at the routers, which would result in different delays at the links of the machines (assuming that delay is part of the cost metric). In addition, the metric values can vary if frequency division multiplexers/modems divide the bandwidth on the link unevenly in the two directions. For example, the bandwidth from R3 to R4 could be 64 kbps and the bandwidth from R4 to R3 could be 128 kbps.

Also note that no costs are associated with the ports emanating from the networks to the routers, nor are there costs associated with the host interfaces to the routers. OSPF does not assume that a network or host computer is capable of participating in the shortest path operations. Notwithstanding, a network or host can participate in the operations by the same methods used by the routers (if the network administration allows a network or host to become involved in the operation). In this context, a convenient way to view the directed graph is to remove the network from the picture and then look at the arrows between the two routers.

Figure 8.13 depicts the directed graph of our hypothetical network. The direction of the arrows represents the cost of the path from a router to another router. The arcs with no value are explained in the previous paragraph. You might notice that only one directional arrow is drawn from the routers to the hosts. In accordance with the rules of OSPF directed graphs, the figure shows what are known as *point-to-point networks*, in which a network is joined by a single router or a single pair of routers. This situation is depicted by the connection having one arrow in the direction of the host.

Based on the values obtained with the directed graph, OSPF creates a pruned tree, representing the shortest (best) path between a

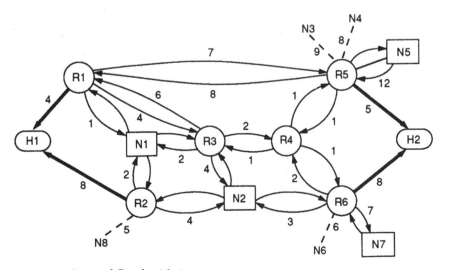

Figure 8.13 Directed Graph with Arcs.

router and all the other nodes. Each router develops its own tree, and the router acts as the root in performing these calculations. Eventually, after messages have been exchanged between the routers and the topological database has been built, the tree provides the destination to any network or host within the autonomous system.

In these examples, routers R2, R6, and R5 are responsible for providing connections to other autonomous systems. As explained earlier, these routers make their connections known to the other routers in the autonomous system through type-1 or type-2 metrics.

Finally, Figure 8.14 shows the pruned tree as viewed by R1. It is quite similar to the tree developed in the previous discussion of algorithm A, except that the nodes are relabeled as routers, networks, and hosts, and no costs are associated with the output ports of the networks and hosts.

The tree and an accompanying topological database provide R1 with a route to all hosts and routers in the autonomous system. Once again, the arcs from N1 to R2 and N1 to R3 are emphasized. No values are associated with these arcs because OSPF is designed as a gateway protocol. The direction of these arcs shows that the network does not furnish information to the routers. In a sense, the routers establish virtual connections between themselves across transit networks. In this example, N1 is a transit network. Certainly these connections are significant as far as the least-cost-path value is concerned. In such a situation, the link state advertisement for a network (N1) must be generated by one of its attached routers, which is identified as the designated router for that network.

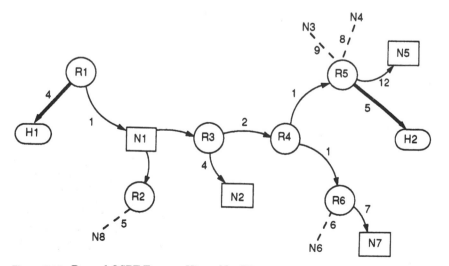

Figure 8.14 Pruned OSPF Tree, as Viewed by R1.

Based on this discussion, imagine the topological database that is built by R4. Indeed, you might want to experiment with Figure 8.13 and draw the pruned tree as viewed by R4. To assist you in this exercise, the routing table for R4, based on Figure 8.12, is shown in Table 8.4. (The host entries, H1 and H2, are usually not stored at a remote router.)

OSPF data structures

OSPF operates with five data structures, which contain the information needed by OSPF to perform its operations. The data structures discussed in this section are:

- Protocol data structures
- Area (and backbone) data structures
- Interface data structures
- Neighbor data structures
- Routing table structures

A useful way to view these data structures is depicted in Figure 8.15. The data structures are as follows:

- The protocol data structure consists of high-level data structures used in the autonomous system.
- The area data structures contain information about the area.
- The interface data structure contains information on the router-to-network operations.

TABLE 8.4   R4 Routing Table

Destination	Next hop	Distance metric
H1	R3	7
H2	R5	6
N1	R3	3
N2	R6	4
N3	R5	10
N4	R5	9
N5	R5	13
N6	R6	7
N7	R6	8
N8	R3	8
R1	R3	3
R2	R3	3
R3	R3	1
R5	R5	1
R6	R5	1

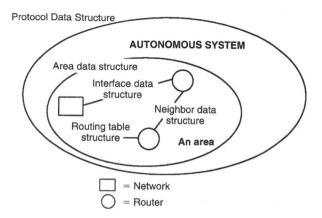

Figure 8.15 OSPF Data Structures.

- The neighbor data structure contains information on the router-to-router operations.
- The routing table structure is stored at the routers and contains information for routing an IP packet.

The *protocol data structure* is a high-level OSPF data structure that provides the following information and services:

Router ID. The 32-bit identifier of the autonomous system router

Area structure pointers. ID to each area with which the router is concerned

Backbone structures pointer. ID to the backbone structure, which is the same as an area structure

Virtual links configured. ID of the router at the other end of virtual circuits

External routes list. List of routes external to this autonomous system

Routing table. Contains an entry for each destination to which the router can forward traffic

The *area data structure* provides the following information and services:

Area ID. The identifier of the area

Address ranges. A list of IP addresses that define the area. A network is associated with an area depending on its IP address value

Router interfaces. The ID of those router interfaces that belong to the area

Advertisements lists. Description of the following information:
  Network links. Advertisements of each router connected to a network
  Summary links. Advertisements from border routers of routes with the autonomous system
  Router links. Advertisements to routers in the area

Shortest path tree. The pruned tree, with this router as the root, is based on the Dijkstra method described earlier in this chapter

Authentication type. The type of authentication (none, simple password) used in this area

The *interface data structure* describes the router and network connection. The interface belongs to the area in which the network resides. The following information and services are provided by the interface data structure:

Interface type. type of attached network—broadcast, multiaccess (such as a packet-switched network with two or more routers), point-to-point, or virtual.

State. current state of the interface (down, waiting, etc.). (OSPF works with states and state transition diagrams.)

IP address. the IP address for this interface.

IP mask. subnet mask for this interface.

Area ID. area associated with the network.

HelloInterval. time between a router issuing Hello packets on this interface.

DeadInterval. time at which the machine considers a router down and will not accept Hello packets.

InfTransDelay. estimated time to send an update packet on this interface.

Router priority. priority of the router on this interface (highest priority becomes the designated router for this network).

Hello timer. interval at which the Hello packet is launched (every HelloInterval seconds).

Wait timer. interval at which this interface looks for a designated router (every DeadInterval seconds).

Neighboring routers. list of all routers attached to this network.

Routers. IDs of designated router and backup router.

Output cost(s). metric cost of sending traffic on this interface, possibly based on each IP TOS.

RxmInterval. timer of issuing link state advertisement retransmissions.

Authentication key. value to verify an authentication field in the OSPF header.

Neighbor data structure. This data structure is used between neighboring routers to control router roles and backup operations. The following information and services are provided by the neighbor data structure:

State. states of the neighbor communications process (down, exchange, etc.). (Neighbor routers operate with states and state transitions machines.)

Inactivity timer. reveals that a Hello packet has not been received from this neighbor.

Master/slave. relationship of the neighbor routers.

Sequence number. values used to coordinate exchange of packets between neighbors.

Neighbor ID. neighbor router ID.

Neighbor priority (PRI). router priority used to select a designated router and its backup router.

IP address. neighbor router's IP address.

Routers. IDs of neighbor's designated router and designated backup router.

Lists. three lists are used to manage link state advertisements (link State Retransmission for advertisements not yet ACKed, Database Summary for advertisements that constitute the area's database, and Link State Requests for advertisements still needed from a neighbor to synchronize the database).

The OSPF *routing table structure* is used by IP packet forwarding. It contains the entries in our previous example (Table 8.4) along with other values. The entries in the table are as follows:

Destination. The destination's IP address (and mask)

Destination type. A network, border, or boundary router

Type of service. Possibly a separate set of routers for each TOS

Area. Area whose link information led to this entry in the table (multiple entries are possible if two border routers share common areas)

Path type. Intra-area, inter-area, or external-to-autonomous systems

Cost. Full cost to the destination

Next hop. Next hop (router) for the datagram

Advertising router. Used for inter-area and autonomous system links

OSPF packets

This section describes the formats of OSPF packets. OSPF runs over IP and relies on IP for fragmentation services for large OSPF packets. In addition, some OSPF packets are multicast. OSPF requires the reservation of two multicast addresses:

ALLSPFrouters. Multicast address reserved for all routers that support OSPF (its value is 224.0.0.5)

ALLrouters. Address reserved for the designated router and a designated backup router (the address value is 224.0.0.6)

RFC 1010 identifies the OSPF with IP protocol number 89. The OSPF routing protocol packets are always sent in an IP datagram with the IP TOS value equal to zero. It is recommended that OSPF packets be treated as high-priority traffic and given precedence over regular IP traffic. The IP precedence field is useful in this situation.

The OSPF packet header. Figure 8.16 illustrates the 24-octet OSPF packet header. Each OSPF packet is appended with this header. The *version* number describes which version of the protocol is currently used (currently, version 2). The *type* field identifies the type of packet. It can contain one of the following values:

1. Hello
2. Database description
3. Link state request
4. Link state update
5. Link state ACK

The packet-length field indicates the length of the field in octets, including the OSPF header. The router ID field contains the identification of the source of the packet. The area ID identifies the area from which the packet is transmitted. The checksum field performs an IP-type checksum on the entire packet, including the authentication field. The authentication type (AUType) identifies the type of authentication that is used. Presently, two authentication types are used: 0 for none and 1 for a simple password. Finally, the authentication field contains the value used by the authentication scheme. The authentication field can be established on a per-area basis.

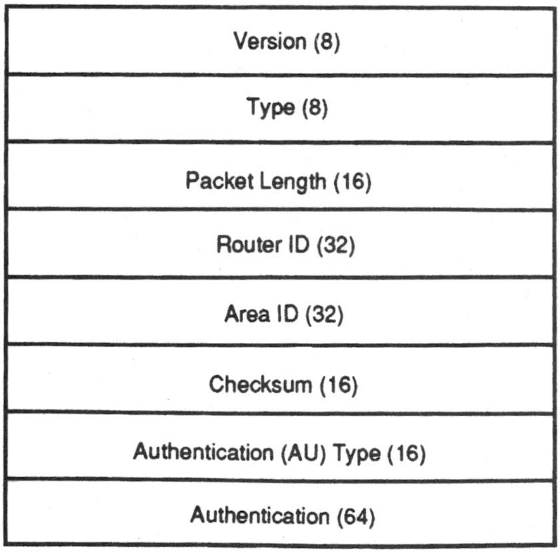

| Version (8) |
| Type (8) |
| Packet Length (16) |
| Router ID (32) |
| Area ID (32) |
| Checksum (16) |
| Authentication (AU) Type (16) |
| Authentication (64) |

Figure 8.16 OSPF Packet Header.

The link state advertisement header.   OSPF uses one other header type, the link state advertisement header. This header constitutes the topological database. Its purpose is to identify each advertisement between the routers. The format for the header is shown in Figure 8.17. All link state advertisements must use this header, which consists of 20 octets.

The LS age field contains (in seconds) the time since the link state advertisement originated. The options field contains IP TOS values supported by the sender. The LS type describes the type of link advertisement, which further defines a format for the advertisement (discussed shortly). This field can be set to the following values:

1 Router links (data on router-to-area interfaces)
2 Network links (data on router-to-network interfaces)
3 Summary link (data IP network)
4 Summary link (data on autonomous system border router)
5 AS external link (data on destinations external-to-autonomous system)

The link state ID field identifies that portion of an internet being described in the advertisement. Its contents can take values to depict router IDs and IP network numbers; the value depends on the LS type field.

The advertising router field identifies the originating router for the link state advertisement. The LS sequence number is used to sequence the advertisements in order to detect duplicate or old pack-

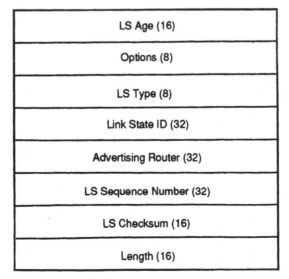

Figure 8.17 Link State Advertisement Header.

ets. The LS checksum field is used to error-check the contents of the packet. Finally, the length field contains the size of the advertisement, in octets, including the 20-octet header.

The Hello packet. The Hello packet is used in OSPF to perform operations between adjacent neighbors. Parameters in the Hello packet allow router neighbors to agree on operating parameters, such as common network mask, the Hello interval, and the dead interval.

The contents of the Hello packet are depicted in Figure 8.18. The OSPF header is required for the packet. The next field is the network mask, which is associated with the interface. The Hello interval (HelloInt) field contains a value representing the number of seconds before the router sends another Hello packet. The options field contains the IP TOS values supplied by the sender. The dead interval (DeadInt) field contains a value that describes the number of seconds before a router is declared down. The router priority (Rtr Pri) field defines if a router is designated as a backup. If this field is set to zero, the router is not allowed to become a designated backup router. The designated router field contains the identity of the router for the network in question. If this value is set to zero, there is no designated router. The backup router field contains the identity of the designated backup router for the network in regard to the advertising router. Finally, the repeating fields designated neighbor router ID contains the ID of each router that has recently sent Hello packets on the network. *Recently* is defined by the value in the DeadInt field.

OSPF Header (192)
Network mask (32)
HelloInt (16)
Options (8)
Rtr Pri (8)
DeadInt (32)
Designated/Backup router (64)
Neighbor Router ID, 1 to *n* fields (32)

Figure 8.18 Hello packet for OSPF.

Figure 8.19 illustrates the operations when a router has received a Hello packet. Upon receiving this packet, the OSPF logic performs editing checks on the IP and OSPF headers. If any errors occur, the packet is discarded and processing stops. If no errors occur, OSPF checks the network mask, Hello interval, and DeadInt fields for proper matches with the configuration at this interface.

If "no mismatches" occur, OSPF checks for the source of the Hello packet. If the source is not currently contained in its neighbor data structure, it creates a skeleton neighbor data structure for this

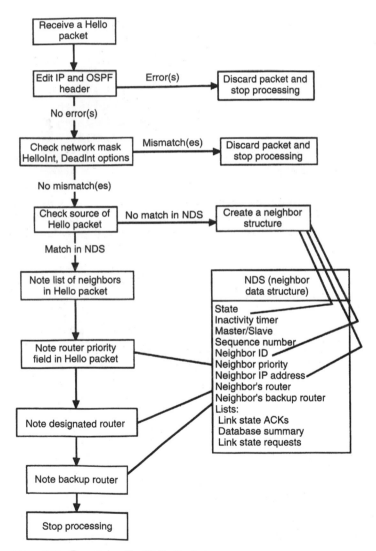

Figure 8.19 Processing the Hello Packet.

source. The creation of the neighbor structure at this point consists of inserting the neighbor ID, the state of the interface, and the neighbor IP address. If there is a "match in neighbor data structure (NDS)," OSPF examines and stores the list of neighbors contained in the Hello packet. OSPF then examines the router priority field in the Hello packet and stores this information in the neighbor data structure. Additionally, it notes the designated router and backup router, and stores this information in the neighbor data structure.

Once the Hello packet has been processed, OSPF then executes logic to establish or reestablish designated routers (DRs) and designated backup routers (DBURs). This process is shown in Figure 8.20. First, OSPF discards any ineligible routers (those routers that have a priority value of 0). Then all attached routers are examined in relation to the information received in the Hello packets. Two major steps are involved in establishing routers and backup routers. In step 1 of Figure 8.20, the designated backup router is chosen by examining the priority field relating to that router. In step 2, the designated router is established. Note that if no router has declared itself to be the designated router, the backup designated router is promoted. Steps 1 and 2 are then repeated to redesignate the backup router. The logic is designed to allow a smooth transition when either a backup or designated backup router fails in an internet. It is possible that a router could, for a time, be designated as both as a router and a backup router. Once this router detects that the primary router is inoperable, however, the logic requires that it remove itself as a designated router.

The database description packet. The purpose of the database description packet is to initialize a database at a router. The database packet can contain information on either part of the topological database or the entire topology. These packets are managed through a master/slave relationship. One of the routers is designated as a master and the other becomes a slave. The master sends polls in the database description packets, which must be acknowledged by database description responses.

The format of the database description packet is illustrated in Figure 8.21. The OSPF header is required for this packet. The options field was described earlier, and the next two octets are reserved and set to zero. Three bits are used in the next octet, labeled the *I bit*, *M bit*, and *MS bit*. The I bit, when set to zero, indicates that the packet is the first in a sequence of packets to follow. The M bit is the "more data" bit. When set to 1, it means that more database description packets follow. The MS bit designates the master/slave. When set to 1, it indicates that the originating router of the packet is the master. When set to 0, the originating router is the slave.

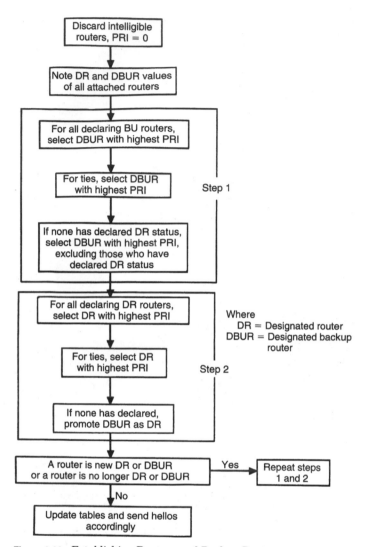

Figure 8.20 Establishing Routers and Backup Routers.

The DD sequence number (NR) is used to sequence the packets between the master and the slave. The number is incremented by 1 with each transmission of a packet. The remainder of the packet field repeats the number of advertisements for each piece of the topological database. The link state type, link state ID, advertising router, LS sequence number, LS checksum, and LS age have been described previously in this chapter.

The link state request packet. The purpose of the link state request packet is to request additional information about a topological data-

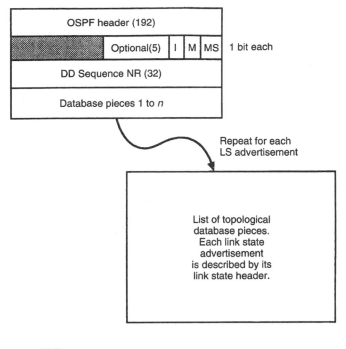

 = Reserved and set to 0

Figure 8.21 1 Database Description Packet.

base from a neighbor (see Figure 8.22). Typically, this packet is exchanged when it is discovered that pieces of the database are missing or out of date. The contents of this packet are the OSPF header and repeating fields for LS type, link state ID, and advertising router.

Link state update packets. Link state update packets provide four types of updates:

- Router links
- Network links
- Summary links
- AS external links

Each of these four types of update packets contains a different format. Figure 8.23 provides an example how these packets are used: a router that has three links in an internet, labeled link 1, link 2, and link 3. Additionally, each link is labeled with the required TOS. Link 1's TOS requires low delay and high reliability. Link 2 requires high

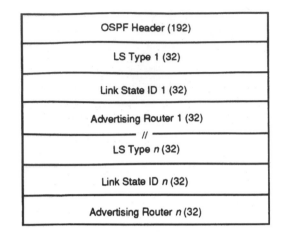

| OSPF Header (192) |
| LS Type 1 (32) |
| Link State ID 1 (32) |
| Advertising Router 1 (32) |
| // |
| LS Type n (32) |
| Link State ID n (32) |
| Advertising Router n (32) |

Figure 8.22   3 Link State Request Packet.

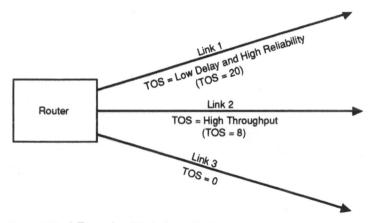

Figure 8.23   3 Example of Link State Update.

throughput. Link 3 has no additional TOS beyond the default value of 0.

When a link-state refresh timer expires or when a link state changes, the router advertises this information to its neighbors through these four types of packets. The advertisement is sent to neighbors, and then to other neighbors. Eventually, all advertisements are flooded throughout the area. Figure 8.24 shows the principal advertisement packet of OSPF, designated as the *router link advertisement packet*. This figure illustrates how information is repeated for each link of the router and each TOS feature on each link.

The OSPF header is placed in front of the packet, as are the number of advertisements. Each router in an area originates an advertise-

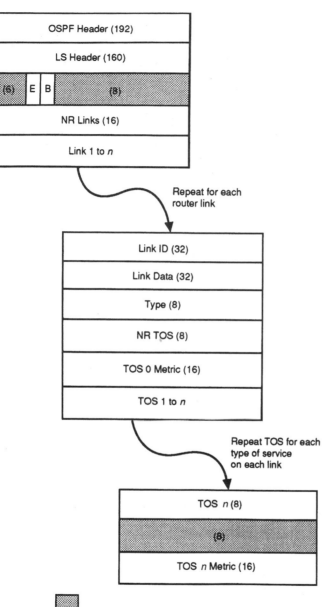

= Reserved and/or set to 0

Figure 8.24 Router Link Advertisement Packet.

ment to describe the state and cost of the router's links in its respective area.

The E bit set to 1 identifies the router as an area boundary router. The B bit set to 0 identifies the router as border router. The NR links depict how many links are advertised in this packet. The link ID describes the object to which the link connects, and its value depends upon the link's type. The link data field value also depends on the link's type field. The type field can be any of the following:

- Point-to-point interface with another router
- Interface to a transit network
- Interface to a subnetwork
- Interface to a virtual link

The NR TOS field contains the number of TOS metrics for the link. The TOS 0 metric is the cost of using this link for TOS 0, which must always be included.

Finally, the figure shows repeating sets of fields designated as *TOS n* and *TOS n metric*, which are contained in the packet for each TOS value for each link. In the example, two sets of these fields would exist for link 1, one set for link 2, and none for link 3.

Figure 8.25 depicts the remaining three formats for the link state update packets. These three formats (starting at the top of the figure) are used to advertise network links, summary links, and AS external links. Most fields in these three formats have been discussed previously in this chapter. The forwarding address field identifies the address that receives data traffic for the advertised destination. The external route tag is not defined in the specification, but can be used by AS boundary routers.

The link state acknowledgment packet. OSPF requires that link state advertisements be acknowledged, so the final OSPF packet is the link state acknowledgment packet (shown in Figure 8.26). The fields are largely self-descriptive and have been discussed previously.

OSPF vs. RIP

You might be left with the impression that, with all its functions, OSPF must use a lot of resources. The actual link bandwidth consumed by OSPF is less than RIP. After all, it makes selected advertisements. On the other hand, OSPF consumes more memory than RIP, but the use of area partitioning can save memory. In general, OSPF consumes less CPU time than RIP because of RIP's frequent updates. More information is available in RFC 1245 and RFC 1246.

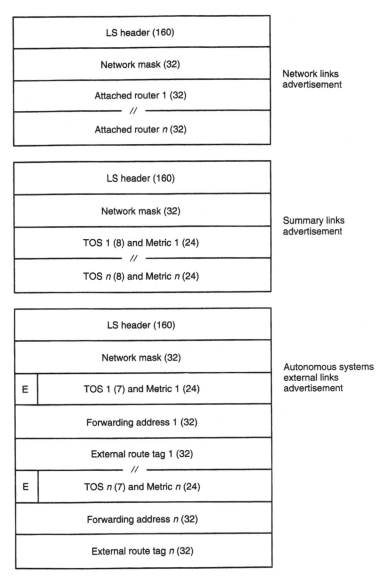

Figure 8.25 Link State Update Packets.

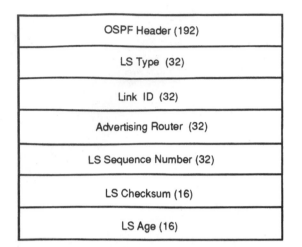

| OSPF Header (192) |
| LS Type (32) |
| Link ID (32) |
| Advertising Router (32) |
| LS Sequence Number (32) |
| LS Checksum (16) |
| LS Age (16) |

Figure 8.26   Link State Acknowledgment Packet.

Summary

The internet system provides a number of protocols that provide routing and reachability information between gateways and autonomous systems and within autonomous systems. EGP is widely used in many systems, and GGP is an older example of a core gateway protocol. Internal gateway protocols are varied, and many systems use RIP. Without question, the OSPF protocol represents a significant improvement in internetworking operations.

The Major Application Layer Protocols

This book focuses on the lower layers of the TCP/IP protocol suite, but to round-out the discussion of TCP/IP, this chapter will examine the application layer protocols that are used by many internet installations. Some of these protocols are very rich in functions, and a full explanation of their operations would require an extensive discourse. My goal, rather, is to provide a general overview of the major services they offer to an end user.[1]

In most vendor products, executing these protocols is an easy matter, usually no more complex than entering one or a few terminal commands, or clicking on an icon on the computer screen. This part of the description is best left to the vendor-specific user manuals. This chapter concentrates on the architecture of these protocols rather than their execution.

The Telnet Protocol

To begin this discussion, imagine that a manager is responsible for a computer operations center. A host computer in the operations center is tasked with supporting the communication operations among many terminals that have different characteristics. Say a user at a DEC terminal needs to communicate with a user at a Hewlett-Packard terminal. Communication in this case is not so easy. Both devices use different screen control and keyboard control characters, and both use different line protocols for managing traffic on the communications link.

---

[1]I have chosen not to rehash the Internet application layer in detail because hundreds of books have been published on the subject.

255

If the host computer needs to support a wide variety of terminals, precious resources are consumed in machine CPU cycles to resolve protocol differences, and designing and coding supporting software to translate the protocols can be a very expensive undertaking. The manager of the computer operations center must spend a great deal of time and expend considerable resources developing or acquiring systems that provide translation facilities between different machines.

Telnet provides some solutions to these problems. For example, it defines a procedure that permits host computers to learn about the characteristics of terminals attached to other hosts with which they communicate. Equally important, Telnet provides conventions for negotiating a number of functions and services for a terminal-based session between two machines. This approach ameliorates the protocol conversion problem because the negotiating machines have the option of not using a service that is not supported by both machines. Telnet does not perform any protocol conversion between different machines; rather, it provides a mechanism to determine the characteristics of the machines and a means of negotiating the interworking of the machines in order to exchange data.

The Telnet protocol allows a program on a host machine (called the *Telnet client*) to access the resources of another machine (called the *Telnet server*) as if the client were attached locally to the server (see Figure 9.1). Although Telnet provides a variety of features, some people call the standard a *remote login* protocol because it supports a remote device's login with a host machine. Be aware that other "remote login" protocols exist besides Telnet. For example, the SUN workstation has a remote logging (Rlogin) procedure.

Network virtual terminal

The Telnet standard is based on the idea of a network virtual terminal (NVT). The term *virtual* is used because an NVT does not actually exist; it is an imagined device that provides a standard means of representing a terminal's characteristics. The idea is to relieve host com-

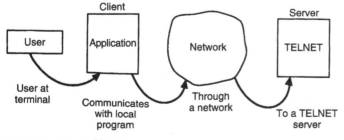

Figure 9.1   Telnet Model.

puters from the task of maintaining characteristics about every terminal with which they communicate. With the Telnet standard, both the user and server devices are required to map their terminal characteristics into the virtual terminal description. The end result is that the devices appear to communicate with the NVT because both parties provide a complementary mapping.

The Telnet protocol, similar to other virtual terminal protocols, allows the communicating machines to negotiate a variety of options to be used during the session. The server and client are required to use a standard set of procedures to establish these options. I will examine these options during the analysis of the Telnet protocol.

Using negotiated options means there is a possibility that host machines can provide services beyond those provided by the virtual terminal. Moreover, the Telnet model does not restrict negotiated options solely to those stipulated in the protocols. Rather, Telnet allows different conventions beyond Telnet specifications to be negotiated.

Telnet RFCs

Internet standards include several Requests for Comments (RFCs) that describe Telnet options that can be negotiated. Table 9.1 provides a list of Telnet option codes, along with their numbers and the relevant RFCs, if available. Do not assume that all these options are provided in each vendor product; many Telnet products do not support all available options.

Figure 9.2 shows how the options can be negotiated between two parties. One party can begin the negotiation by inquiring to another party about a particular option (function x in the figure). The response in this figure is that the responding party can support the option. Then the initiating party asks for the characteristics of the option from the responding party, and the responding party sends information about the option. This information describes characteristics of the responding party's terminal or other operating requirements.

Messages flowing between the two parties must adhere to a Telnet message format (called the *command structure*). For example, the initial signal of "do you support?" or "will you support?" is established by special Telnet codes *do* or *will* In turn, the responder must return a Telnet code (in this example, *will*).

Table 9.2 lists the names of the codes, the numeric values placed in the Telnet message, and a brief description of their meaning. These functions are common across almost all terminal-based applications, so Telnet defines a standard means of representing them. Here are six of them:

TABLE 9.1   Telnet Option Codes

Number	Name	RFC
0	Binary transmission	856
1	Echo	857
2	Reconnection	NIC 15391
3	Suppress go ahead	858
4	Approximate message size negotiation	NIC 15393
5	Status	859
6	Timing mark	860
7	Remote controlled trans and echo	726
8	Output line width	NIC 20196
9	Output page size	NIC 20197
10	Output carriage-return disposition	652
11	Output horizontal tabstops	653
12	Output horizontal tab disposition	654
13	Output form feed disposition	655
14	Output vertical tabstops	656
15	Output vertical tab disposition	657
16	Output line feed disposition	658
17	Extended ASCII	698
18	Logout	727
19	Byte macro	735
20	Data entry terminal	732
21	SUPDUP	736
22	SUPDUP output	749
23	Send location	779
24	Terminal type	930
25	End of record	885
26	TACACS user identification	927
27	Output marking	933
28	Terminal location number	946
29	3270 regime	1041
30	X.3 PAD	1053
31	Window size	1073

Interrupt process (IP).   Allows a system to suspend, interrupt, abort, or terminate a user process. For example, it allows a user to terminate an operation to get out of an endless loop.

Abort output (AO).   Allows an application to run to completion but not send the output to the user's workstation. This function also clears output that is stored but not yet displayed.

Are you there (AYT).   A useful operation to invoke if you want to know that the application is executing. Typically, the AYT function is invoked if a user has not received messages for an extended time.

Erase character (EC).   Enables the user to delete a character in a stream of data. In its simplest form, it can be used to edit data on a screen if input mistakes are made.

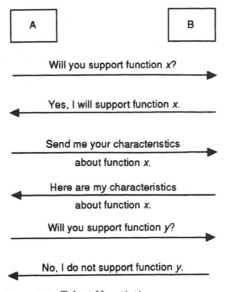

Figure 9.2   Telnet Negotiations.

TABLE 9.2   Telnet Command Codes

Code name	Value	Meaning
SE	240	End of subnegotiation parameters
NOP	241	No operation
Data mark	242	The data stream portion of a sync
Break	243	BRK character
Interrupt process	244	The IP function
Abort output	245	The AO function
Are you there	246	The AYT function
Erase character	247	The EC function
Erase line	248	The EL function
Go ahead	249	The GA function
SB	250	Subnegotiation of the indicated option
Will (option code)	251	Begin performing, or confirmation that device is now performing the indicated option
Won't (option code)	252	Refusal to perform or continue to perform the indicated option
Do (option code)	253	The request that the other party perform, or confirm that you expect the other party to perform, the indicated option
Don't (option code)	254	Demands that the other party stop performing, or confirm that party is no longer expecting the other party to perform, the indicated option
IAC	255	Interpret as command

Erase line (EL). Allows a user to delete an entire line for editing purposes.

Go ahead (GA). Allows the session to follow a half-duplex transmission sequence.

In addition to those described in Table 9.2, Telnet has a number of codes for manipulating hard-copy output on a printer. The codes are quite similar to their virtual terminal protocols, such as the ITU-T X.3 PAD Recommendation. These codes perform operations such as horizontal tab (HT), vertical tab (VT), form feed (FF), backspace (BS), Bell (BEL), line feed (LF), and carriage return.

Telnet commands

The Telnet data unit is called a *command*, and the format is depicted in Figure 9.3 (the commands were described in Table 9.2, and the options in Table 9.1). If three bytes are used, the first byte is the *interpret as command* (IAC) byte, which is a reserved code in Telnet. It is also an escape character because it is used by the receiver to detect whether incoming traffic is a Telnet command. The next byte is called the *command code* and is used in conjunction with the IAC byte to describe the type of command. The third byte is called the *option negotiation* code. It defines a number of options to be used during the session.

Example of Telnet commands

You can study the RFCs listed in Table 9.1 if you want to gain an in-depth understanding of the many functions of Telnet terminals. This section provides an example of one of these functions, echo.

Echoes are used in practically all workstation environments to allow the data entered on the keyboard to be placed (echoed) onto the screen. In some situations, the echo occurs only locally; that is, the terminal keyboard entry is echoed to the screen. In others, the echo is sent to the receiving machine and then echoed back to the transmitting machine. The particular implementation depends on the type of hardware and software that exists on the workstations.

The Telnet echo option allows two users to determine how echoing will occur during the session. The command format for the echo is as

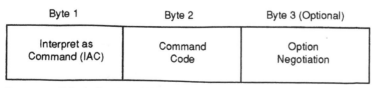

Byte 1	Byte 2	Byte 3 (Optional)
Interpret as Command (IAC)	Command Code	Option Negotiation

Figure 9.3 Telnet Command Format.

follows (the values in parentheses represent the IAC, command code, and option negotiation parameter that was explained in Figure 9.3 and Table 9.1):

```
IAC WILL ECHO (255 251 1)
```

This command allows a user to begin echoing the characters it receives over the connection back to the sender of the data characters. Conversely, the command:

```
IAC WON'T ECHO (255 252 1)
```

specifies that the sender of this command either will not echo, or wishes to stop echoing the data characters it is receiving back to the sender. Another command is used for a request that the receiver of the command begin, echoing. It takes the form:

```
IAC DO ECHO (255 253 1)
```

The last Telnet echo command is used by the sender to require the receiver of the command to either stop or not start echoing characters that it receives over the connection. This is formatted as:

```
IAC DON'T ECHO (255 254 1)
```

The Telnet echo option defaults to *won't echo* and *don't echo.* That is, no echoing is done over the connection. Another commonly used option is the transmit binary, in which the data stream is interpreted as 8-bit binary images. To request permission to use this service, the sender issues:

```
IAC WILL TRANSMIT-BINARY (255 251 0)
```

The sender of the next command, if he or she does not want the connection to be operated with the transmit binary option, issues:

```
IAC DON'T TRANSMIT-BINARY (255 254 0)
```

All the Telnet operations are conducted in a manner similar to these examples. Thus, the protocol is simple and easy to implement.

Rlogin

Rlogin is a simpler remote login protocol than Telnet, because it is designed to operate only between UNIX-based hosts. Therefore, options need not be negotiated, since the communicating parties know about each other. Rlogin is documented in RFC 1282.

Rlogin works with the client-server arrangement. After a simple logon session, the client sends one byte at a time to the server. The server echoes back the character to the client. Rlogin has a simple flow-control mechanism, and is performed by the client. When a user keys in ASCII START or STOP key combinations (Ctrl–Q Ctrl–S), the client starts or stops terminal output. The characters are also used to control the server. If a Ctrl–S is sent by the terminal user, the server stops. But remember that traffic might already be in the network, so you might continue to see traffic scroll down your screen.

Rlogin also permits the client to change the server window during an ongoing session. A few other options are available, but Rlogin is very simple and was not designed to offer many features.

Figure 9.4 shows some examples of Rlogin operations. In event 1, the client sends the byte 0 to the server. This operation begins a handshake between the client and server. After receiving an ACK (in event 2), the client sends an ID for the client host, the server ID, the type of terminal used by the client, and the terminal speed (event 3).

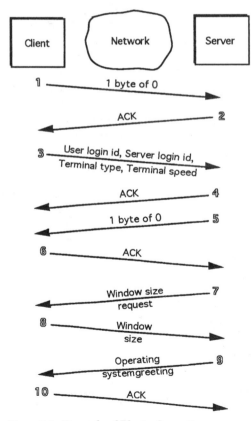

Figure 9.4 Example of Rlogin Operations.

Events 4, 5, and 6 continue the handshake. In events 7 and 8, the client and server negotiate the window size that will be used for the session. Finally, in events 9 and 10, operating system parameters are exchanged.

Trivial File Transfer Protocol (TFTP)

TFTP is appropriately named because is a simple file transfer protocol. It is not as complex as FTP, nor does it have as many functions. It does not consist of a lot of code, nor does it consume much memory; consequently, it can be used on small machines.

TFTP has no security provisions or user authentication provisions. Indeed, it has very little end-to-end reliability because it rests on the user datagram protocol (UDP). It does not use TCP, but TFTP nonetheless has some integrity checks, supports timers, and retransmission capabilities.

Typically, the transmitter sends a fixed block of data (512 bytes) and waits for an acknowledgment before sending the next block. This type of operation is known as a *flip-flop protocol* because the transmitter must wait for an acknowledgment from the receiver before it sends the next block of data.

Each block is numbered sequentially, and the acknowledgment field contains the number of the block that has been acknowledged. The end of a message is detected is marked by a fragmented block that is less than 512 bytes.

This protocol is not designed to be robust. Almost any type of problem will cause a termination of the connection. However, it does provide some error messages, and it supports time-outs to detect when messages have been lost. Generally, errors occur if:

- One party is unable to satisfy a request (for example, the format of the request is ill-formed or a file cannot be located)

- A file can be found, but the request cannot be fulfilled because the servicing party does not have sufficient resources

- Other errors have occurred (such as a duplication of the request)

TFTP is not used extensively today, although some vendors have brought it into their product line to ease compatibility problems. For example, IBM's TCP/IP product line for its personal computers implements TFTP to allow interaction between AIX and PC DOS machines.

TFTP and other protocols

As discussed earlier, TFTP runs over UDP. Since a user datagram header is encapsulated into an IP PDU, TFTP can rely on these lower-layer protocols to provide their services. For example, TFTP uses the UDP source and destination ports to map the two TFTP users onto the file transfer session. This operation is accomplished with *TFTP transfer identifiers* (TIDs). They are created by TFTP and passed to the UDP, which places them in the port identifier fields of the datagram.

TFTP uses port binding, which is discussed in Chapters 1 and 7. To review, the initiator of the file transfer (say host A) selects a value for the source TID. The source TID is set to any value as determined by source A. The destination TID is the well-known port number 69, assigned to TFTP. When host B returns an acknowledgment to the TFTP connection request, its source TID is the value 69, and its destination TID is the same identifier as host A's source TID.

TFTP packets

TFTP supports five types of PDUs, which are called *packets* in the standard:

- Read request (RRQ)
- Write request (WRQ)
- Data (DATA)
- Acknowledgment (ACK)
- Error (ERROR)

The names of the packets describe their functions. The *read request* (RRQ) packet requests a read operation on a foreign file. Conversely, the *write request* (WRQ) requests modification to a file. After receiving one of these requests, the foreign system might return an *acknowledgment data unit* (ACK), which contains the block number of 0. After these handshaking operations have occurred, the *data* packets are transmitted. They contain sequence numbers that identify each block of data, and the block numbers are sequentially numbered from a value of 1. The *error* packet contains information about problems that occurred during the operation.

The structure of these control packets is shown in Figure 9.5. The *opcode* (operation code) contains the values to identify the type of packet. In RRQ and WRQ packets, the opcode field is followed by the filename field. It identifies the file that is to be retrieved (typically performed with GET <remote filename> [<local filename>]), or the name of the file that is to receive the data (PUT <remote filename> [<local filename>]).

The mode field signifies the mode of transfer that is to take place during the operation. As established in RFC 783, three modes are supported in TFTP:

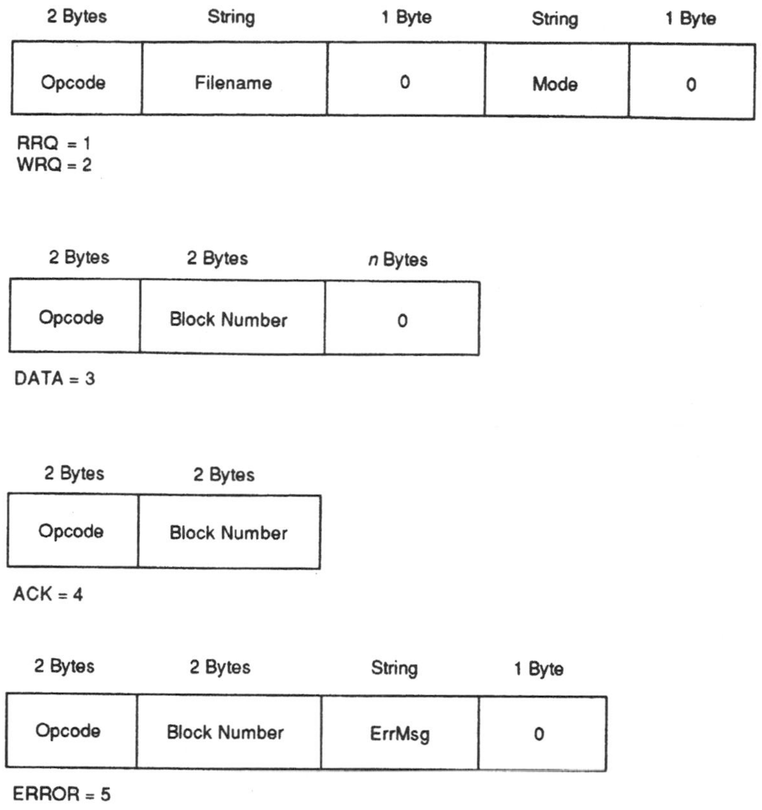

2 Bytes	String	1 Byte	String	1 Byte
Opcode	Filename	0	Mode	0

RRQ = 1
WRQ = 2

2 Bytes	2 Bytes	*n* Bytes
Opcode	Block Number	0

DATA = 3

2 Bytes	2 Bytes
Opcode	Block Number

ACK = 4

2 Bytes	2 Bytes	String	1 Byte
Opcode	Block Number	ErrMsg	0

ERROR = 5

Figure 9.5 TFTP Packets.

NetASCII.   USA Standard Code for Information Interchange

Byte.   Eight-bit bytes or binary data

Mail.   Traffic goes to a user rather than to a file, but the code is still NetASCII

The block number in the data packet begins with the value 1 and is incremented by 1 with each succeeding packet transmittal. The data field is a fixed-length block of 512 bytes. The last block in the file transfer contains between 0 and 511 bytes of data (and is labeled 0 in the figure).

The acknowledgment packet also contains a block number field. This field acknowledges the transmitted data using the same value that was received in the block number in the data packet. The error packet contains an ErrMsg field to describe six types of errors:

0.   Not defined

1. File not found

2. Access violation

3. Disk full or allocation exceeded

4. Illegal TFTP operation

5. Unknown transfer ID

Figure 9.6 shows the handshake and transfer operations between two machines using the TFTP standard. The initial handshaking activities are accomplished with the WRQ and ACK transactions. Data are then sent and acknowledged as depicted in the third and fourth boxes of the figure.

File Transfer Protocol (FTP)

The Internet standards include a more powerful and widely used file transfer protocol, called the *file transfer protocol* (FTP). FTP defines procedures for the transfer of files between two machines.

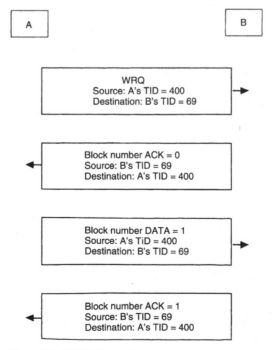

Figure 9.6   TFTP Operations.

FTP is rather unusual in that it maintains two logical connections between machines. One connection is used for the login between the machines and uses the Telnet protocol. The other connection is used for data transfer. The concept is shown in Figure 9.7. The end user communicates with a *protocol interpreter* (PI), which governs the control connection. The PI must transfer information between the user and the PI's *file system*. Commands and replies are transmitted between the user PI and the server PI. As depicted in the figure, the other machine's (server's) PI responds to the Telnet protocol in managing connections.

During the file transfer, data management is performed by the other logical connection, called the *data transfer process* (DTP). Once the DTP has performed its functions and the user's request is satisfied, PI closes the connection.

FTP also permits transfers between a device other than the original server and client. This operation is typically known as a *third-party transfer*. As shown in Figure 9.8, a client opens a connection to two remote machines that both act as servers. The purpose of such a connection is to request that the client be given permission to transfer files between the two servers' file systems. If the requests are approved, one server forms a TCP connection with the other server

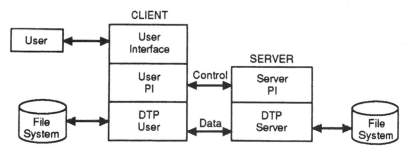

Figure 9.7   FTP Model.

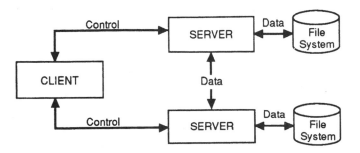

Figure 9.8   FTP Third-Party Transfer.

and transfers data across the sending FTP and TCP modules, and into the receiving FTP module.

Data types

FTP is somewhat limited both in its capability to support different types of data representation and in negotiating the use of these types between machines. FTP users can specify the type to be used in the transfer (for example, ASCII or EBCDIC). ASCII is the default, and FTP requires that all implementations support ASCII code. EBCDIC is also supported and used rather extensively in data transfer between mainframe host computers.

Both ASCII and EBCDIC use a second parameter to indicate if the characters will be used for format control purposes. For example, carriage control (CR), line feed (LF), vertical tab (VT), and form feed (FF) can be defined as control characters during the FTP session.

FTP also supports the transfer of bit streams, which it calls *image types*. With this operation, the data are sent in continuous bit streams. For the actual transfer, they are packed into 8-bit bytes. Most operations use image types for transmitting binary images, and therefore most FTP implementations support the image type.

A local type is also supported. This type is transferred in bytes whose size is determined by a parameter called *byte size*. FTP requires that the byte size value be a decimal integer.

FTP commands and replies

The FTP uses a number of commands for preliminary identification, password authentication, and the ongoing file-transfer operations. Table 9.3 lists the acronyms for these commands and a brief description of their functions.

FTP also describes a number of replies, used for the correct file transfer between two processes. As the name suggests, these replies are invoked as a result of FTP commands. The replies consist of a three-digit number followed by some descriptive text. The first digit can take the values from 0 to 5. This value identifies the five major types of replies. Table 9.4 lists the major types of replies and a brief description of their functions.

The y value of the reply codes can be coded to contain additional information about the nature of the reply. The type of reply in this code is identified by five values, 0 through 5; these values define status commands, syntax errors, authentication commands, control, data connection commands, etc. Table 9.5 lists and describes these codes.

The third digit defines an even finer level of detail about the meaning of the reply. These codes are numerous and beyond the scope of

TABLE 9.3   FTP Commands

Commands	Function
USER	Identifies the user; required by the server
PASS	User password; preceded by USER
ACCT	User account ID
CWD	Change working directory
CDUP	Change to parent directory
SMNT	Mount a different file system data structure
QUIT	Terminate connection
REIN	Terminate connection and start another
PORT	Port address
PASV	Request for passive-open
TYPE	Representation type (ASCII, EBCDIC, etc).
STRU	File structure = file, record, or page
MODE	Transfer mode = stream, block, or compressed
RETR	Transfer copy of file to other party
STOR	Accept data and store it
STOU	Accept data and store it under different name
APPE	Accept data and append it to another file
ALLO	Allocate (reserve) storage for operation
REST	Restart marker (checkpoint) at which transfer restarts
RNFR	Old pathname of file to be renamed
RNTO	New pathname of file to be renamed
ABOR	Abort previous FTP command and associated data transfer
DELE	Delete specified file at the server site
RMD	Remove directory
MKD	Create (make) a directory
PWD	Return (print) name of current working directory
LIST	Transfer list of directories, files, etc., to DTP
NLST	Transfer a directory listing to user site
SITE	Provide services specific to user site
SYST	Query to determine type of operating system at server
STAT	Return a status over the control connection
HELP	Retrieve helpful information from the server
NOOP	No operation

this book, but I will provide an example of their use shortly. I encourage you to refer to RFC 959 for more information on this level of detail about FTP reply codes.

Sequence of operations in an FTP session

FTP follows several well-ordered steps to effect a data transfer between two users. These steps are discussed in this section in the order in which they occur.

Remote host login (1). Before data transfer can occur between two users, the login operation must be completed. One of the functions of this login is to ensure that passwords, authorization codes, and other

TABLE 9.4   FTP Reply Codes

Value code	Function
1yz	A positive preliminary reply that means the command action is being initiated. The invoker of the command can expect another reply before proceeding to a new command.
2yz	A positive completion reply that informs the invoker that the command action has been completed successfully, and a new request can be initiated.
3yz	A positive intermediate reply signifying that the command has been accepted, but the action is in a hold state because the performer needs additional information.
4yz	A transit negative completion reply signifying that the command is not accepted and an action did not take place. It also signifies a temporary error condition, and the action can be requested again.
5yz	A permanent negative completion reply stating that the action did not occur, the command is not accepted, and it is not expected that the reinitiation of the command will have any better success.

TABLE 9.5   Additional FTP Reply Codes

Value code	Function
x0z	Identifies a syntax error; syntax is correct but the command makes no sense
x1z	Replies to requests for information, such as status
x2z	Replies that refer to connection management
x3z	Replies for authentication and accounting commands
x4z	Not specified
x5z	Replies on the status of file server system

security features have been satisfied. At a minimum, a user must have an acceptable user name and password available for the other host machine. During the login process, it is possible to change some tables that control the data transfer. This is a very useful function if a user wants different support services for different connections.

Directory definition (2).   This feature might not be needed, but once the control connection is available, you might need to change a directory to manage the space in which the data will reside.

File transfer definition (3).   Using the directory, this third operation defines the file to be transferred through a list of subcommands. FTP supports a very wide repertoire of subcommands. The most common are GET and PUT subcommands, which allow the file to be copied from the remote host to a local file system, or from the local file system to the remote host.

Mode transfer definition (4).   The next step in the FTP file transfer process involves defining the type of mode to be used during the transfer. Basically, this step entails defining how the data are to be represented and how the bits will be transferred. FTP supports several subcommands to support these operations:

Block. This parameter preserves the logical record within the file. It transfers the file in the same format as it was input to the transmitting module.

Stream. This mode is a default mode for the transfer. It is quite efficient because it sends no block control information. Stream mode does not care what kind of data is transmitted, so it is code- and block-transparent.

TYPE. This mode is used with IMAGE, ASCII, and EBCDIC parameters.

ASCII. This is a default transfer mode for TYPE.

EBCDIC. EBCDIC is used frequently between hosts that use EBCDIC characters, such as IBM-type machines.

IMAGE. This mode supports the transfer of contiguous binary bits packed in 8-bit bytes. It is the most widely used method for transferring straight binary data.

Starting the data transfer (5). This step can begin with many of the FTP commands. For example, the retrieve command could be used to begin operations, or the append command could be used to add records to an existing file.

Stopping the data transfer (6). This is a rather simple step involving the FTP QUIT subcommand. The subcommand disconnects the host running the FTP operations. You might want to issue the CLOSE subcommand instead, however, which does not cause a disconnection. If you CLOSE, FTP stays active and another user can begin a new FTP session with the OPEN subcommand.

Examples of FTP operations

In this section, I will provide examples of the FTP protocol in order to summarize FTP operations and the FTP overview information you have seen so far. FTP is similar to several other internet protocols in that it is state-driven. Consequently, it is useful to illustrate and explain several state diagrams with examples. The following definitions apply to all the examples:

B. The operations begin.

W. The protocol machine is waiting for a reply.

E. The operation was created in error.

S. The operation was a success.

F. The operation was a failure.

Each operation is depicted with reply codes emanating from the function boxes. The reply codes are coded as 1yz, 2yz, 3yz, 4yz, and 5yz, which were discussed earlier in the chapter. The yz values give more specific information about the replies.

The general notation for these figures is shown in Figure 9.9. The figure shows the code CMD, which begins the operation. This command creates a wait state, after which reply codes signify the success or failure of the operation. With this in mind, let us move to a discussion of several of the operations of FTP.

Refer again to Figure 9.9, which illustrates a state diagram modeled for many of the FTP operations. The model in Figure 9.9 supports the following commands: ABOR, DELE, CWD, CDUP, SMNT, HELP, MODE, NOOP, PASV, QUIT, SITE, PORT, SYST, STAT, RMD, MKD, PWD, STRU, and TYPE. (Refer to Table 9.3 for a brief description of these commands.) You can simply insert one of the commands into the command notation (CMD) in the figure, and follow the remainder of the flow chart to determine possible outcomes.

Figure 9.10 shows a similar state diagram, only reply code 1 entails the protocol machine returning back to a wait-to-reply state. This diagram supports the following commands: APPE, LIST, NLST, REIN, RETR, STOR, and STOU.

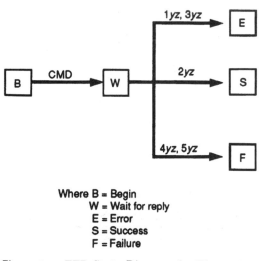

Where B = Begin
       W = Wait for reply
       E = Error
       S = Success
       F = Failure

Figure 9.9 FTP State Diagram for Elementary Operations.

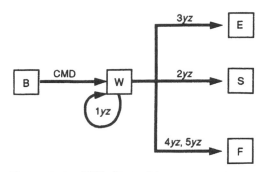

Figure 9.10 FTP State Diagram for Other Options.

The last example, Figure 9.11, shows a rather complex state diagram, which depicts the operations in state transitions for the login procedure. As depicted in the figure, the operation begins with the issuance of a USER message. Subsequently, the password (PASS) and accounting (ACCT) messages are issued to determine if the login is a success, failure, or error.

Example of a file retrieval

Figure 9.12 shows an example of a file retrieval. The top part of the figure depicts the permissible replies that can be returned from a retrieve (RETR) command. The bottom part of the figure shows the sequence of the replies. RFC 959 uses the following convention for documenting reply sequences: preliminary replies are listed first, followed by suc-

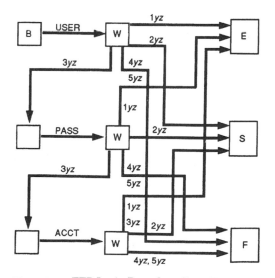

Figure 9.11 FTP Login Procedure State Diagram.

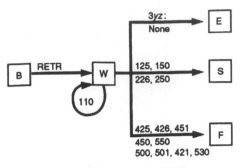

Command-reply sequence for RETR:

RETR
   125, 150

   (110)
   226, 250
   425, 426, 451
   450, 550
   500, 501, 421, 530

Figure 9.12   Example of Retrieve Operations.

ceeding replies (indented under the preliminary replies) and, finally, positive and negative completion replies. To help analyze Figure 9.12, the reply codes for RETR are listed in Table 9.6. Remember that many other reply codes are defined in the FTP standard. (See Box 9.1.)

Simple Mail Transfer Protocol (SMTP)

The SMTP standard a widely used upper-layer protocols in the Internet Protocol stack. As its name implies, SMTP defines how to transmit messages (mail) between two users.

TABLE 9.6   Codes Relevant to Figure 9.12

Code	Meaning
125	Data connection already open; beginning the transfer
150	File status correct; about to open data connection
110	Remark marker reply
226	Closing data connection; action was successful
250	Request action successfully completed
425	Cannot open data connection
426	Connection closed; action aborted
451	Local error; action aborted
450	Requested action not taken; file unavailable (e.g., busy)
550	Requested action not taken; file unavailable (e.g., not found)
500	Syntax error; command cannot be interpreted
501	Syntax error; parameters cannot be interpreted
421	Service not available; closing control connection
530	Not logged in

Type:	ASCII, Nonprint
Mode:	Stream
Structure:	File, record
Commands:	USER, QUIT, PORT, TYPE, MODE, STRU, RETR, STRO, NOOP

Default values as follows:

TYPE:	ASCII, Nonprint
MODE:	Stream
STRU:	File

Box 9.1 Minimum Implementation of FTP.

SMTP uses the concept of spooling, which allows mail to be sent from a local application to the SMTP application, which stores the mail in a device or memory. Typically, once the mail arrives at the spool, it is queued. A server checks to see if any messages are available and then attempts to deliver them. If the user is not available for delivery, the server might try later. Eventually, if the mail cannot be delivered, it will be discarded or returned to the sender. This concept is known as an *end-to-end delivery system* because the server attempts to contact the destination to deliver, and it keeps the mail in the spool for a period of time until it has been delivered.

SMTP is found in two RFCs. RFC 822 describes the structure for the message, which also includes the envelope. RFC 821 specifies the protocol that controls the exchange of mail between two machines.

SMTP model

Figure 9.13 illustrates a general model of SMTP. The operations begin with the sender SMTP establishing communications with the receiver SMTP. Before mail transmission, the two SMTP entities

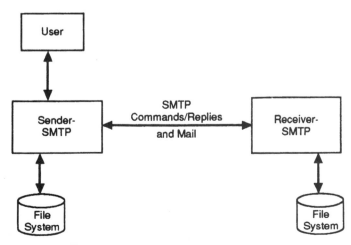

Figure 9.13 SMTP Model.

might exchange passwords or other authentication signals. Then the sender transmits a special command called MAIL, which gives the sender's identification and some other information for the mail exchange. The receiver must return an acknowledgment to the MAIL command. In SMTP, this acknowledgment is written as 250 or, in some documents, 250 OK. Regardless of the format, acknowledgment means that the requested mail action was completed.

The next step in the procedure is to transmit an RCPT command in order to identify the destination of the message. Again, an acknowledgment is required from each potential receiver.

The third step in the process is to issue the DATA command. This message is sent by the sender SMTP to alert the receiver(s) that a message is forthcoming. The data are then transmitted, line by line, until the sender sends a special sequence of control characters to signal the end of the message. At this time, the server can choose to terminate the process with a QUIT command.

Address field format

The sender SMTP uses a standard format for its sending address and receiving address fields. They take the form:

```
local-part@domain-name
```

An SMTP name thus follows the Domain Name System (DNS) concept, and some systems use the same server facility to derive an IP address from this name. In practice, this format scheme could appear as:

```
Jones@beta.aus.edu
```

where the local person's name is Jones and beta.aus.edu is the domain identifier for the person. The local-part@domain-name can take other forms to designate the following:

- A direct connection (user@host)
- A mail receiver located at a non-SMTP host via a mail gateway (user%remote-host@gateway-host)
- A relay between more than two hosts (@host-b@host-c@host-d)

Examples of SMTP operations

Figure 9.14 shows a simple operation of two SMTP users exchanging mail. The left side of the figure shows the sender establishing the connection. The receiver responds with 220 OK. The HELLO command is

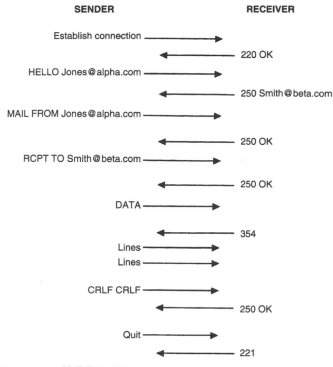

SENDER RECEIVER

Establish connection ⟶

⟵ 220 OK

HELLO Jones@alpha.com ⟶

⟵ 250 Smith@beta.com

MAIL FROM Jones@alpha.com ⟶

⟵ 250 OK

RCPT TO Smith@beta.com ⟶

⟵ 250 OK

DATA ⟶

⟵ 354

Lines ⟶

Lines ⟶

CRLF CRLF ⟶

⟵ 250 OK

Quit ⟶

⟵ 221

Figure 9.14 SMPT Mail Transaction.

used as an identifier exchange between the two machines. The MAIL FROM command tells Smith@Beta.com that a new mail transaction is beginning. The receiver uses this command to clear its buffers, reset state tables, and prepare for the message. Then the RCPT command gives the forward path address of the receiver. In this example, it is Smith@Beta.com, which replies with 250 OK. The DATA command informs the receiver that message contents follow. The response is 354, which means to start mail input and end it with CRLF CRLF.

The data are transmitted, and the end of transmission is signaled with CRLF CRLF. The receiver responds with 250 OK and the connection is taken down with QUIT and the responding 221, which means the server is closing the connection.

Figure 9.15 shows examples of other types of SMTP mail exchanges. The top part of the figure illustrates the verification command (VRFY). Its purpose is to confirm the name of the receiver. In this example, JSmith should return a full name and a fully specified mailbox. The second operation in Figure 9.15 depicts how SMTP can confirm an identity in a mailing list. The respondents should return full names and fully specified mailboxes.

■ Parent and child windows are managed through *stacks*. This approach is hierarchical in nature in that a child window rests beneath a parent window. In turn, a child window can be a parent window above other child windows. The rationale for this approach is to provide a means for subwindows to be visible on the screen when their parent is on top of the child's stack.

The xlib module is not the only available interface to X. A number of tool kits are available to mask the application from xlib, and they never use xlib directly.

The X Window system protocol

Client applications and the server communicate with each other through the X Window system protocol. Four types of messages are used:

Request.   An instruction to the workstation server to perform an action, such as drawing a line.

Reply.   This is sent from the server in response to a request (or for requests).

Event.   This is used by the server to inform the application of changes that affect the application (e.g., a user clicking a mouse or a foreign application changing a window).

Error.   This is sent to the client application by the server if something is wrong (e.g., the user selects an execution of a program that consumes more memory than is available).

The formats for these messages are shown in Figure 9.17. The request format contains major and minor opcodes of one octet each.

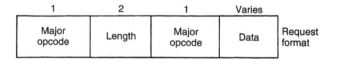

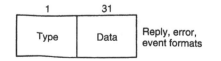

Figure 9.17   X Window System Protocol Message Formats.

The length field is two octets, and the data field is variable. The reply, error, and event formats contain one octet for the type field and a 31-octet data field.

Many messages on X do not warrant a reply. For example, a "move mouse" message is a one-way request. Additionally, these one-way messages are often buffered and sent in a *batch stream*. This approach allows a user to issue an xlib request and go on to other operations. On the other hand, a round-trip transaction with a returned request requires that the application wait for the reply.

An event message is sent only if an application has solicited the type of event being sent. This approach is quite important in that it allows an application to receive only relevant events.

The display connection

X Window applications must establish a display connection before they can communicate. The application uses an X request called *XOpenDisplay* from the xlib library to establish a connection with a workstation. The workstation and xlib exchange information with each other while establishing the connection, then xlib creates a *display structure* that contains the necessary configuration data for proper communication between the application and the workstation. A reply to XOpenDisplay returns a pointer to the display structure.

After a *display connection* has been established, the application and workstation are ready to work. Of course, the nature of the work depends on the application. For example, if the application wants to know what window the mouse pointer is in, it issues the *XQueryPointer* call to xlib. The position is returned in a reply.

As another example, suppose the application wants to move the screen cursor (in contrast to it being moved by the mouse user). Issuing the *XWarpPointer* moves the cursor pointer in accordance with the arguments supplied to the call by the application.

These are specific examples of X operations; on a more general level, applications use standard X requests to operate on the following objects (resources):

Windows. The rectangular image on a screen that identifies the manipulated resource (user applications, database, file, etc.)

Graphic contexts. The look of objects (line size, boldness, etc.).

Color. The translation of application commands to colors on the screen.

Fonts. Shape, size, style of text.

Pixmaps.   Hiding displays for later use (a cut and later paste, for example).

Cursors.   The look of the cursor and its movement

It should be helpful to examine a few examples of X events, generated to inform an application about something that happened. These examples are far from being all-inclusive; they show only mouse-related events.

A *ButtonPress* event is generated each time a mouse user presses a button (or buttons) on the mouse (when the pointer is within a specified window). The opposite holds true for the generation of a *ButtonRelease* event. The *MotionNotify* event is generated when the pointer moves within a specified window. It can be generated with mouse manipulation or program control.

I have only touched the surface of the capabilities of the X Window system. Many books and articles are available on the system, and RFC 1198 (FYI:6) provides more information and contact points within the Internet.

Remote Procedure Call

Remote procedure call (RPC) is a widely used software module developed by Sun Microsystems, Inc. It can be used on almost all UNIX-based systems, and greatly facilitates the distribution of applications to multiple machines. RPC is published in RFC 1057.

RPC is a remote subroutine call program. It allows a caller program, referred to as a *client*, to send a message to a *server*. The caller program then waits for a reply message. This call message includes parameters that define what is to be performed at the remote site. In turn, the reply message contains the result of the procedure call.

RPC can be implemented on either a TCP or a UDP transport layer. UDP does not provide reliability, so it is up to the end-user application to provide for retransmissions, time-outs, and other transport-layer mechanisms. The RPC call message contains only three fields: remote program number, remote program version number, and remote procedure number.

The purpose of *remote program number* is to identify a group of procedures, such as a database system or a file system. Sun Microsystems administers numbers in the range of 0–1*fffffff*. They are intended to be identical for all installations. The procedures are actually macros or cataloged procedures, such as a read or write, and are identified with *remote procedure numbers*. Within the procedures, it might be necessary to change the system, in which case a *remote version number* is assigned as different releases are placed into production.

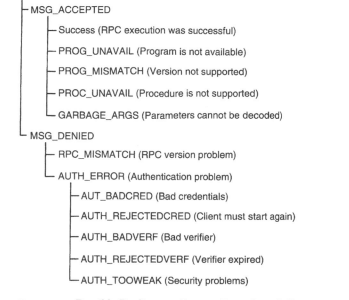

Possible RPC replies

—MSG_ACCEPTED

— Success (RPC execution was successful)

— PROG_UNAVAIL (Program is not available)

— PROG_MISMATCH (Version not supported)

— PROC_UNAVAIL (Procedure is not supported)

— GARBAGE_ARGS (Parameters cannot be decoded)

—MSG_DENIED

— RPC_MISMATCH (RPC version problem)

— AUTH_ERROR (Authentication problem)

— AUT_BADCRED (Bad credentials)

— AUTH_REJECTEDCRED (Client must start again)

— AUTH_BADVERF (Bad verifier)

— AUTH_REJECTEDVERF (Verifier expired)

— AUTH_TOOWEAK (Security problems)

Figure 9.18 Possible Replies to a Remote Procedure Call.

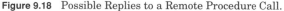

The RPC reply message is quite simple. It provides the status of a procedure call, with the replies shown in Figure 9.18.

Network File System

The Network File System (NFS) was also developed by Sun Microsystems, Inc., to allow computers to share files across a network or networks. It is published in RFC 1094. NFS is computer-independent and is also independent of lower layers, such as the transport layer, because it rests above the RPC.

NFS consists of two other protocols, the *mount protocol* and the *NFS protocol*. The purpose of the mount protocol is to identify a file system and the remote host to be accessed. The NFS protocol is responsible for performing the file transfer operations.

The NFS server procedures

An NFS server performs its operations through several procedures. These procedures are *stateless*, in that no state tables are maintained to track the progress of the procedures' operations. This approach might seem a bit strange. After all, file reading and especially writing are inherently state-oriented (sometimes called "stateful") because the operations must be tracked. NFS solves the problem by assuming that any required state-oriented services are implemented in other protocols. A user application could therefore contain the state-oriented logic (file locks, write positions, etc.) and call NFS for the use of its procedures. The procedures of NFS are similar to other network transfer or management protocols. A user can invoke procedures to perform the following:

- Create, rename, or remove a file
- Get attributes of files
- Create, read, or remove a file directory
- Read or write to a file
- Perform other procedures

The user application is responsible for keeping track of the position in the file where reading and writing is to occur. For example, the NFS read file procedure, NFSPROC_READ, requires the application to furnish the position in the file where the reading is to begin, as well as the number of bytes to be returned in the reply.

Remote Exec Daemon

The remote exec daemon (REXECD) allows the execution of the REXECD command on a remote host through a TCP/IP-based network. The client is required to perform the REXECD processing. REXECD is designed to handle commands issued by host machines and delegate these commands to slave machines for job execution. REXECD is responsible for authenticating the user (if a user ID/password is used). It also performs automatic login functions to the host. The protocol rests above TCP in the IP suite. IBM systems extensively use REXECD. IBM's VM, AIX, and DOS machines can run this protocol.

PING

PING is a very simple protocol that uses the User Datagram Protocol (UDP) segment. Its principal operation is to send a message and simply wait for it to come back.

PING is so named because it is an echo protocol and uses the ICMP echo and echo-reply messages. Each machine operates with a PING server whenever IP is active on the machine. PING is used principally by system programmers for diagnostic and debugging purposes. It is very useful because it provides the following functions:

Loopback ping   Verifies the operation of the TCP/IP software

Ping address Determines if a physical network device can be addressed

Ping remote IP address Verifies whether the network can be addressed

Ping remote host name Verifies the operation of a server on a host Refer to Chapter 6 for more information on this protocol.

Host Monitoring Protocol

The host monitoring protocol (HMP) collects information from host computers in an internet. Typically, the information is used by a network control center (NCC) to determine the performance and status of hosts. HMP uses the term *monitoring entity* to describe a monitored host and *monitoring host* to describe what would typically be the NCC. One host is able to monitor another.

Earlier implementations of HMP were used by NCCs to collect network information from gateways, cluster controllers, and other network entities. Some implementations have been used simply to exchange information between host machines.

HMP is a connectionless protocol. It operates at the transport layer over IP and ICMP. This approach does not preclude other layer suites; for example, HMP could rest over logical link control (LLC) type 1, 2, or 3 in a LAN. The idea of HMP is based on the realization that certain information needs to be exchanged between hosts and hosts and NCCs. First, the monitored entity might need to send unsolicited traffic to a monitoring center. One action that comes to mind is sending alarms from a monitored host. Second, the monitoring host (the control of the NCC) might need to gather information from the monitored entity for log control management. Finally, the NCC might need to set certain control parameters at the monitored host and ascertain if these control parameters were set and carried out successfully. To meet these needs, HMP is designed to collect three classes of data.

Spontaneous events are captured by the monitoring entity. These events are called *traps* in the Internet. Typically, a trap would be on something deemed important enough to warrant the NCC's attention. Trap messages must contain identifiers to indicate the report, time, host, and, of course, any data relevant to the trapped message.

The second type of data collected by HMP deals with the current status of a host machine. *Status information* is topical, and not necessarily collected over a long period of time. HMP accomplishes this action by sending a typical poll message to a host. The poll requires the host to respond with its latest status information.

The third type of data collected by HMP is *long-range data*, such as performance data over a period of time. Unlike status information, all this data is important because it is used to analyze the performance of the network and the host.

Discard Protocol

This protocol is also useful as a diagnostic tool. As its name implies, it discards any data it receives. The usefulness of this protocol might initially escape you. Typically, it is used by the receiver to analyze received data. The data is likely not actual end-user data, but data introduced at the transmitting entity for network tuning considerations. Therefore, instead of passing this data to an upper layer, the discard protocol discards it.

The discard protocol is used with TCP when the discard server listens for the connections on TCP port 9. After the connection is established, any data coming in on this port is discarded. The discard service is also provided for UDP. The server listens for data on UDP port 9. Upon receiving the data, the datagram is discarded.

Finger

Finger is a very simple protocol for obtaining information about users logged on to a machine. The information given to an inquiring user depends entirely on the specific implementation of the finger. Typically, when the client sends a command, a list of users currently logged on that host is provided in response. Be aware, however, that the implementation of finger varies, as does the information provided in the retrieval. Typical information retrieved with finger is the name of the user, the job title of the job running on the machine, the interface to the user (the terminal being used), the location of the workstation. Finger is now published as RFC 1196 and RFC 1288, which has clarified some ambiguities about the protocol.

Network Time Protocol

Chapter 6 discussed the use of an Internet Control Message Protocol (ICMP) time stamp option in which communicating machines such as gateways and hosts coordinate their clocks. The question that remains is, how do these machines obtain their timing information? After all, who can say that one gateway has a more accurate clock than another? This section, which discusses the network time protocol (NTP), published in RFC 1119, provides the answer to this question. In addition to RFC 1119, you might want to refer to RFCs 956 and 957. I highly recommend that you read RFC 1119 if you need more detailed information on clocking protocols, algorithms for smoothing the clock, how to develop clock offsets, and how to estimate round-trip delays for synchronizing clocking values.

NTP operation is depicted in Figure 9.19. Clocking information for a network is provided through the primary time server, designated as a *root*. The time server obtains its clocking information from master sources. In the United States, this is usually one of four sources:

Fort Collins, Colorado.   Station WWV operated by the National Institutes of Standards and Technology (NIST), using high-frequency (HF) transmissions

Kauai, Hawaii.   Station WWVH operated by NIST, also operating with HF transmissions

Boulder, Colorado.   Station WWVB, operating with low-frequency (LF) transmissions

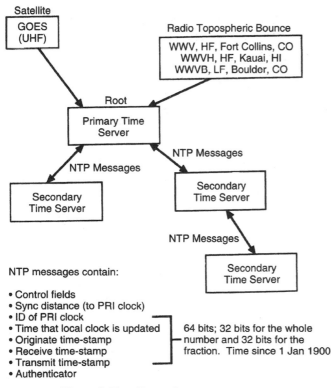

Figure 9.19 Network Time Protocol.

Geosynchronous Orbiting Environmental Satellite (GOES).   Operated by NIST in the ultra-high frequency (UHF) range

These master clocking sources are used by the primary time server to derive accurate clocks. Other countries might have their own clocks to provide clocking over large areas. Most of these clocks provide very accurate clocking synchronization on the order of less than 1 millisecond. Local clocks are even more accurate. Part of the problem with obtaining absolutely accurate clock information stems from the variable propagation delays resulting from different atmospheric conditions, interrupt latencies at the machines, and small oscillator drifts in the clocks.

The primary time server, upon receiving clocking information from a master clocking source, uses the NTP protocol to coordinate clocks at the secondary time servers. Secondary time servers can in turn provide clocking for other secondary time servers. The accuracy of the clocking decreases as NTP messages are propagated through the clocking hierarchy. Although Figure 9.19 shows one primary time server servicing an internet, this need not be the case. Multiple primary time servers can service clocking within the network.

The NTP messages contain, as one might expect, *time stamps* that are used by the primary and secondary time servers to calculate clock offsets and correct clocking inaccuracies. (Several *control fields* are contained in the NTP message; they are not discussed here because they are beyond the scope of this discussion.) The *sync distance* is an estimate of the round-trip propagation delay to the primary clock, as seen by the originator of the NTP message. The *ID of the primary clock* contains the unique identifier of the primary time server. The next four fields contain the following time stamp information:

Time local clock updated.   Time that the originator of this message has had its local clock updated

Originate time stamp.   Time that this message was originated

Receive time stamp.   Time that this message was received

Transmit time stamp.   Time that this message was transmitted after receiving it

All time stamps are 64 bits in length, with 32 bits reserved for a whole number and 32 bits for the fraction. Time stamps are benchmarked from January 1, 1900. Does the 32-bit field provide enough space for growth? Most definitely. The value 2^{32} provides magnitudes well beyond what should be needed in the future. The last field is the authenticator. It is an optional field, used for authentication purposes.

NTP uses port 37 and can operate above UDP or the TCP. Be aware that the information retrieved and displayed to the user on a terminal is not very usable as is. For example, the value gives the number of seconds since January 1, 1900, midnight (GMT). Consequently, the date of January 1, 1980 GMT at midnight would be retrieved and displayed as 2,524,521,600. Of course, you could write or obtain a simple program to translate this notation into a user-friendly format.

Daytime

Daytime is similar to the time protocol, except that it returns times that are easier to use. The returned string is an ASCII text. The information returned from the daytime protocol is usually displayed in the format weekday, month day, year, time zone. This protocol is used quite often in internet standards when machine-readable protocol is not required (as in the time protocol discussed previously).

Point-to-Point Protocol

The point-to-point protocol (PPP) was implemented to solve a problem that has evolved in the industry during the last decade. With the rapid growth of internetworking, several vendors and standards organizations have developed a number of network-layer protocols.

IP is the most widely used of these protocols, but machines such as routers typically run more than one network-layer protocol. While IP is a given on most machines, routers also load network-layer protocols developed by companies such as Xerox, Apple Computer, and SUN. Thus, machines communicating with each other might not know which network-layer protocols are available during a session.

Also, until the advent of PPP, the industry did not have a standard means of defining a serial link or point-to-point encapsulation protocol, such as the capability that exists on a LAN with an Ethernet Ethertype field or link service access points (LSAPs). The encapsulation protocol carries or encapsulates a network-layer PDU in its information (I) field and uses another field in the frame to identify which network-layer PDU resides in the I field. The PPP standard solves these two problems.

PPP encapsulates network-layer datagrams over a serial communications link. The protocol allows two machines on a point-to-point communications channel to negotiate the particular types of network-layer protocols (such as IP) to be used during a session. After this negotiation occurs, PPP carries the network-layer PDUs in the I field of an HDLC-type frame. This protocol supports either bit-oriented synchronous transmission or asynchronous (start/stop) transmission. It can be used on switched or dial-up links, but requires full duplex capability.

PPP is divided into three major components. The first component deals with the HDLC frame and how it is used to encapsulate datagrams in the I field of the frame. The second major component of PPP is the link control protocol (LCP), which establishes the link, tests the link for various quality-of-service features, configures it, and releases the link. The third major component is a generic family of network control protocols (NCPs) for establishing which network-layer protocols are to be used for the connection.

PPP supports the simultaneous use of different network protocols. For example, the protocol allows two users to negotiate the simultaneous use of IP, Digital's DECnet IV network layer, IPX, and XNS.

The PPP PDU uses the HDLC frame as stipulated in ISO 3309-1979 (and amended by ISO 3309-1984/PDAD1). Figure 9.20 shows this format. The flag sequence is the standard HDLC flag of 01111110 (hex 7e). The address field is set to all 1s (hex ff), which signifies an all-stations address. PPP does not use individual station addresses because it is a point-to-point protocol. The control field is set to identify an HDLC unnumbered information (UI) command. Its value is 00000011 (hex 03). The I field contains the user data (the datagram) for the protocol that is identified in the protocol field.

Once negotiations have occurred between two stations and these stations agree on the network-layer protocols that will be used, the information field actually contains the datagram. For negotiations, the protocol value is set to a leading 8, 0, or C (as discussed in the next paragraph). The I field contains the control values that perform various negotiations. The maximum default length for the I field is 1500 octets. Other values can be used if the PPP implementors so agree. The frame check sequence (FCS) field is used for error detection. As with most HDLC FCS checks, the calculations are performed on the address, control, protocol, and I fields.

The protocol field identifies the PDU that is encapsulated into the I field of the frame. The values in this field are assigned through RFC

Flag	Address	Control	Protocol	Information (I field)	FCS	Flag

```
      Flag = 01111110
   Address = 11111111
   Control = 00000011
  Protocol = See RFC 1060
Information = Network layer PDU
       FCS = 16 bits
```

Figure 9.20 PPP Frame Format.

1060. On a more general note, the field values are assigned initially in accordance with the values in this figure. As suggested in the figure, values beginning with a 0 identify the network protocol that resided in the I field; values beginning with 8 identify a control protocol to negotiate the protocols that will actually be used; and a leading value of C identifies the protocol as LCP.

LCP supports the establishment of the connection and allows for certain configuration options to be negotiated. The protocol also maintains the connection and provides procedures for termination. To perform these functions, LCP is organized into four phases:

Phase 1. Link establishment and configuration negotiation

Phase 2. Link quality determination

Phase 3. Network layer protocol configuration negotiation

Phase 4. Link termination

PPP requires that LCP be executed to open the connection between two stations before any network-layer traffic is exchanged, which consists of a series of message exchanges called *configure packets*. After these packets have been exchanged and a configure-acknowledge packet has been sent and received between the stations, the connection is considered to be in an open state and datagrams can be exchanged. LCP confines itself to link operations. It does not understand how to negotiate the implementation of network-layer protocols. Indeed, it does not care about the upper-layer negotiations relating to network protocols.

The PPP frame I field carries the link control protocol packet. The protocol field in the frame must contain hex C021 to indicate that the I field carries link control protocol information. The format for the field is shown in this figure. The *code field* must be coded to identify the type of LCP packet encapsulated into the frame. For example, the code would indicate if the frame contained a configure request, which would likely be followed by a configure ACK or NAK. Additionally, the code could indicate an echo request data unit. Naturally, the next frame would probably identify the echo reply.

Multilink PPP

In recent years, many manufacturers have developed link-level protocols to manage more than one link. The advantages are obvious. First, additional throughput can be achieved; second, a faulty link can be replaced easily by a predefined back-up link.

In 1984, X.25's layer-two LAPB was amended to include provisions for multilink procedures (MLP). The MLP protocol is quite similar to SNA's transmission groups. LAPB is based on ISO 7776.

In an MLP configuration, stations communicate through more than one communications channel. Each single-link channel behaves in its conventional manner, and MLP adds one additional component: a sequence number for all the multilinks. This sequence number allows you to manage the windows and flow control across all the links identified to the multilink. The flow control, sequencing, and window management of MLP closely follow the concept of individual single links. The main difference is MLP's management of multiple physical links as if they were one logical link.

The Internet's PPP multilink operation is similar to the multilink protocol described in ISO 7776 and LPBD, but there is no requirement for acknowledged-mode operation on the link layer, although that is optionally permitted.

As stipulated in RFC 1717, PPP multilink is based on the LCP option that permits a system to indicate to a peer that it is capable of combining multiple physical links into a logical multilink (also known as a *link set* or *trunk*).

Obtaining Internet Services

The Internet supports other messaging systems. The post office protocol (POP) provides remote access to a mailbox. POP stores messages until a POP user agent accepts delivery of the traffic. Two POP agents (a user agent and a message transfer agent) can be remotely located. The POP port is 109. POP services are available from several Internet service providers through either dial-up or leased line connections.

The network news transfer protocol (NNTP) is another messaging store-and-forward service. NNTP identifies news groups and transfers news articles between the news groups. The NNTP port is 119. You might have some of these systems available through local Internet service provider. Check with your network administrator.

The World Wide Web (WWW)

One of the most popular applications used in the Internet is the World Wide Web (WWW). Initially implemented as a text-only browser, the Web has evolved into a multifunction text and graphical browser. There are thousands of Web sites throughout the world, housing an untold number of Web pages.

The Web is not a separate system from the Internet; it is an application that runs on the Internet. In its simplest form, it is a set of protocols that are exchanged between a user machine (called a *client*) and another user machine in the network (called a *server*). The system uses the concept of a Web page to organize the information at a Web site. A Web site can contain many pages linked together in a single retrievable package. The information can be organized in a hierarchical tree structure, as a linear search or a completely random search through pages.

Information is created in the Web through what is called the *markup language*. These are not programming languages such as C or Fortran; they consist of meta data that is embedded in documents to describe how the documents are formatted. You might want to explore mark-up languages further by examining the hypertext mark-up language (HTML), which is a specific implementation of the standard generalized mark-up language (SGML).

The Web also uses another concept called *hyperlinks*, which allow you to navigate through a document or move from one document to another. The coding of an HTML command embedded in a document allows users to move from one document to another. Hyperlinks allow users to initiate a request from their computer to retrieve a page on the same Web server or a remote server, depending on the need. These specific pages are identified by what is called the *uniform resource locator* (URL).

Browsing Packages (Netscape)

As stated at the beginning part of this chapter, hundreds of books are available on internet application-layer protocols, especially browsers and systems such as WWW. You need only walk into the Internet section of a technical bookstore to find books on these subjects. One example of a software package used on the WWW is Netscape Navigator. I cite this program because it was one of the first commercially successful systems and, as of this writing, is the most widely used WWW browser in the commercial industry. Netscape was developed by Netscape Communications Corporation and is available through commercial packages or under certain licensing agreements, free of use, to educational and nonprofit institutions. Check your company policy to see if there are arrangements for you to use Netscape. Certain sites on the Internet make the software available for downloading.

Netscape operates on either a SLIP or PPP connection, and various platforms such as Windows and Macintosh. Unlike earlier browsers, Netscape is very user-friendly and does not require a technical background to use the system. It can also be run in conjunction with FTP by issuing special commands to the software.

Java

To conclude this brief description of popular Internet browsing architectures, I should mention Java. As you learned earlier, the WWW

TABLE 10.1   Common Internet RFCs for Network Management

1052	IAB recommendations for the development of internet network management standards
1155	Structure and identification of management information for TCP/IP-based internets
1213	Management information base for network management of TCP/IP-based internets: MIB II
1157	A simple network management protocol (SNMP)
1441	Introduction to SNMPv2
1142	SNMPv2 SMI
1095	CMIP over TCP/IP (CMOT)
1085	ISO presentation services over TCP/IP-based internets or the lightweight presentation protocol (LLP)

- RFC 1155 contains common definitions and identifies information used on TCP/IP-based networks. It is similar in intent to the OSI Network Management Standard IS 7498-4 and IS 10040.

- RFC 1213 contains information dealing with an IMIB. This document is the second release of the MIB, and is known as MIB II.

- The other important document is RFC 1157, which describes the SNMP.

Although subsequent RFCs contain additional information on the use of SNMP, RFC 1215 (how to define traps for use with the SNMP) and RFC 1187 (bulk table retrieval with SNMP) are useful documents for ancillary information. Additionally, RFC 1212 (concise MIB definitions) is a very useful document that provides information on producing MIB modules. RFCs 1095 and 1085 deal with the CMOT and the lightweight presentation protocol (LPP). As stated earlier, the CMOT approach has not proven to be successful, but it is listed in this table if you want to analyze it for historical reasons.

Table 10.1 also lists two RFCs that pertain to version 2 of SNMP (SNMPv2). Be aware that several other RFCs are published on SNMPv2, but you should read RFC 1121 and RFC 1142 before the others. All RFCs can be obtained from many sources (your Internet host or access node, for example) using anonymous file transfer protocol (FTP) or e-mail.

Layer Architecture for Internet Network Management

Figure 10.1 depicts the internet layers for network management standards. Note that the SNMP forms the foundation for the management architecture. The network management applications found at the top are not defined in internet specifications. These applications consist of vendor-specific network management modules such as fault management, log control, security, and audit trails. As illustrated in the

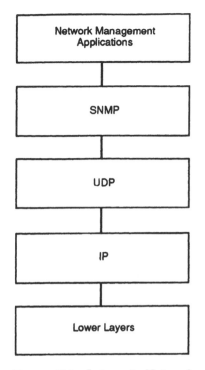

Figure 10.1 Internet Network Management Layers.

figure, SNMP rests over the user datagram protocol (UDP). UDP, in turn, rests on top of IP, which then rests on the lower layers (the data link layer and the physical layer).

The Internet Naming Hierarchy

Network elements within an internet have many common characteristics across subnetworks, vendor products, and individual components. It would be quite wasteful for each organization to spend precious resources and time using ASN.1 (and modified ASN.1) to describe these resources. Therefore, the Internet provides a registration scheme wherein resources can be categorized and identified within a registration hierarchy. This concept is founded on the ISO/ITU-T naming convention, which identifies objects and entities within a system.

Figure 10.2 shows the ISO and internet registration tree for the Internet MIB. At the root level, three branches identify the registration hierarchy as ITU-T (0), ISO (1), or joint ITU-T/ISO (2). As this chapter is concerned with internet activities, Figure 10.2 shows the ISO branch in more detail. Notice branch 3, labeled IE-ORG. The next

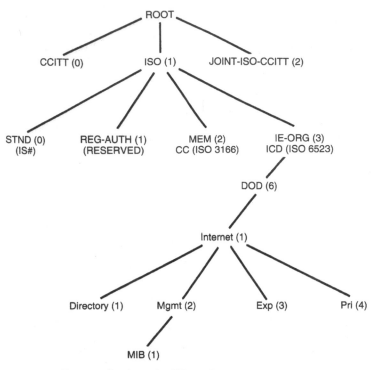

Figure 10.2   Internet Registration Hierarchy.

branch identifies the Department of Defense (DOD) with the value 6. Under this hierarchical tree, an internet has a value of 1. Within the internet hierarchy are four nodes. One is labeled management (Mgmt) with a value of 2. Finally, the leaf to this node is labeled MIB (1).

The registration hierarchy permits the assignment of unique identifiers to objects, also called *variables*. (*Managed object* is a general term used to identify any internet-managed resource, such as a router, TCP connection, or an IP address table.) The identifier is derived by concatenating the numbers associated with each node in the tree. In Figure 10.2, the internet MIB is identified by 1.3.6.1.2.1.

Structure of Management Information

Structure of management information (SMI) describes the identification scheme and structure for the managed objects in an internet. The SMI document deals principally with organizational and administrative matters. It leaves the task of object definitions to the other network management RFCs.

SMI describes the names that identify managed objects (the network resources). These names are *ASN.1 object identifiers* and use the naming convention depicted in Figure 10.2. Referring to Figure 10.2, the Directory (1) subtree is currently reserved. It is anticipated that this subtree will determine how the emerging OSI directory services (X.500) will interface with an internet.

Mgmt (2) identifies the managed objects in the network. This subtree is managed by IAB, and the numbering is delegated by IAB to other managed objects. Each definition in the tree is named as an object identifier, which is a unique identifier of a managed object.

Exp (3) identifies objects used in experimental endeavors. Again, the authority for naming through this subtree rests with IAB.

Finally, Pri (4) tree permits private enterprises to register their own managed objects. The tree is still administered by IAB, but the private enterprise, upon receiving the node of the tree, can define new MIB objects within the hierarchy. The IAB recommends, however, that all private names be registered under one authority.

Parts of the SMI standard are written in ASN.1-type coding, but the syntax for SMI is simpler than that for ASN.1. The objective of this approach is to provide a less rigorous convention for describing managed objects in an internet. I will shortly examine the syntax rules for defining SMI objects. For the present, you need concern yourself only with the types of managed objects defined in these standards.

SMI syntax and types

Internet standards use ASN.1 constructs to describe the syntax of object types, but the full ASN.1 set is not allowed. The primitive types permitted are: integer, octet string, object identifier, and null. In addition to the primitive types, the constructor types "sequence" and "sequence of" are also allowed. The SMI standard defines other object types. Listed below are some examples, but the list is not all-inclusive of the allowed types:

Network Address.   This type allows you to choose from among the internet family of protocols. The type is defined in the modified ASN.1 notation as CHOICE, and allows a developer to choose the protocol within the family. Presently, only the internet family is identified.

IP Address.   This address defines the Internet's 32-bit address. The ASN.1 notation is an octet string.

TimeTicks.   This type represents a non-negative integer that records events such as the last change to a managed object, the last update to a database, etc. The SMI standard requires that it represent a time increment in hundredths of a second.

Gauge. The SMI definition for this type is a non-negative integer that can range from 0 to 2^{31-1}. The gauge definition does not permit counter wrap-around, although its value can increase or decrease.

Counter. This defined type is described as a non-negative integer, again ranging from 0 to 2^{31-1}. This type differs from gauge in that the values can be wrapped around and can only increase.

Opaque. This defined type allows a managed object to pass anything as an octet string. It is so named because the encodings are passed transparently.

The Management Information Base

The internet network management structure is organized around object groups, of which 10 have been defined. Figure 10.3 depicts the composition of these object groups. Note that several of the object groups are discussed in this book, notably IP, ICMP, TCP, UDP, and EGP. Each of these object classes is defined further in the internet MIB. RFC 1213 provides a detailed description with the modified ASN.1 notation for each of the groups.

An organization is not required to implement all MIB object groups. Certainly, if you are using exterior gateways, the External Gateway Protocol (EGP) group is mandatory. If an organization implements UDP at the transport layer, however, it might not need to implement the TCP group. The decision to deploy MIBs depends on the type and nature of the network, and the applications supported by the network. These standards do require that if an object group is supported, all elements in that group must be supported.

The object groups consist of *objects*, also called *variables*. An object is anything deemed important enough to manage in the network (e.g., a packet switch, PBX, or modem). For the internet MIB, each object must have a name, syntax, and encoding.

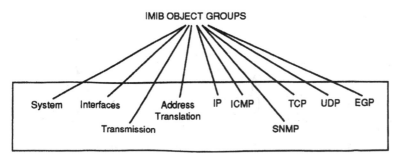

Figure 10.3   MIB Object Groups.

The name is an *object identifier*, which must be identified through the internet registration hierarchy naming conventions, described earlier in this chapter. Using OSI terms, an object is also defined by a type and an instance. The object type and object instance (in conformance with OSI conventions) serve to unambiguously identify an object. Internet network management standards do not use all OSI terms, but they are still relevant. The syntax for each object uses ASN.1. As stated earlier, not all ASN.1 constructs are permitted. I will describe those that are used later in this chapter.

The third aspect of an object is its encoding, which describes how the object type is represented through the object type's syntax. In addition, encoding deals with how an object type is coded (represented) while being transmitted on the network communications channel. The encoding is done in conformance with the basic encoding rules (BER) of ASN.1.

Overview of the object groups

Each object group (Figure 10.3) is described briefly in this section. Be aware that this general explanation is to give you only an idea of the major operations of the groups. You will need to study RFC 1213 to appreciate the full functions supported by the MIB definitions. The *system* object group describes:

- The name and version of the hardware, operating system, and networking software of the entity
- The hierarchical name of the group
- When the management portion of the system was reinitialized (in time)

The *interfaces* object group describes the:

- Number of network interfaces supported
- Type of interface operating below IP (e.g., LAPB or Ethernet)
- Size of datagram acceptable to the interface
- Speed of the interface (in bps)
- Address of the interface
- Operational state of the interface (up, down, etc.)
- Amount of traffic received, delivered (unicast or broadcast), or discarded, and the reasons

The *address translation* group describes the address translation tables for network-to-physical address translation. This group will eventually become obsolete, as its functions now reside in the IP group. The *IP* group describes:

- If the machine forwards datagrams
- The time-to-live value for datagrams originated at this site
- The amount of traffic received, delivered, or discarded, and the reasons
- Information on fragmentation operations
- Address tables, including subnet masks
- Routing tables, including destination address, distance metrics, age of route, next hop, and protocol from which route was learned (RIP, EGP, etc.)

The *ICMP* group describes the:

- Number of the various Internet Control Message Protocol (ICMP) messages received and transmitted
- Statistics on problems encountered

The *TCP* group describes the:

- Retransmission algorithm and maximum/minimum retransmission values
- Number of TCP connections the entity can support
- Information on state transition operations
- Information on traffic received and sent
- Port and IP numbers for each connection

The *UDP* group describes the:

- Information on traffic received and sent
- Information on problems encountered

The *EGP* group describes:

- Information on traffic sent and received and problems encountered
- The EGP neighbor table
- Addresses to neighbors
- The EGP state with each neighbor

The *transmission* group was added to the second release of MIB (MIB II). This group contains MIBs, object groups, and objects that pertain to unique transmission systems. For example, a transmission group has been defined for the cell-based technology ATM.

The *SNMP* group was also added to MIB II. It contains 30 objects used with simple network management protocol (SNMP). Most of the objects deal with error-reporting capabilities and are explained later in this chapter.

Table 10.2 lists and briefly describes the objects for the system object group. Similar tables could be created for each group, but this level of detail is beyond the scope of the book. This table is included only to give you an idea of MIB definitions. (Refer to my book *Network Management Standards* for a listing of all internet objects.)

All Internet objects are described further with certain *key words* (reserved words). Five notations describe the format of a managed object:

Object descriptor. As the name implies, this describes the object in ASCII text.

Syntax. The syntax describes the bit-stream representation of the object.

Definition. This notation describes the managed object in text to aid human readability.

Access. This notation describes whether the managed object is read-only, write-only, read/write, or not accessible.

Status. This notation describes whether the version is mandatory or optional and if the object is obsolete.

TABLE 10.2   System Group

Function: The system group provides general information about managed objects. This group must be implemented for all objects.

sysDescr	An octet string to describe the object, such as hardware, operating system, etc.
sysObjectID	An OBJECT IDENTIFIER to identify the object uniquely (with naming hierarchy values) within the naming subtree
sysUpTime	In TimeTicks, the time since the object was declared up and running (reinitialized)
sysContact	An octet string to identify the person/organization to contact for information about the object
sysLocation	An octet string containing the location of the object
sysServices	An integer value that describes the service(s) offered by the object, based on the location of the service within a layer

Templates to describe objects

All object definitions are defined with templates and ASN.1 code. The template format is shown in Figure 10.4. (The fields in the figure were listed and described in the previous section.)

Each of the 10 object groups in Figure 10.3 is defined in RFC 1213 with the standard template format. It is of little value to repeat these templates here, since they consume almost 50 pages. Each group was described briefly in the previous section of this chapter to give you an idea of the principal functions of each group. This section shows one example of the templates taken from the interfaces object group.

Figure 10.5 shows the template for a leaf entry of a registration tree for TCP/IP interfaces. (Be aware that several intermediate nodes are not included in this example.) The notation of ifType {IfEntry 3} means that IfType belongs to parent IfEntry 3 in the tree.

The syntax clause describes the abstract syntax (in ASN.1) of the object type. As the entry shows, the physical, data link, and subnetwork interfaces that exist below IP are described and assigned an integer value. Thus, two machines that exchange information about the interface supported below the IP layer are required to use these values. For example, ifType = 6 must be used to identify an Ethernet interface.

Definition of high-level MIB

Figure 10.6 depicts the RFC 1213 ASN.1 notation for MIB groups. The code can be understood in the context of the objects illustrated in Figure 10.3 and the naming hierarchy tree in Figure 10.2. The IMPORTS statement designates that a number of definitions are imported from RFC 1155. All objects are tagged as object identifiers and defined with yet another name within the naming tree ({mgmt1}, {mib 1}, etc.).

OBJECT:
  A name for the object type, with its
  corresponding OBJECT IDENTIFIER

Syntax:
  The ASN.1 coding to describe the syntax
  of the object type

Definition:
  Textual description of the object type

Access:
  Access options
Status:
  Status of object type

Figure 10.4 Template for IMIB Object Type Definitions.

OBJECT:
   ifType {if Entry 3}
Syntax:
  INTEGER {
    other (1),   –none of the following
    regular1822 (2),
    hdh1822 (3),
    ddn-x25 (4),
    rfc877-x25 (5),
    ethernet-csmacd (6),
    iso88023-csmacd (7),
    iso88024-tokenBus (8),
    iso88025-tokenRing (9),
    iso88026-man (10),
    starLan (11),
    proteon-10Mbit (12),
    proteon-80Mbit (13),
    hyperchannel (14),
    fddi (15),
    lapb (16),
    sdic (17),
    t1-carrier (18),
    cept (19),   –european equivalent of T-1
    basiclsdn (20),
    primarylsdn (21),
            –proprietary serial
–... and others not shown,
    }

Definition:
  The type of interface...immediately "below"
  the IP in the protocol stack.
Access:
  read-only
Status:
  mandatory
Note: ...means some of the material of RFC is omitted.

Figure 10.5 Interface Type (iType) Template.

RFC1213-MIB ::= BEGIN

IMPORTS
    mgmt, NetworkAddress, IpAddress, Counter, Gauge, TimeTicks
    FROM RFC1155-SMI;
    OBJECT-TYPE
      From RFC-1212;

mib-2   OBJECT IDENTIFIER ::= {mgmt 1}

   system   OBJECT IDENTIFIER ::= {mib-2 1}
   interfaces   OBJECT IDENTIFIER ::= {mib-2 2}
   at   OBJECT IDENTIFIER ::= {mib-2 3}
   Ip   OBJECT IDENTIFIER ::= {mib-2 4}
   icmp   OBJECT IDENTIFIER ::= {mib-2 5}
   tcp   OBJECT IDENTIFIER ::= {mib-2 6}
   udp   OBJECT IDENTIFIER ::= {mib-2 7}
   egp   OBJECT IDENTIFIER ::= {mib-2 8}
-- cmot   OBJECT IDENTIFIER ::= {mib-2 9}
   transmission OBJECT IDENTIFIER ::= {mib-2 10}
   snmp   OBJECT IDENTIFIER ::= {mib-2 11}
   END

Figure 10.6 High-Level MIB Definition.

The SNMP

SNMP owes its origin to decisions made by the IAB in early 1988. At that time, the IAB met to discuss methods to develop network management protocols to operate on TCP/IP-based networks. The result of that meeting was the decision to develop two parallel management systems, SNMP and CMOT.

SNMP is designed to be a simple, short-range solution to network management on the Internet. It is based on an earlier protocol called the Simple Gateway Monitoring Protocol (SGMP). Refer to RFC 1028 for a description of this earlier protocol.

SNMP products began to appear on the marketplace in late 1988 and early 1989. In 1988, the MIB to support SNMP was also published. In September of 1988 at Interop '88, several announcements were made regarding implementations of SNMP. As the standard matured, other RFCs were released to further define its operation. In early 1989, RFC 1098, titled *SNMP over Ethernet*, was published. Today, SNMP is widely implemented over many networks and vendor products.

SNMP administrative relationships

SNMP version 1 architecture uses a variety of terms that were explained earlier in this chapter. As shown in Figure 10.7, entities residing at management network stations and network elements that communicate with each other using the SNMP standard are called SNMP *application entities*. Pairing application entities with SNMP agents (explained shortly) makes for what is called an *SNMP community*. Each community is identified by an Internet hierarchical name.

SNMP messages originate with SNMP application entities, so they belong to the SNMP community that contains the application entity. These messages are termed *authentic SNMP messages*. Authenti-

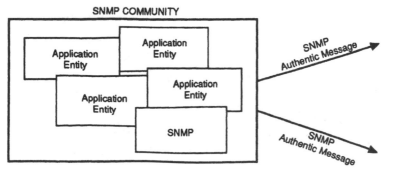

Figure 10.7 SNMP Community.

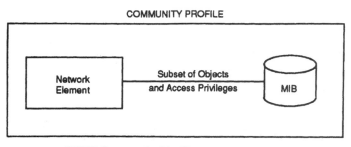

Figure 10.8   SNMP Community Profile.

cation schemes identify the message and verify its authenticity. This process is called an *authentication service*.

Figure 10.8 provides a view of other administrative relationships for SNMP. An SNMP *network element* uses objects from the Internet MIB. The subset of objects pertaining to this element is called an SNMP *MIB view*. In turn, an SNMP *access mode* represents an element of the set (for example, read-only elements or write-only elements). Pairing the SNMP access mode with the MIB view is called the SNMP *community profile*. In essence, the profile specifies access privileges for an MIB view. These relationships are determined by the SNMP community pairing, by developing profiles called SNMP *access privileges*. These access privileges then provide directions on how SNMP agents and network elements can use the MIB.

Example of an SNMP operation

Figure 10.9 shows an example of how the operations of SNMP work. In this illustration, a network control center (which could be a host computer, gateway, or any other machine) communicates with an IP gateway that contains an IP *agent*. The agent performs SNMP operations and accesses the MIB residing at the gateway. In turn, the IP agent can use SNMP messages to communicate with the network control. These messages (explained in a later section) support operations

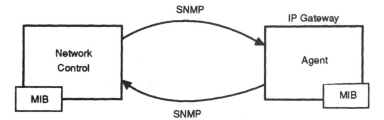

Figure 10.9   SNMP Operations Between Agent and Network Control.

such as obtaining information regarding operations, changing information, and issuing unsolicited messages in the event of alarms.

The data operated on by these messages are defined by the IMIB and also illustrated in Figure 10.9. In a typical environment, network control contains the MIB for all its managed resources (objects). It is not necessary for each agent to store the full MIB; rather, each agent stores that portion of the MIB relevant to its own operation. In this example, the IP gateway agent would have the MIB entries pertaining to IP routing tables, address translation, ICMP operations, and other tasks with which a gateway becomes involved. The gateway would not need to store the TCP MIB object group because TCP might not reside in a gateway. (Actually, in most gateways, TCP is used because these gateways use network application-layer protocols, such as Telnet.)

SNMPv1 and SNMPv2

Internet task forces have been working on an enhanced version to SNMP for the past couple of years. In the summer of 1993, SNMP version 2 was entering its final changes and is now a published standard.

SNMPv2 is a substantial improvement over SNMPv1. Perhaps the biggest change has been the improvement of security mechanism deficiencies that existed in SNMPv1. For example, SNMPv2 provides authentication and integrity services that allow the receiver of a message to authenticate the originator of the message. This approach uses a private encryption key concept and will be implemented in the U.S. by Data Encryption Standards (DES).

SNMPv2 has also improved access controls. For example, reads, writes, and specific MIB views have been improved over SNMP 1. Moreover, a security and privacy feature was added to SNMPv2 that guarantees that messages have not been tampered with. Encryption options are available for each SNMPv2 message, but all these features need not be implemented in one package. Vendors and implementors can implement any of the three major parts of security: authentication and integrity, access controls, and security and privacy.

SNMPv2 also provides mechanisms for coordinating the activities of multiple SNMPv2 managers. For example, locking mechanisms are now available to prevent managers from writing to the same agent. Gateways are also provided that allow SNMPv2 traffic to move to intermediate points between managers. Traps now have confirmation options, so an agent can issue an alarm and receive confirmation that the alarm was received correctly. Another major improvement is the addition of a *get bulk* operation that allows one SNMPv2 message to access multiple objects in an MIB, and an *inform request* operation, which permits SNMP managers to communicate with each other.

SNMP PDUs

SNMP uses simple operations and a limited number of PDUs to perform its functions. Seven PDUs are defined in the standard:

Get request. This PDU accesses the agent and obtains values from a list. It contains identifiers to distinguish multiple requests, as well as values to provide information about the status of the network element.

Get next request. This PDU is similar to the get request, except it permits retrieval of the next variable in an MIB tree.

Get response. This PDU responds to the get request, get next request, and set request data units. It contains an identifier that associates it with the previous PDU. It also contains identifiers to provide information about the status of the response (error codes, error status, and a list of additional information).

Set request. This PDU describes an action to be performed on a managed element. It is typically used to change the values of a variable or table.

Trap. Trap allows the network object to report on an event at a network element or change the status of a network element.

Get bulk. This operation allows an agent to access table columns and rows with only one get request from the user.

Inform request. This operation allows managers to communicate with each other.

All SNMP PDUs have a common coding format based on ASN.1. and are shown in Figure 10.10. The figure has been greatly simplified, assuming you are not familiar with ASN.1. I have replaced some of the ASN.1 code with ASN.1 comments, which are preceded by a double dash (--).

The request-ID field distinguishes between different requests in the PDUs. The ErrorStatus coding provides a list that describes the type of error being recorded. This list is accessed through the error-index field, which is listed below the error-status field. The error-status field provides values for reporting problems.

The VarBind sequence identifies the name of the managed element and any associated value. The VarBindList is a list of values that sets the variable bindings. Be aware that SNMP uses the term *variable* to

```
PDUs =
  CHOICE {
  --Allows a choice of the various SNMP PDUs
  --followed by a tag to identify each PDU on the channel
  }

PDU =
  SEQUENCE {
    request-ID
      Integer 32,

    error-status       --sometimes ignored
      INTEGER {
        noError(0)
        tooBig(1)
        --and 17 other errors
      },

    error-index        --sometimes ignored
      INTEGER (0..max-bindings),

    variable-bindings   --values are sometimes ignored
      VarBindList
  }
  --variable binding
  VarBind =
    SEQUENCE {
      name
```

Figure 10.10 SNMP PDUs.

describe an instance of a managed object; the term *VarBind* simply describes the pairing of a variable to the variable's value. The VarBindList, therefore, contains a list of the variable names and their corresponding values.

SNMP MIB managed objects

MIB II contains managed objects pertaining to the SNMP group. They are summarized in Table 10.3.

CMOT

CMOT was also designed by the Internet Engineering Task Force (IETF). It was based on ISO network management standards and can be used to run on a connection-oriented transport layer (such as TCP) or connectionless layer (such as UDP).

CMOT layers

The CMOT architecture is depicted in Figure 10.11. If you are familiar with OSI, you should be quite at ease with this illustration. Notice that the OSI association control service element (ACSE) is used in the

TABLE 10.3   SNMP Group

Function: The SNMP group provides information about SNMP objects, principally statistics relating to traffic and problems/error conditions. All these objects have a syntax of Counter, with the exception of the entry snmpEnableAuthTraps, which is an integer.

snmpInPkts	An indication of the number of packets received from the layer below SNMP.
snmpOutPkts	Identifies the number of packets delivered from SNMP to the layer below.
snmpInBadVersions	Indicates the number of PDUs received with an erroneous version.
snmpInBadCommunityNames	Indicates the number of PDUs received with unidentifiable or unauthenticated community names.
snmpInASNParseErrs	Indicates the number of PDUs that could not be parsed to ASN.1 objects and vice versa.
snmpInBadTypes	Indicates the number of PDUs received that were indecipherable types.
snmpInTooBigs	Indicates the number of PDUs received with the tooBig error status field.
snmpInNoSuchNames	Indicates the number of PDUs received with an error status in the NoSuchName field.
snmpInBadValues	Indicates the number of PDUs received with an error status in the badValue field.
snmpInReadOnlys	Indicates the number of PDUs received with an error status in the readOnly field.
snmpInGenErrs	Indicates the number of PDUs received with an error status in the genErr field.
snmpInTotalReqVars	Indicates the number of MIB objects that have been retrieved.
snmpInTotalSetVars	Indicates the number of MIB objects that have been changed/altered.
snmpInGetRequests	Indicate the number of respective PDUs that were received.
snmpInGetNexts *snmpInSetRequests* *snmpInGet Responses* *snmpInTraps*	
snmpOutTooBigs	Indicates the number of PDUs sent with the tooBig field.
snmpOutNoSuchNames	Indicates the number of PDUs sent with the nosuchName field.
snmpOutBadValues	Indicates the number of PDUs sent with the badValue field.
snmpOutReadOnlys	Indicates the number of PDUs sent with the readOnly field.
snmpOutGenErrs	Indicates the number of PDUs sent with the genErr field.
snmpEnableAuthTraps	Describes if traps are enabled or disabled. This value can be read or written.
snmpOutGetRequests *snmpOutGetNexts* *snmpOutSetRequests* *snmpOutGetResponses* *snmpOutTraps*	Indicate the number of respective PDUs that were sent.

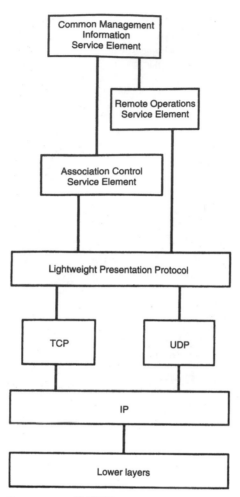

Figure 10.11   CMOT Layers.

application layer to provide services to network management ASEs. The remote operations service element (ROSE) is also used.

The figure also shows an additional layer, called the Lightweight Presentation Protocol (LPP). Because TCP and UDP were not developed with OSI service definitions, LPP interfaces the OSI application service elements to TCP/UDP modules. In the spirit of OSI, the next lower level, which is the IP, is transparent to the CMOT applications in the upper layers.

Lightweight Presentation Protocol (LPP)

RFC 1085 contains the specifications of LPP. The formal title is "ISO Presentation Services on Top of TCP/IP-Based Internets." LPP is necessary in the CMOT protocol stack because of the presence of ACSE and ROSE, which need certain services of the OSI presentation layer. LLP provides these services using the following OSI presentation-layer service definitions:

- P-CONNECT
- P-RELEASE
- P-U-ABORT
- P-P-ABORT
- P-DATA

The following well-known port numbers are used between LPP and TCP/UDP:

163/tcp. CMOT Manager

163/udp. CMOT Manager

164/tcp. CMOT Agent

164/udp. CMOT Agent

CMOT has had a difficult time in the Internet and in most internets. Most implementors are not interested in becoming involved in object-oriented systems. Additionally, SNMP has been easier to implement on request. In contrast, CMIP requires a very "intelligent" agent because of its many features. I think a CMOT-type solution will gain favor, however, if for no other reason than people realizing the value of a more powerful network management protocol. The use of CMIP is growing, but it is usually found in large, complex networks such as BellCore's SMDS networks and a number of commercial SONETs. These implementations run CMIP over a full OSI stack, not TCP/IP.

Summary

Internet network management standards are widely used in both local and wide area networks. The internet MIB defines internet-managed objects and how they can be manipulated. SNMP is the most prevalent network management standard in the industry. CMOT has received very little support thus far in the industry.

Operating TCP/IP
with Other Protocols

This chapter provides several examples of how TCP/IP can be stacked with other protocols. The initial focus of this discussion is on LAN stacks, but subsequent discussions examine WANs, the Integrated Services Digital Network (ISDN), and the Signaling Digital Hierarchy (SDH).[1] In these later examples, TCP/IP stacks are replaced by the OSI Transport Protocol, class 4 (TP4) and Connectionless Network Protocol (CLNP).

The first examples show the encapsulation and decapsulation process of the PDUs on the left and right sides of the figures. For simplicity, later examples eliminate these notations. Each stack of protocols represents the protocols operating in each machine. In Figure 11.1, for example, the left stack is in one machine and the right stack is in another.

At first glance, it might seem that the placement of TCP/IP with other protocols is relatively simple. The concept is made somewhat more complex, however, by the following three requirements:

---

[1]SDH is known in North America as the Synchronous Optical Network (SONET).

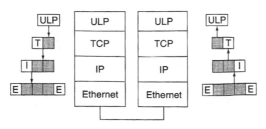

Figure 11.1   Minimum TCP/IP LAN Stack.

- What services are needed in each layer?
- Are these services available?
- Do the layers perform redundant services?

In some vendor products, stacking is rather lazy and haphazard, resulting in degraded throughput and response time, as well as considerable function redundancy.

Several of the protocol stackings covered in this chapter are described in internet RFCs. Others are not published in standards, but rather implemented through specific vendor products. I have used still others with clients.

A Minimum TCP/IP and LAN Stack

Figure 11.1 shows the familiar TCP/IP stack. It is a simple and efficient implementation using Ethernet at the lower layer to connect two stations on a LAN.

The ULPs consist of vendor software and end-user applications. It is a good idea to check vendor products in considerable detail to determine their functions, ease of use, and overhead in relation to the functions provided by the TCP and IP operations.

A Word About Operating System Dependency

Figure 11.2 adds an operating system notation to emphasize that how these protocols communicate with each other depends on how the operating system manages the interfaces between the layers in each machine. For example, a UNIX operating system provides interfaces of these layers that are different than DOS. Notwithstanding, the two machines' ability to communicate with each other (as shown in Figure 11.2) does not require the operating systems to be compatible. The essential requirement is that the PDUs exchanged between the machines in the peer layers are understandable and invoke complementary functions in each machine.

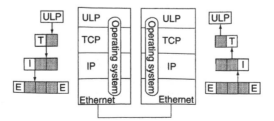

Figure 11.2 Operating System Dependency.

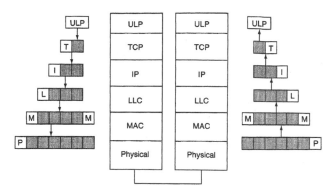

Figure 11.3   IEEE 802 Stack.

TCP/IP over LLC

Figure 11.3 shows a common LAN stack (discussed in Chapters 2 and 3) in which *logical link control* (LLC) and *media access control* (MAC) have been placed between IP and the physical layer. Typically, this approach uses LLC type 1, which is a connectionless data link protocol. The use of the LLC header is valuable because it provides destination and source service access points (SAPs) that identify users of the layer above LLC. Of course, in this simple example, the user layer above LLC is IP. A common approach for the IP/802 configuration is to use the address resolution protocol (ARP) to map a 32-bit Internet address to a 16- or 48-bit IEEE 802 address.

A few implementations, especially IBM Token Rings, support the full repertoire of the LLC standard by using LLC type 2 (LLC2) in the stack. Unnumbered information (UI) commands, exchange identification (XID) commands and responses, and test (TEST) commands and responses must be supported. Additionally, when an XID or TEST command is received with a response flag, the destination and source SAP addresses must be swapped and the relationship of the P and F bits must be preserved. That is, a P bit solicits an F bit in all cases.

IP need not run over LLC2 in a LAN, and the LLC1 protocol provides useful features with UI exchange, XID, and TEST frames. Running LLC1 under TCP/IP is an efficient approach, because this "lean" LLC can rely on TCP to perform sequencing, flow control, and acknowledgment operations. Additionally, using source and destination SAPs provides a very useful service for IP. For some applications, TCP might be considered overkill if the LAN operations already experience high throughput and integrity. You might consider replacing TCP, which is discussed in the next section.

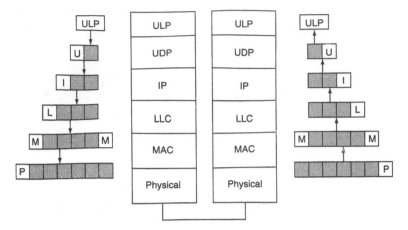

Figure 11.4 Using UDP in Place of TCP.

Replacing TCP with UDP

Figure 11.4 shows a slightly different stack in which the User Datagram Protocol (UDP) replaces the Transmission Control Protocol (TCP). This stack can be quite useful because of its simplicity and because it still provides the integrity of traffic typically offered by TCP if certain changes are made.

The biggest change is to provide traffic integrity with ULP or LLC, but I will first discuss the use of LLC. In effect, LLC2 provides a connection-oriented link protocol, which ensures the delivery of traffic to the receiving LLC. Like TCP, LLC2 provides sequencing, flow control, and window control capabilities by establishing a Set Asynchronous Balanced Mode (SABM) link configuration, placing some of the TCP functions below IP. This approach entails risks because LLC does not have a graceful close. Some means must be taken at a ULP to take care of connection management (closing). Of course, ULP can provide for acknowledgments, sequencing, and flow control. If the upper-layer applications operate with these features, then UDP is a good choice for the transport layer.

You need to weigh the trade-offs of achieving connection-oriented services at LLC or the ULP level. Again, check out the vendor's ULP carefully, because some LLC2 and ULP connection-oriented services might perform overlapping functions.

A word of caution on LLC2 Link layer protocols such as LLC2 use fixed timers to resolve a nonresponse from a station that is supposed to acknowledge the reception of traffic. Upon sending traffic, an LLC2 entity will start a timer. If a response is not received within the timer value, the timer expires and the traffic is retransmitted. The timer is configured by the network implementor and it does not vary, which works well enough on a LAN or LANs connected together. This approach might not work well, however, if LANs are interconnected through WANs, which might experience wide and variable delays. The LLC2 timer is not adept enough to handle this type of operation. Consequently, LLC1 is a better choice for LAN-WAN-LAN internetworking. It has no timer; it lets TCP handle the time-out operations. As you learned in Chapter 7, TCP's adjustable timers provide a better approach.

NetBIOS over TCP or UDP

Figure 11.5 shows a typical stack for personal computer-based networks that use IBM's NetBIOS. The illustration shows NetBIOS used above TCP or UDP. NetBIOS is designed principally to interconnect PC applications. It locates application resources, establishes a connection between these applications, receives data between the applications, and then terminates the connections. NetBIOS provides both connection-oriented and connectionless modes. All the resources managed by NetBIOS are referenced by a 16-character name, and applications are registered through this name. NetBIOS is reached through an internet's well-known port numbers (described in Chapter 7) as follows:

Port 137.   NetBIOS name service

Port 138.   NetBIOS datagram service

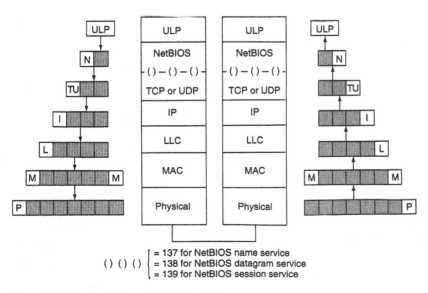

Figure 11.5   Personal Computer Network Layers.

Port 139.   NetBIOS session service

NetBIOS supports the NetBIOS Name Server (NBNS) node. In some installations, the NBNS is mapped to the internet Domain Name System (DNS). NetBIOS contains a scope identifier that identifies machines that operate under a specific NetBIOS area. Stacking NetBIOS and TCP typically uses a NetBIOS name with its scope identifier to map to an internet DNS. One of the services provided in this stack is the name discovery, in which an IP address can obtain an associated NetBIOS name. After obtaining addresses through the naming services, a NetBIOS session can be established. It consists of three phases:

1. Establishing a session in which IP addresses and TCP ports are mapped to the remote entity.
2. Exchanging NetBIOS messages.
3. Closing the session by the other entity.

To establish a session, an entity must listen on a well-known service port for incoming NetBIOS session requests. The NetBIOS session server accepts requests for the end-user application. It is important to note that the TCP connection must be open before NetBIOS services can occur. NetBIOS session occurs with a request packet containing called and calling IP addresses, as well as called and calling NetBIOS names.

For a close operation, an end user requests of NetBIOS that the session be closed. Typically, the system obtains a TCP graceful close. If the graceful close does not occur successfully and the TCP connection remains open, NetBIOS closes the NetBIOS session itself.

IP over NetBIOS

Figure 11.6 shows yet another possibility with NetBIOS. In this scenario, IP datagrams are encapsulated in NetBIOS packets. This implementation represents a minimum service stack wherein NetBIOS is run with connectionless services.

The principal consideration for this stack is the address mappings between IP and NetBIOS. NetBIOS names must reflect the IP address; part of the NetBIOS address space is coded IP.*xx.xx.xx.xx*. The IP indicates an IP over NetBIOS operation, and the *xx.xx.xx.xx* represents the IP address. Broadcast addresses are coded as IP.FF.FF.FF.FF.

This stack provides connectionless services at IP, NetBIOS, and LLC. Consequently, any connection-oriented services for sequencing, flow control, data integrity, etc. must be addressed by the ULPs. As another option, LLC2 could be configured, which would provide a

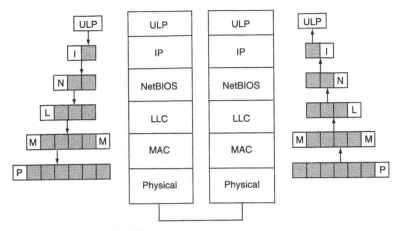

Figure 11.6 IP over NetBIOS.

minimal level of data integrity, sequencing, and flow control. I recommend, however, that the connectionless services be provided in a ULP and that LLC be kept simple and efficient.

XNS over IP

Figure 11.7 shows a simplified version of the widely used Xerox Network System (XNS) stack. XNS was developed in the 1970s and 1980s by the Xerox Corporation for use in some of its product lines. In most instances, the protocols were designed to work with Ethernet LANs. Xerox has made the XNS software available to the public, and the stacks have found their way into many other vendors' products. The lower layers come as no surprise. XNS also uses the IP protocol. At the layer above IP, XNS uses the *Sequenced Packet Protocol*, which has some of the functions of TCP (but it is not as functionally rich).

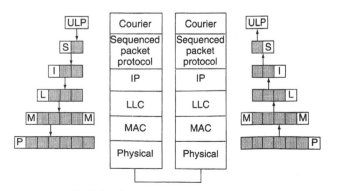

Figure 11.7 XNS Stack.

Figure 11.7 also shows the *courier* protocol resting in the ULP layer. The courier entity provides general services associated with the OSI presentation and session layers. It also supports procedure calls in which a request for a service is made to another entity. The results are returned, signifying the success or failure of the service request.

The figure also shows IP residing in the stack. The term used by XNS to define a set of complementary protocols is *internet transport protocols.* Note that all of these complementary protocols might not be implemented in this module. They deal with functions such as error reporting (similar to ICMP) and the error protocol (similar to the echo function of ICMP). Additionally, the XNS IP layer typically uses the routing information protocol (RIP) for the exchange of routing information between routers, gateways, and host machines.

IP Router Stacks

Figure 11.8 shows the stacks of an IP router. In this example, the router connects two LANs; one is an 802.3 CSMA/CD network and the other is an 802.5 token-ring network. The stacks at the router vary, depending on which port is being managed. Notwithstanding, the only difference in the stacks exists at the physical and MAC layers; LLC and IP remain the same. The operations associated with this stack are covered in more detail in Chapters 2, 3, and 5.

Relationship of IP and LAN Bridges

Figure 11.9 shows two LANs connected through a *bridge.* In this situation, IP does not exist at the bridge. The *MAC relay entity* is respon-

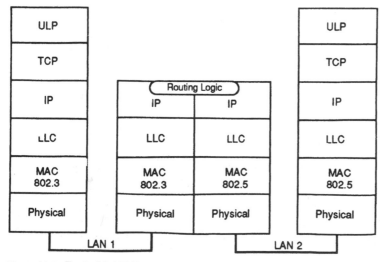

Figure 11.8 Typical LAN Router.

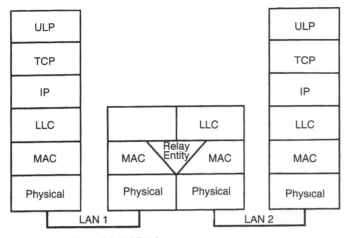

Figure 11.9 Typical LAN Bridge.

sible for routing traffic between the two ports (that is, the two networks). You might wonder why LLC is located at the bridge, since its principal function is to provide an interface from the upper layers into MAC. The reason is that IEEE 802.1 MAC bridges allow the traffic to move from either the incoming MAC port across the relay entity to the outgoing MAC port or from MAC into its LLC for bridge management functions. Once the traffic arrives at the LLC located in the gateway, traffic can be passed back down to MAC or to the relay entity for operations such as bridge learning and bridge forwarding. In any event, LLC is required for all 802 MAC bridges.

IP and X.25

IP and X.25 can connect in various ways:

- LANs
- Public Data Networks
- Amateur packet radio

IP, X.25, and LANs

Figure 11.10 shows the use of X.25 on a LAN. In this example, OSI TP4 is placed on top of IP, which is in turn stacked on X.25's network layer (called *packet layer procedures* or *PLP*). The LAN station does not invoke lower-layer X.25 services, such as Link Access Procedure Balanced (LAPB) or the V Series interfaces. Rather, it encapsulates the X.25 packet into the LLC and MAC PDUs for transport to the gateway. At the gateway, the traffic traverses the stacks in reverse

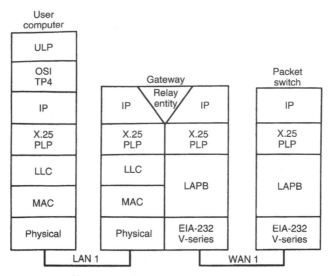

Figure 11.10   X.25 on a LAN.

order. At the X.25 PLP layer in the gateway, the X.25 packet header maps a logical channel relationship between the user computer and the left side of the protocol stack in the gateway. IP is then invoked to perform its functions at the gateway, after which the gateway relays the traffic to the proper output port. In this example, the LAPB data link control frame encapsulates the X.25 packet, and the traffic is transmitted through EIA-232 or a V Series interface to the WAN packet switch. This stack works, but it is awkward.

Notice that the X.25 packet layer procedures are invoked on both links: between the router and the LAN station, and between the router and the packet switch. In effect, this operation requires that the router maintain two connections. A better implementation is for the router to accept X.25 traffic from the user device and pass it transparently to the packet switch. Therefore, the router does not participate directly in the connection between the user station and packet switch. Of course, the router must still examine the packets and forward them to the proper machine.

IP, X.25, and Public Data Networks (PDNs)

The placement of X.25 on a LAN is not very common. More typically, a user host computer connects with X.25 to the packet switch of a Public Data Network (PDN). Figure 11.11 shows the layers for this configuration. RFC 877 has established a few simple rules for the X.25-IP and X.25-packet switch interfaces:

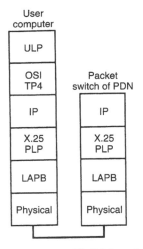

Figure 11.11 IP, X.25, and
a Public Data Network.

- A virtual circuit is handled as usual: on demand. When the host computer receives a datagram by the X.25 module, it sends a call request packet to the switch. Upon receiving a call connected packet, the host transmits the IP datagram in the X.25 user data field of the X.25 packet.

- The first octet of the call user data field of the call request packet must contain hex CC to signify that IP is running on X.25.

- Megabit operations are allowed.

- Unless negotiated otherwise, the maximum size of the IP datagram is 576 octets.

IP, X.25, and amateur packet radio

Another possibility for an IP-X.25 combination is to encapsulate X.25 packets into IP datagrams. This technique supports the AX.25 protocol, which runs on the amateur packet radio system.

The procedure is very simple. One AX.25 packet is encapsulated into one IP datagram. LAPB flags are not used, nor is zero-bit stuffing and unstuffing. LAPB Cyclic Redundancy Checks (CRCs) are included, as well as LAPB address and control fields. Otherwise, AX.25 maintains all other LAPB and X.25 fields.

Using IPX with UDP/IP Networks

The Internet Packet Exchange protocol (IPX) is Novell Netware's IP-type product. It is derived from the XNS protocol. Because Netware is so widely implemented, a short discussion is appropriate to show how IPX traffic can be carried through internet networks. As shown in Figure 11.12, the stacking arrangement is from the top layer to the bottom layer as follows: ULP, IPX, UDP, IP, then lower-layer protocols (typically, LANs such as IEEE or Ethernets).

IP and UDP headers are not affected by this stacking arrangement. The principal consideration for this stack concerns address mappings. An IPX address space consists of a network number and a host number. The network number is four octets and the host number is six octets. This combined number is used by IPX to route each IPX packet to its destination. Like the IP scheme, once the network number has fulfilled its function of reaching the destination network, the host number routes the traffic to the host attached to the destination network. For the IPX UDP/IP interface, RFC 1234 requires that the first two octets of the host number be set to 0 and the last four octets represent the node's IP address. This approach provides an easy method to handle unicast transmissions by simply discarding the first two octets of the host number.

The maximum transmission unit (MTU) for IPX is 576 octets. For this stack, the resulting PDU will be 604 octets:

$$\text{IPX of }576 + \text{IP header of }20 + \text{UDP of }8 = 604$$

All implementations supporting this stacking arrangement must be able to receive an IP packet of 604 octets.

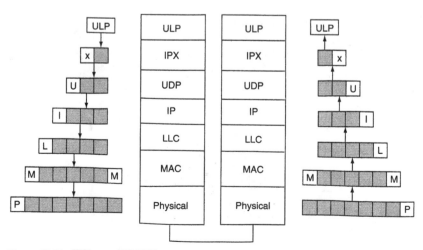

Figure 11.12   IPX over UDP/IP.

Transmitting 802 LLC Traffic over IPX Networks

A different approach, depicted in Figure 11.13, is to transmit IEEE 802 type-1 LLC traffic over IPX networks. This is a fairly common implementation for organizations that have configured their LANs with IPX. It provides a convenient method of continuing to use IPX over an 802 LAN card.

The protocol stacking arrangement is as follows, from higher layer to lower layer: ULP, TCP, IP, 802.2 LLC, IPX, then the physical layer. RFC 1132 has established two rules for this protocol stacking arrangement, First, address mapping between IP addresses and IPX addresses is performed using ARP, but the IPX physical address is 10 octets (four bytes for IPX network address and six bytes for the IPX host address). Second, this protocol stacking arrangement does not use the IPX checksum.

Transmitting IP Datagrams over FDDI Networks

The layer arrangement for this service is identical to the services described earlier in Figure 11.3. The only difference is that FDDI contains two sublayers at the physical layer, which is completely transparent to IP and 802.2 LLC. The mapping arrangement for the physical and network addresses is in conformance with the internet specifications described in Chapters 2 and 3.

The FDDI standard permits a maximum frame size of 4500 octets. After preambles and the LLC/SNAP (Logical Link Control/Subnetwork Access Protocol) header, 4470 octets are available for user data.

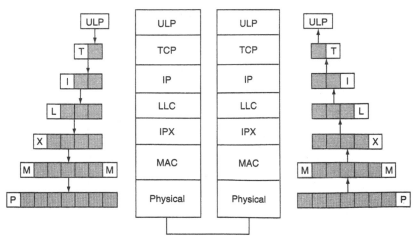

Figure 11.13   802 LLC over IPX.

RFC 1188 makes an exception in this case in that it defines 4096 octets for data and 256 octets for headers at the layers above MAC. Gateways supporting FDDI must be able to accept packets this large and, if necessary, perform fragmentation operations. Additionally, although hosts can accept large packets, it is recommended that they not send datagrams greater than 576 octets unless they know the receiving host can support a larger size.

Addressing schemes on FDDI networks are quite similar to those discussed earlier for other IEEE 802 networks. The only restriction is that interworking IP and ARP over FDDI requires the use of a 48-bit physical level address.

As you might expect, IP over FDDI requires using 802 LLC1 using the conventional LLC frames: UI, XID, and TEST. Be aware that IEEE specifies its control values with the least significant bit first (the "little endian"). Internet Protocols are just the opposite and document their control fields in "big-endian" order. This difference presents no problem as long as users working with IEEE and internets understand the documentation.

IP over Switched Multimegabit Data Service

Switched Multimegabit Data Service (SMDS) is a public network offering packet-switched connectionless service. Its purpose is to support high throughput with low delay, as well as large PDUs of up to 9188 user octets. SMDS provides no explicit flow-control mechanisms; rather, it has a subscriber-to-network and a network-to-subscriber access class enforcement mechanism, which provides for congestion control in the network.

IP can rest on top of an SMDS network by interfacing into the IEEE 802 LLC sublayer. In turn, LLC rests on top of the SMDS layers. This arrangement is straightforward because the interface protocol into SMDS is based on the IEEE 802.6 metropolitan area network (MAN) distributed-queue dual-bus (DQDB) MAC protocol. This protocol has a rich MAC convergence function that allows connectionless services such as LLC1 and IP to be encapsulated into the DQDB PDU.

The concept of IP over SMDS is based on using an SMDS to support multiple logical IP subnetworks (known as LIS). Each LIS is managed by separate administrative authorities, but uses the common SMDS for communications. For LIS configuration, all stations within the LIS are accessed directly from one SMDS. This method requires that all LIS members have the same IP network and subnetwork numbers. Communications for stations outside LIS are performed through an IP router. An SMDS group address is used to identify all members within the LIS, which permits SMDS to deliver traffic to the LIS members.

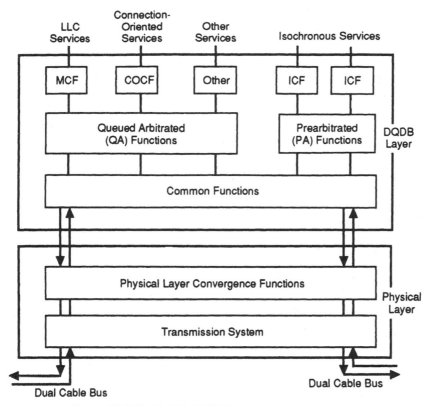

Figure 11.14   IP over SMDS with 802.6 DQDB.

The layering arrangements for this stack are shown in Figure 11.14. The IP interface occurs through the media convergence function (MCF), which interfaces directly into LLC. The queued arbitrated (QA) functions define the procedures for sharing the DQDB. Resting beneath QA are functions common to both queued-arbitrated and prearbitrated (PA) functions. PA functions are not relevant to this discussion, but are used for asynchronous services, such as voice and video. The physical layer provides the ongoing cabling and physical transmission for the dual cable bus. As you might expect, the services with this stack are quite common to other services that use LLC. The use of LLC1 frames is the same as for protocol stacks, discussed earlier in this chapter.

OSI's Transport Protocol Class 0 over TCP

Figure 11.15 shows the stacking arrangement to run OSI's TP class 4 (TP0) over TCP. You might wonder why such a stacking arrangement would be desirable, but the principal advantage is that it provides a

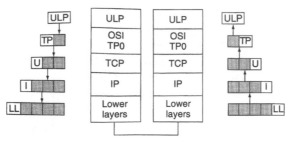

Figure 11.15   OSI Transport Class 0 over TCP.

convenient and easy access to the upper layers of the OSI model, and it allows an organization to continue using the widely used TCP/IP suite. Additionally, TP0 is a minimal level of service for the transport layer, so you don't risk redundancy of function when implementing both OSI's transport layer with TP0 and the Internet's TCP.

In the OSI model, a connection between a transport layer user and the transport layer is achieved through service definitions, also known as *primitives*. These are defined in ITU-T's X.214 and ISO's 8072 standards. For using the stack in this scenario, RFC 1006 defines mapping these OSI primitives to receive TCP service. The OSI transport layer does not work with a client-server approach, so an OSI indication primitive is used instead of a server listening on a well-known port. The mapping between TCP and TP0 occurs through OSI service definitions. Table 11.1 lists these mappings as well as mappings of the parameters between the network service and TCP.

OSI Connectionless Transport Layer over UDP

This section describes a similar approach to Figure 11.15, except that connectionless services are used, both at the OSI layer and the inter-

TABLE 11.1   Mapping TP0 and TCP

TP0 ↔ Network layer definitions	TCP service
N-CONNECT.request	Open completes
N-CONNECT.indication	Passive Open (Listen) finishes
N-CONNECT.response	Listen finishes
N-CONNECT.confirmation	Open (Active) finishes
N-DATA.request	Send data
N-DATA.indication	Data ready

TP0 ↔ Network parameter	TCP parameter
Called address	Server's IP addresses
Calling address	Client's IP address
Data (NDSU)	Data
Others	Ignored

net layer. The scheme is almost identical to that described in the previous section, except that no connection-oriented services are invoked. Rather, the OSI network services of N-UNITDATA.request and N-UNITDATA.indication are the only services permitted between connectionless OSI and UDP. The parameter mapping is also quite simple. The source and destination addresses in the OSI layer map to the called and calling IP addresses for UDP services. User data maps directly to the UDP user data. Any other fields that exist in the OSI model are ignored. The stacking arrangement is quite simple, as depicted in Figure 11.16.

TCP/IP over ISDN

Figure 11.17 shows a typical protocol stack for interfacing a user workstation to a packet switch through an ISDN node. The traffic is transmitted from the user computer across the ISDN *R reference*

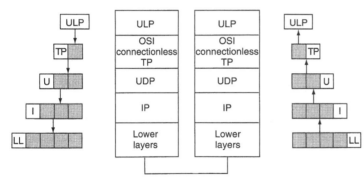

Figure 11.16 OSI Connectionless Transport Layer over UDP.

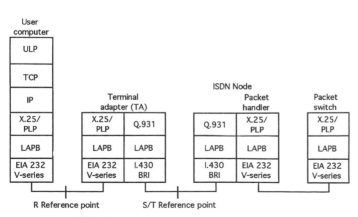

Figure 11.17 ISDN Connections.

point and the *terminal adapter (TA)* stack, which maps the X.25 layers according to X.25 specifications. Operations take place on the right side of the TA. The TA uses ISDN layers to establish proper D and B channel operations to the ISDN node across the *S/T reference point.* Although not depicted in this figure, after the three layers of ISDN are operational, the terminal adapter dequeues the X.25 traffic and transports it transparently through the ISDN layers to the ISDN node. At the ISDN node, the traffic is passed up through the ISDN layers and then passed off to an ISDN *packet handler* (which, in the real world, is nothing more than a packet switch). The packet handler assumes the functions of X.25 and sends the packet down through the X.25 stack to communicate with the network packet switch.

TCP/IP over Frame Relay or ATM

The placement of TCP/IP over Frame Relay or ATM is an effective approach for internetworking frame-relay networks with TCP/IP-based workstations. Because Frame Relay and ATM do not guarantee the delivery of all traffic, TCP acts as the "last line of defense" to ensure that crucial user traffic is accounted for between the two end-user stations. Since this subject is of such keen interest in the industry, Chapter 14 is devoted to it.

Summary

TCP/IP exists in a wide variety of standards and vendor products. Most implementations are based on the layered protocol approach, in which TCP/IP is encapsulated into other PDUs or other protocols are encapsulated into TCP segments and IP datagrams.

Chapter

12

Network Security

This chapter provides a general description of the subject of network security. Private and public key encryption schemes are explained, followed by a discussion of Pretty Good Privacy (PGP) systems. The chapter concludes with a discussion of the security features of IPv6.

Private and Public Encryption Systems

Two forms of encryption are used to obtain security in an internet: private and public key encryption.

Private key encryption

In its simplest form, private key encryption requires that the sender and receiver of a message use one value (key) to "scramble" and "unscramble" the traffic, respectively. These keys are called *private keys*, because they are known and shared only between the sender and receiver, or (usually) between a known and trusted community of senders and receivers.

In 1977, the U.S. Government published the Data Encryption Standard (DES). It was established in conjunction with IBM and released to the general public with the goal of providing a standardized cryptography algorithm for the industry. DES is based on an encryption algorithm that changes plain text with so many combinations that it should be difficult to figure out the plain text even if numerous copies were available.

The DES provides a key of 65 bits, of which 56 bits are used directly by the DES algorithm and 8 bits are used for error detection. There are over 70 quadrillion (70,000,000,000,000,000) possible keys of 56 bits in length. Obviously, a tremendous amount of computer power is needed to break this key. It can be done, however, with high-speed computers. Notwithstanding, the objective of the DES is not to provide absolute security, but rather to provide a reasonable level of security for business-oriented networks.

The 56-bit key is too short for some applications. For example, a high-speed computer can search all 2^{56} possible (72,057,594,037, 927,936) in less than four hours. Systems are now available, however, that use longer keys. One system, called triple DES, performs three encryptions with DES by using two keys. Triple DES yields a key of 112 bits.

The problem with a private key is just that: it must be held privately between the two communicating parties. Party A and party B have a shared key that no one else knows. However, if these parties need to communicate with another party, say party C, then two more secret keys are needed: A $\leftrightarrow$ C and B $\leftrightarrow$ C.

With n parties to be "fully meshed," n $(n-1) \div 2$ keys are needed. To place this problem into perspective, the Internet has over 20 million users. For any two Internet users to communicate with each other would require 200 trillion keys. Each user would have to keep a file of 20 million keys, or somehow exchange, in secret, the secret key with selected parties—clearly an impossible task. This problem gave rise to public key systems.

Public key encryption

In contrast, public key encryption allows one of the keys, the public key, to be made known to the public—hence, the name *public key encryption*. This public key is created during the same invocation of an algorithm that creates another value, the private key. (Actually, more than two keys are created, but this generic example will focus on two keys). Therefore, public and private keys are the result of the same function instance.

Because of this relationship, public key encryption permits the sharing of a public key, yet security is obtained by limiting knowledge of the private key to the entity that invoked the algorithm producing the private key. The private and public keys can encrypt and decrypt traffic.

Public encryption systems can distribute private keys. For example, assume that party A chooses a secret key and sends it to party B by encrypting it with the public part of party B's key, which is stored in a public directory. In turn, party B decrypts the message with party B's private part, thus obtaining party A's private key. The process is reversed for A to obtain B's private key.

The best known public key system is the RSA algorithm, named after its inventors (Ron Rivest, Adi Shamir, and Len Adleman of

MIT). It works as follows. Party A selects two large prime numbers (p and q) and calculates n = p × q. Next, party A chooses a random integer e, 1 n. The value e must have no integer divisors > 1 that are in common with p − 1 or q − 1. Party A publishes the (n,e) pair, but not the (p,q) pair. Thus (n,e) is the public key and (p,q) is the private key.

Assume that party B now has A's public key (n,e). Party B encrypts a message, m, into a cipher, c, to send to party B:

$$c = m^e \ (\text{mod } n) \ \ 0 \le c < n$$

Party A decrypts the ciphered message c as follows:

$$m = c^d \ (\text{mod } n)$$

where d is A's secret decryption exponent. The value d is computed correctly from e only if p and q are known:

$$ed = (\text{mod } p - 1)$$

$$ed = 1 \ (\text{mod } q - 1)$$

because c and d are multiplicative inverses:

$$(m^e)^d = m^{ed} = m^1 = m$$

In 1977, Rivest, Shamir, and Adleman issued a challenge to the industry to break the RSA 129-digit code (which is equivalent to a 429-bit key). It was expected that the code could not be broken for many years. In 1994, a task force organized by Bellcore broke the code. The team was able to find two prime numbers multiplied together that resulted in the 129-digit key value. Bellcore claims that it is close to breaking 155-digit keys, which is of considerable concern to companies who moved away from the 129-digit code to a 150-digit code.

As of this writing, efforts are focused on using more digits in the key, and 150- to 230-digit sizes are ranges that are recommended. Several studies show that long keys are quite secure because they require immense computational resources (and time) to break.

The Pretty Good Privacy (PGP) program

PGP is a popular version of the RSA algorithm. It also uses a session key, one that is randomly generated for each message sent onto the communications channel. The following events occur when a message is sent using PGP. First, PGP creates a random key for the message (the session key). It then uses an algorithm (known as the IDEA algorithm) to encrypt the message with the session key. It also uses the RSA algorithm to encrypt the session key with the pubic key of the party that is receiving the message. Finally, it packages the message together with the session key and passes this traffic to an application, such as e-mail.

Each public key is kept in a key certificate, which contains the public key, one or more IDs for the party that created the key, the creation data of the key, and some optional entries (such as digital signatures about the key). A file called the *key ring* contains the public keys of all parties to which a sending party sends messages (known as pubring.pgp). In addition, another file (known as secring.pgp) contains the secret ring (or rings) of the sender. In order to create a key pair (public and private), PGP requires that the creator invent a pass phrase. The purpose of the pass phrase is to decrypt the secret key on the secret key ring. It also prevents a potential hacker from using the secret key since the secret key cannot be used if the pass phrase is not known.

PGP has many other features and can be installed on many operating systems. A number of books are available on PGP. I recommend Simson Garfinkel's *PGP: Pretty Good Privacy* (O'Reilly and Associates, Inc.) as a starter.

SNMPv2 Security

The enhanced security features of SNMPv2 can be obtained in a number of ways. First, a nonsecure minimal agent configuration provides no security or authentication, other than checking the community name against an access privileges profile. This is the same procedure used by SNMPv1. Of more interest is the provision for SNMP message authentication by way of either private or public keys (see Figure 12.1).

As the name implies, a private key encryption protocol requires that both communicating parties (say, party A and party B) use the same key for encrypting and decrypting messages (as shown in the top part of the figure). Therefore, the distribution of these keys must be carefully controlled to prevent any unwanted (other) party from obtaining the keys and intercepting traffic. Typically, party A used one key as input to a function (Efunc in this figure) to encrypt a message and party B uses the same key to decrypt this message (Dfunc in this figure). Party B can use yet another key to encrypt a message, and party A uses this key to decrypt the message.

Using public keys provides a more flexible arrangement. Like the private key operation, the communicating parties own a private key, but each party generates a unique key and does not distribute it to anyone else. With the same function and at the same instantiation of

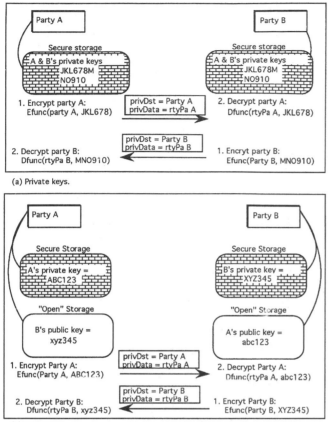

(a) Private keys.

(b) Public keys.

Figure 12.1 SNMPv2 Security.

the function, a public key is also generated. This key is distributed to other parties.

A sending party then uses its private key to encrypt a value (called privacy data, or privData), and places this result in a message along with the unencrypted equivalent value of the privData (called privacy destination or privDst). This activity is shown in the bottom part of this figure as the encrypt function (Efunc).

To authenticate a sending (challenged) party, the receiving (challenger) party executes a decrypt function (Dfunc). First, it uses privDst to obtain information (a proper key) from its local database. It constructs a value with Dfunc using privData as the input to the function. If this value is the same as privDst, the message is accepted as valid. Otherwise, it is discarded without further processing.

IPv6 and Network Security

Earlier in this book I briefly mentioned the security features of IPv6. These features are provided by the authentication header and the encrypted security payload. This section will summarize the IPv6 security features. More information is provided in RFCs 1825, 1826, 1827, 1828, and 1829.

Both authentication and encryption require that the sending and receiving parties agree on a key and a specific authentication or encryption algorithm. Other parameters are set up as well, such as the lifetime of the key.

The authentication header is one of the generic headers defined in the IPv6 standard. It is identified with payload type 51. The syntax of the authentication header is depicted in Figure 12.2. As the figure illustrates, the format for the header is quite simple. It contains the next header indicator in the daisy chain of headers, the length of the header in multiples of 32 bits, a 16-bit reserved field that is currently set to 0s, the 32-bit SPI, and authentication data also coded in 32-bit word increments. The contents of the authentication data field depends on the specific encryption/authentication algorithm and the types of keys that are used. For example, a Pretty Good Privacy system could be employed with the PGP data contained in the authentication data field of the authentication header. However, the RFCs cited previously describe other techniques for encryption and authentication.

MD5

One of the security systems recommended in the Internet is known as *keyed MD5*. It was designed by Ron Rivest, who also participated in the RSA algorithm, and is derived from what is known as *message digest 5 algorithm* (MD5). MD5 is similar to RSA in that it computes on a 128-bit checksum of the message. It combines the message with a secret key and then computes the hash code on the result. Once again, I emphasize that MD5 is only one algorithm and others are equally applicable, such as the PGP system.

Next header	Length	Reserved	
Security parameter index			
Authentication data			
More data			

Figure 12.2 IPv6 Authentication Header.

Be aware that using the authentication header has nothing to do with the data contents of the datagram. These bits remain in the clear and therefore remain vulnerable to monitoring or alteration. Consequently, encrypted security payload features are used to obtain security on the payload of the IP datagram. The method in which the IPv6 payload is encrypted depends, once again, on which algorithm is employed. For example, the data encryption standard or PGP could be used.

Distribution of Keys

There are a wide variety of techniques for key distribution, and it is anticipated that IPv6 will employ more than one method. One proposal is called Photuris and is explained in the RFC cited previously.

As of this writing, security procedures on the Internet are far from settled. Debates still take place on whether or not security should be mandated, as well as which algorithm should be used. In addition, an issue still remains as to where encryption should be performed—in which layer of the internet protocol stack. RFCs are occurring regularly to resolve some of these issues and I encourage you to check your RFC file periodically on this important issue.

Summary

As the Internet and internets become more widely used, security becomes a bigger problem. Today, a wide variety of tools are available to users who need privacy and security. It is not a good idea to use the Internet without some protection. Even individual users should have a virus checker installed on their systems.

13

TCP/IP and Operating Systems

This chapter provides an overview of the relationship of computer operating systems and the TCP/IP suite of protocols. The focus in this chapter is on the UNIX and IBM PC operating systems, due to their prevalence in the industry. Keep in mind that many other interfaces are also available. For example, C function calls and Fortran subroutine calls could be used, as shown in Figure 13.1. The UNIX examples included in this chapter illustrate the implementation of the System V UNIX release from AT&T. The PC explanation focuses on higher-level calls to obtain services for an application layer or a PC keyboard user.

UNIX and TCP/IP

This section provides several examples of the UNIX operating system and its interface with TCP. I cite the 4.3 BSD UNIX interfaces in this

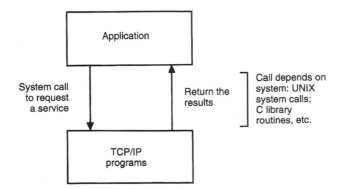

Figure 13.1 Accessing TCP/IP through UNIX calls.

section because of their prevalence in the industry. UNIX was developed at Bell Labs in the late 1960s. It was designed originally for single processor computers and includes many features that make it quite popular among software developers. Principal among those features are its time-sharing capabilities and its system calls, which provide the programmer with easy operations.

Connection-oriented services

The concept of a *socket*, which is discussed several times in this book, is very much a part of the BSD UNIX input/output (I/O) concept. A socket is really nothing more than an end point in the communications process. Unlike some sockets with I/O files, the TCP/IP BSD UNIX concept allows a socket to be created without providing a destination address. A destination address in a later system call creates a final binding between the sending and receiving addresses.

Figure 13.2 shows the system call that creates a socket consisting of three arguments. The *domain* field describes the protocol family (a domain) associated with the socket. It could include, for example, the internet family, PUP family, DEC family, or Appletalk family. The *type* argument stipulates the type of communications desired with the connection. The programmer can establish values to specify a datagram service, reliable delivery service, or a raw socket. The third argument allows the programmer to code the type of service for each of the *protocols* within the protocol family. This argument is required because protocol families usually consist of more than one protocol. The programmer must supply the specific protocol in this argument. If left at 0, the system selects the appropriate protocol within the domain.

The domain values are available in the <sys/socket.h> file. The UNIX domain is AFUNIX; the internet domain is AF_INET. Socket types are also found in the file <sys/socket.h> and are coded in the systems call as SOCK_STREAM for a reliable, stream service; SOCK_DGRAM for a datagram service; and SOCK_RAW for a raw socket that provides access to underlying protocols for communications programmers.

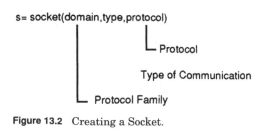

s= socket(domain,type,protocol)

Protocol

Type of Communication

Protocol Family

Figure 13.2 Creating a Socket.

You learned earlier that UNIX lets you create a socket without furnishing addresses for the socket (in UNIX V, called *naming* the socket). Communications cannot occur until local and foreign internet addresses are declared for the association between the communicating entities. In the UNIX domain, local and foreign path names are used. Figure 13.3 shows the system call to establish the local address with the socket. The *bind* call sets up half an association. The first argument in the list is called *s* and contains the integer number value of the socket. The local *name* argument can vary, but usually consists of three values: the protocol family, the port number, and an internet address. The *namelen* argument contains the length of the second argument.

Figure 13.4 shows the next step in mapping the TCP/IP connection between two machines. The *connect* system call allows the programmer to connect a socket to a destination address. As the figure illustrates, *s* (socket number), *name* (destination ID), and *namelen* (name length) are included as arguments. The name parameter identifies the remote socket for the binding.

The asymmetric nature of port bindings allows an easy implementation of a client-server relationship. The server issues a bind to

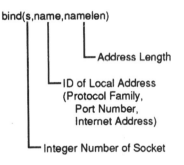

Figure 13.3 Establishing the Local Address.

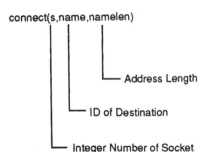

Figure 13.4 Connecting to a Destination Address.

establish a socket for a well-known service, such as file transfer protocol (FTP). It then passively listens for a client to send a connect request to the server's passive socket. If a connection is unsuccessful, an error is returned to the requester. Over 20 error codes are available with the connect call, such as ECONNREFUSE, which signifies the host refusal of the connection because the server process cannot be found given the name furnished, and ETIME OUT, which means the connection attempt took too long.

After a server has set up a passive socket, it listens for requested incoming connections (this function is supported only for reliable stream delivery). This operation is performed with the *listen* system call, which takes the form shown in Figure 13.5.

The parameter *s* is the socket on which connections will occur; the *backlog* parameter establishes the maximum queue size for holding incoming connection requests. If the queue is full, an incoming connection request is refused with an indication of ECONNREFUSED. Other error codes associated with listen are:

EBADF. *s* is invalid

ENOISOCK. *s* is not a socket

EONOTSUPP. Socket does not support a listen operation

After the listen has been executed, the accepting entity (usually a server) must wait for connection requests. It uses the *accept* system call for this operation. The accept pulls the first entity in the queue to service and takes the form shown in Figure 13.6.

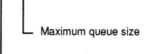

Figure 13.5 Listen Call.

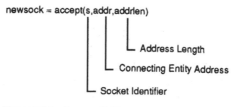

Figure 13.6 Accept Call.

The *s* parameter is the listening socket, the *addr* parameter contains the *sockaddr* of the connecting entity, and *addrlen* is the length of the address. If the operation succeeds, a new file descriptor, *ns*, is allocated for the socket and the new descriptor is returned to the requester.

After all these system calls have executed successfully, the application entities can exchange data. Data exchange is accomplished through the *write* system call depicted in Figure 13.7. The call is quite simple. It contains three arguments:

- The socket identifier (descriptor)
- The buffer (buf), which is a pointer in memory containing the user data
- The length field (sizeofbuf), which determines the length of the buffer search for the user data

To receive data, the *read* system call is invoked. Its format is illustrated in Figure 13.8. You will probably see the repetitive aspects of the design of the system calls. This call contains the socket identifier (descriptor), the identification of the buffer (buf) in which the data will reside, and the length indicator (sizeofbuf) that describes the number of bytes to be read.

Other input/output calls

Input/output can also be achieved with the following calls:

send.   s, buf, sizeofbuf, flags

recv.   s, buf, sizeofbuf, flags

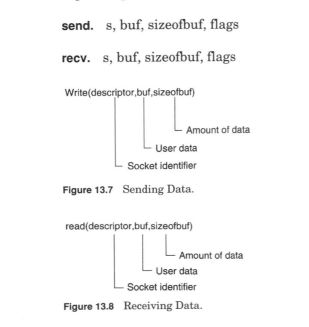

Write(descriptor,buf,sizeofbuf)

— Amount of data
— User data
— Socket identifier

Figure 13.7 Sending Data.

read(descriptor,buf,sizeofbuf)

— Amount of data
— User data
— Socket identifier

Figure 13.8 Receiving Data.

The only difference between these calls and the write and read calls is the extra *flags* parameter. It allows the programmer to use some other options in receiving or sending data to or from a connected socket. The flags field (established in the <sys/socket.h> file) can be set to signify the following:

MSG_PEEK.   Examine the next message without reading it

MSG_OOB.   Receive out-of-band (urgent) data

MSG_DONTROUTE.   Send data but do not actually route them (for diagnostic/maintenance purposes)

Two other input calls are available. The *recvfrom* call requests input on a socket either in a connected or unconnected state. Its form is:

```
recvfrom (s, buf, len, flags, from, fromlen)
```

Two other parameters are present with this call. The *from* parameter holds the message sender's address. The *fromlen* parameter returns the length of the sender's address. The *recvmsg* call can also be used to receive input on an unconnected socket. It has fewer parameters than recvfrom and takes this form:

```
recvmsg (s, msg, flags)
```

The *msg* parameter defines a structure that includes the address and the size of the incoming message and some authentication entities.

Datagram services

Two other calls similar to *recvfrom* and *recvmsg* are *send to* and *sendmsg*, respectively, except they send data rather than receive it. The send to and recvfrom calls are used with UDP datagram services. In addition, a connect call is permitted with UDP operations to map a socket to a destination address. Accept and listen are not used with UDP.

Closing a connection

A socket can be closed if it is no longer needed with the following system call:

```
close (s)
```

Data can, however, continue to be sent and/or delivered even after the close is issued (check with your vendor for this feature). After some period of time, the data are discarded. If the user does not want to send or receive any more data, it can issue:

```
shutdown (s, how)
```

where the parameters for *how* are:

0. Not interested in receiving data

1. No more data will be sent

2. No more data will be sent or received

Other system calls

I have reviewed the most commonly used UNIX system calls for invoking TCP/IP services. Several others are available and warrant an explanation (the parameters for these calls are not included in this general explanation):

select. Multiplex input/output operations on more than one socket

gethostbyname. Obtain host name (usually its domain name)

sethostbyname. Set host name

getpeername. Obtain the name of a peer connected to a socket

gethostbyaddr. Obtain internet address of the host

getsockname. Obtain a socket and its associated local address

getnetbyname. Obtain network name

getnetbyaddr. Obtain network address

getprotobyname. Obtain protocol name

getprotobynumber. Obtain protocol number

All the UNIX calls are not included; several others are available for domain sources, mapping and swapping network numbers, and obtaining information on servers and clients.

Example of programs to invoke UNIX-based TCP/IP services

Figure 13.9 shows an example of a program using UNIX calls to open a socket, read it, and close. Figures 13.10 and 13.11 show examples of reading and sending datagrams. These examples are from *UNIX SYSTEM V, Release 4, Programmers Guide: Network Interfaces* (Prentice Hall, 1990) and are reprinted with the permission of Prentice Hall.

PC Interface Program

PC vendors offer a number of interface programs to invoke TCP/IP services and internet applications services. This section highlights several user commands available in the IBM Interface Program. Further information is available in IBM manual number SC23-0812-0.

While studying this section, note how easily user commands work with this interface program. Granted, the parameters associated with the commands require a user to have a firm grasp of how the TCP/IP protocols operate. In this context, a "user" of this interface is a system/communications programmer. An end-user interface (with friendly screen menus and blinking color lights) is beyond this discussion. Note that IBM uses the syntax diagram shown in Figure 13.12 to document many of its products, including the material in this section.

Sending mail through SMTP

The *netmail* command supports transmitting user mail through Simple Mail Transfer Protocol (SMTP) to another user or users. Figure 13.13 shows the syntax of the command. The *mail_file* parameter identifies the file to be sent. The *rcpt* parameters use internet naming convention for the user host. The repeat arrow signifies that more than one user can be identified.

An example of an entry on a PC in which the PC user wants to send mail in the file called "sales memo" to UBlack at ACME.COM. would appear as:

```
$ netmail sales memo UBlack@ACME.COM
```

Sending a file through TFTP

Figure 13.14 shows the syntax for a user command to transfer files between hosts with the Trivial File Transfer Protocol (TFTP). The *action* parameter is coded as:

wrp. Writes the file designated as *localname* into the file system of the foreign host designated as *foreignname*

```
#include <sys/types.h>
#include <sys/socket.h>
#include <netinet/in.h>
#include <netdb.h>
#include <stdio.h>
#define TRUE 1
/*
   *This program creates a socket and then begins an infinite loop. Each time
   *through the loop it accepts a connection and prints out messages from it.
   *When the connection breaks, or a termination message comes through, the
   *program accepts a new connection.
   */
main()
{
     int sock, length;
     struct sockaddr_in server;
     int msgsock;
     char buf[1024];
     int rval;
     /*Create socket.*/
     sock = socket (AF_INET,SOCK_STREAM,0);
     if (sock < 0){
                     perror (''opening stream socket'');
                     exit (1);
     }
     /*Name socket using wildcards.*/
     server.sin_family = AF_INET;
     server.sin_addr.s_addr = INADDR_ANY;
     server.sin_port = 0;
     if(bind(sock,(struct sockaddr*)&server, sizeof server)<0){
                     perror(''binding stream socket'');
                     exit(1);
     }
     /*Find out assigned port number and print it out.*/
     length = sizeof server;
     if (getsockname (sock, (struct sockaddr*)&server,
       &length) < 0){
                     perror (''getting socket name:);
                     exit(1);
     }
     printf(''Socket port#%d\n'', ntohs (server.sin_port));
     /*Start accepting connections. */
     listen(sock, 5);
do{
             msgsock = accept(sock, (struct sockaddr*)0,(int*)0);
```

Figure 13.9 Accepting an Internet Domain Stream Connection.

```
          if (msgsock = -1)
                    perror (''accept'');
          else do {
                    memset(buf, 0, sizeof buf);
                    if ((rval = read(msgsock, buf, 1024)) < 0)
                            perror(''reading stream message'');
                    if (rval = 0)
                            printf(Ending connection\n'');
                    else
                            printf(''-- > %s \n'', buf);
          } while (rval! = 0);
          close(msgsock);
} while (TRUE);
/*
   *Since this program has an infinite loop, the socket ''sock'' is
   *never explicitly closed. However, all sockets will be closed
   *automatically when a process is killed or terminates normally.
   */
   exit (0);
```

Figure 13.9   Continued

```
#include <sys/types.h>
#include <sys/socket.h>
#include <netinet/in.h>
#include <stdio.h>

/*
   *The include file <netinet/in.h> defines sockaddr_in as follows:
   *struct sockaddr_in(
   *      short sin_family;
   *      u_short sin_port;
   *      struct in_addr sin_addr;
   *      char sin_zero [8];
   *);
   *
   *This program creates a datagram socket, binds a name to it, then
     reads
   *from the socket
   */
main()
{
          int sock, length;
          struct sockaddr_in name;
          char buf[1024];

          /*Create a socket from which to read.*/
          sock = socket (AF_INET, SOCK_DGRAM,0);
          if (sock < 0){
                    perror (''opening datagram socket'');
                    exit (1);
```

Figure 13.10   Reading Internet Domain Datagrams.

```
#include <sys/types.h>
#include <sys/socket.h>
#include <netinet/in.h>
#include <netdb.h>
#include <stdio.h>

#define DATA ''The sea is calm, the tide is full...''

/*
   *Here I send a datagram to a receiver whose name I get from the command
   *line arguments. The form of the command line is:
   *dgramsend hostname portnumber
   */
main(argc, argv)
         int argc;
         char*argv[];
{
         int sock;
         struct sockaddr_in name;
         struct hostend *hp, *gethostbyname();

         /*Create socket on which to send. */
         sock = socket(AF_INET, SOCK_DGRAM,0);
         if(sock<0){
                  perror(''opening datagram socket'');
                  exit(1);
         }
         /*
            *Construct name, with no wildcards, of the socket to send to.
            *gethostbyname returns a structure including the network
             address
            *of the specified host. The port number is taken from the
             command
            *line.
            */
         hp = gethostbyname (argv[1]);
         if (hp == 0){
                  fprintf(stdarr, ''%s: unknown host\n'', argv[1]);
                  exit(2);
         }
         memcpy( (char*)&name,sin_addr,(char*)hp- > h_addr,
           hp- > h_length);
         name.sin_family = AF_INET;
         name.sin_port = htons(atoi(argv[2]));
         /*Send message.*/
         if (sendto (sock, DATA, sizeof DATA, 0,
           (struct sockaddr*)&name, sizeof name)<0)
                  perror(''sending datagram message'');
         close(sock);
         exit(0);
```

Figure 13.11   Sending an Internet Domain Datagram.

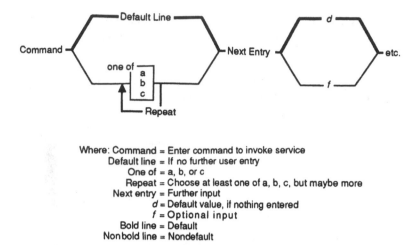

Where: Command = Enter command to invoke service
Default line = If no further user entry
One of = a, b, or c
Repeat = Choose at least one of a, b, c, but maybe more
Next entry = Further input
d = Default value, if nothing entered
f = Optional input
Bold line = Default
Nonbold line = Nondefault

Figure 13.12   Syntax Diagram.

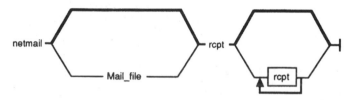

Figure 13.13   netmail Command for SMPT Services.

Figure 13.14   tftp Command for TFTP Operations.

rrg.   Reads the file designated as *foreignname* from the foreign host into the local file designated as *localname*

o.   Overrides or supersedes ongoing local files
The *mode* parameter is coded as follows:

netascii.   File transfer using standard ASCII characters

image.   Transfer files and binary images with no conversion performed

mail. Appending stipulated files to the end of a specified user mailbox; afterward the user can retrieve this information with the PC/UNIX (AIX) mail command

An example of an entry on a PC in which the PC user transfers the binary file /receipts from host4 to /tempreceipts at host10 is as follows:

```
$ tftp -w /receipts host4 /tempreceipts image
```

Sending a file through FTP

Figure 13.15 shows the syntax for invoking FTP operations. This command supports the transfer of files to and from a foreign server. The *xftp* command assumes a packet size of 1576 bytes and a window size of 6 kilobytes. Files are transferred in the standard ASCII format, although other commands are available to request binary transfer. The *-n* parameter provides the user with automatic login, which precludes the user from having to enter an ID and password. The *host* parameter is the name of the client host. The *dbg* parameter is coded into one of four values to request the following services:

0. Obtain trace service messages

1. Obtain error messages

2. Show all receipt packets

4. Show all sent packets

When the commands are executed, the xftp can be followed by several subcommands, which are provided to the user with an xftp> prompt on the screen. The user can then enter subcommands. Several examples of subcommands are the following:

acct. Provides accounting information.

append. Appends a file to another file

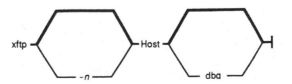
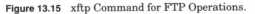

Figure 13.15 xftp Command for FTP Operations.

binary.   Data transferred is binary.

dir.   Displays a listing of the directory

get.   Retrieves a foreign file and stores it at the local host

pass.   Provides password information

put.   Sends a local file on a foreign host.
Here is an example of the xftp operation:

```
$ xftp host 4
... login operations (e.g., Telnet)
xftp > binary
xftp > put/receipts/tempreceipts
... status messages of file transfer
xftp > quit
... user is logged off
```

Using tn to invoke Telnet login services

Figure 13.16 shows the syntax for logging onto a foreign host through the Telnet interface. The *tn* command is used to access a Telnet protocol. Note that several subcommands can be used as part of tn by keying in Ctrl–T and single- character subcommands. These subcommands allow the user to obtain many of the services of Telnet described in earlier chapters, such as "are you theres," breaks, keying in data, establishing echo modes, and displaying status.

The *host* parameter identifies the Telnet connection to the specific host. If this parameter is not supplied, the user is prompted to provide a host name. The *-d* indicates that the debugging option is on, and *-p port* identifies the foreign port number for this connection; otherwise, the system defaults to the Telnet port. A typical example of a Telnet login is as follows:

```
$ tn host 4
... login occurs
... user can enter subcommands
```

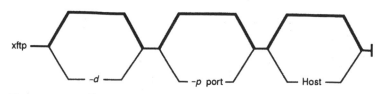

Figure 13.16   tn Command for a Telnet Login.

Retrieving network statistics

The *netstat* command allows an end user to obtain information about the state of the network and the state of connections. The netstat command is depicted in Figure 13.17. Four options are available to obtain these services:

-a. Displays the state of all connections

-i. Displays the state of configurations that are automatically configured (connections that are loaded into the system)

-r. Displays the routing table

-v. Displays statistics about the LAN device driver on this internet interface

The following example is of a user keying in the netstat command to obtain the local IP routing table:

```
$ netstat -r
... routing table is displayed on the screen
```

Using PING to obtain echo services

Figure 13.18 shows the syntax for the PING service. After entering the command PING, the user chooses one of four parameters to obtain the PING service:

-g. a GGP echo request message is sent to a specified host.

-i. An ICMP echo request is sent to a specified host.

-m. A submask is returned for a specified host.

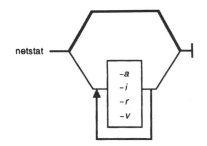

Figure 13.17 netstat Command to Obtain Network Statistics.

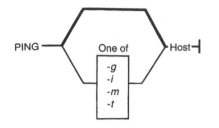

Figure 13.18 PING Command to Obtain Echo Services.

-t. An ICMP-type time stamp request is returned for a specified host.

The following is an example of how a user executes PING to obtain the ICMP time stamp service:

```
$ ping -t host 4
... Information on screen contains the three ICMP time stamp
    values:  originated, received, transmitted
```

Using route to manipulate the IP routing table

Figure 13.19 depicts the syntax to add or remove routes from the IP routing table. The commands *add* and *delete* will add and remove a route, respectively. The *-f* command clears the host gateway table. The *destination* parameter is an IP address identifying a host or network where the route is directed. The *gateway* parameter is an IP address that identifies the next gateway to process the datagram. The following is an example of the route command in which 14.3.2.1 is established as a default gateway:

```
$ route add 0 14.3.2.1
```

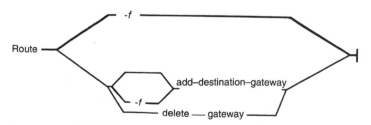

Figure 13.19 ROUTE Command to Add and Remove IP Routes.

Summary

Through the use of operating system calls such as UNIX, a communications programmer can manipulate TCP/IP to open and close sockets, transfer data, obtain name server support, and perform other services. On a higher level, programs such as the IBM Interface Program allow users to obtain the upper internet application-layer services such as file transfer, mail exchange, and remote terminal login without needing to understand more complex operating system calls.

IP, Frame Relay, and ATM

Frame Relay and ATM have been mentioned briefly several times in this book. Since these technologies are now interworking with IP and many systems, it is a good idea to understand their architecture in relation to IP. This chapter describes Frame Relay and ATM and compares these technologies to IP. The approach is to use Frame Relay as the benchmark and compare IP and ATM to this benchmark.

Operations and Architecture

A principal goal of Frame Relay and ATM is to provide a common and standardized interface between different vendor equipment at the user-to-network interface (UNI), as shown in Figure 14.1. Frame Relay and ATM are designed to provide a fast relay service for data applications. This goal is not unique in the telecommunications industry; X.25 and other user-to-network interfaces have the same goal.

The acceptance of Frame Relay and ATM leads to fast, standardized network interfaces. The word *standardized* is important. By

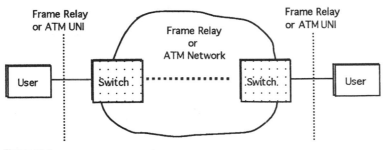

Figure 14.1

using Frame Relay and ATM, the industry can avoid having to use proprietary interfaces.

A Key Difference Between IP and Frame Relay/ATM

One of the key differences between IP and Frame Relay/ATM is the fact that IP is a connectionless technology and both Frame Relay and ATM are connection-oriented. This part of the chapter explains these concepts in relation to IP, Frame Relay, and ATM.

The Frame Relay and ATM approach

In the past, end users operating with terminals and computers communicated with each other through a communications channel called a *physical circuit*. The situation is also true today, and these physical circuits are known by other names, such as *channels*, *links*, *lines*, and *trunks*.

These physical circuits can be configured where two users communicate directly through one circuit, and no one uses this circuit except these two users. In more complex systems, circuits are shared with more than one user. The circuits are terminated at intermediate points through machines that provide relay services to yet another circuit. We learned in this book that these machines are known by names such as *switches*, *routers*, *bridges*, and *gateways*. These machines are responsible for relaying traffic between the two communicating users.

The result of this arrangement is that more than one user shares a physical circuit. Since many communication channels can support more than one user session, the network device (such as the switch) is responsible for placing the traffic of multiple users onto a circuit and removing it at the switches and/or the end-user devices.

The term *virtual circuit* describes a shared circuit (or circuits) where the sharing is transparent to circuit users. Both Frame Relay and ATM use the virtual circuit concept. The term was derived from computer architecture in which an end user perceives that a computer has more memory than actually exists. *Virtual memory* is actually memory on hard disk. Therefore, virtual memory and virtual circuits exist in the mind of the beholder (the user).

A virtual circuit (a service to a network) can be provisioned on a continuous basis. With this approach, the user has the service of the network at any time. This concept is called a *permanent virtual circuit* (PVC). Both Frame Relay and ATM use the virtual circuit concept, and support PVCs.

A PVC is established by creating entries in the network nodes that identify the user. These entries contain a unique identifier of the user, which is known by various names, such as *logical channel, virtual channel identifier* (VCI), and *virtual path identifier* (VPI). A user need only provide this identifier to the network node. The network node examines a logical channel or virtual circuit table to discern what kind of services the user wants and with whom the user wants to communicate.

In contrast to a PVC, a switched virtual circuit (SVC) or call is not preprovisioned. When a user wants to obtain network services to communicate with another user, he or she must submit a connection request message to the network. This message usually identifies the originator. It must identify the receiver, and it might also contain the virtual circuit to be used during the session. This virtual circuit value is simply a label that is used during the communications process. Once the session is over, the value is made available to any other user who wants to "pick it out" of a table. Many networks support another virtual circuit service, which is called by various names (I will use the name *semi-PVC*). With this approach, a user is preprovisioned in that the user is identified to the network as well as the user's end communicating party and the network features to be used during the session. Therefore, the network node contains information about the communicating parties and the type of services desired.

Systems that employ the concepts of virtual circuits discussed in the previous section are connection-oriented. As you just learned, the network maintains information about users, such as their addresses and their ongoing quality-of-service needs. This type of system often uses state tables that contain rules governing the manner in which users interacts with the network. These state tables clarify the procedures between the use and the network, but they do add overhead to the process.

The IP approach

In contrast, systems that do not employ virtual circuits are connectionless systems. As described in Chapter 5, IP fits into this category. Connectionless systems are also known as *datagram systems* and are widely used throughout the industry. The principal difference between a connection-oriented and a connectionless operation is that connectionless protocols (as the name implies) do not establish a circuit for the end-user communication process. Instead, traffic is presented to the service provider in a somewhat ad-hoc fashion. Handshaking arrangements are minimal and perhaps nonexistent. The network service points and network switches (if employed) maintain no ongoing knowledge about the traffic between the two end users (such as state tables). Therefore, datagram services provide no *a priori* knowledge of user traffic, such as a PVC or SVC.

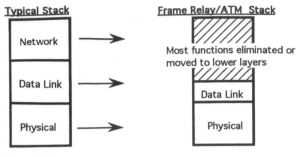

Figure 14.2

Protocol Stacks

Figure 14.2 compares the protocol stacks of Frame Relay and ATM to a conventional data communications network protocol stack, such as X.25 and SNA. Most of the network functions are eliminated or moved to the data link layer. Therefore, a network layer header is no longer used. In addition, many of the conventional data link layer operations are removed, such as sequencing, ACKs, NAKs, and flow control. The reason? To reduce delay and take advantage of current technology, such as faster and relatively error-free networks.

How does IP fit into this stack?

As explained in Chapters 1 and 5 of this book, IP is a layer-3 (network layer) protocol. So you could ask, "What happens to IP in the Frame Relay and ATM stack? Is it gone?" The answer is no. It resides above the Frame Relay and ATM stack. In effect, it is a user layer of the Frame Relay and ATM technologies. I will return to this concept later in the chapter. For now, however, we need to turn to the subject of network interfaces.

Other Interfaces

In addition to UNI, which was explained at the beginning of this chapter, two other interfaces and protocol types might exist in a communications network: the protocol that governs the interface between networks, and the protocol that governs the operations within a network. These three interfaces are shown in Figure 14.3, as well as the common terms associated with the interfaces.

The initial thrust of Frame Relay and ATM has been on the interface between the user and network (the UNI/SNI). However, the network-to-network interface (NNI) or intercarrier interface (ICI) is also quite important, because many organizations that need to communi-

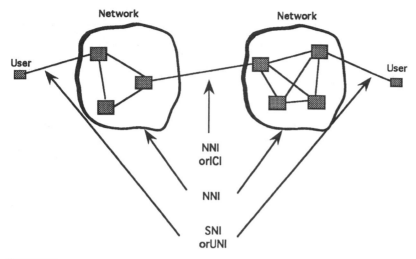

Figure 14.3

cate with each other are connected through different networks. Therefore, Frame Relay and ATM define this interface as well.

Historically, the operations within a data network have been proprietary, and specific to a vendor's implementation. This situation is changing, although most internal operations still remain proprietary and not standardized. While ATM defines this interface, Frame Relay does not. Be aware that the initials NNI might also stand for *network-node interface*, which describes operations that occur between the nodes (switches) within a network.

IP can operate at all three interfaces. It does not become involved with the operations that pertain to Frame Relay and ATM. Although IP is not defined as a UNI, ICI, or NNI protocol, it functions effectively at all three interfaces. Frame Relay operates at the UNI and ICI. ATM and IP operate at the UNI, ICI, and NNI.

Services provided at the interfaces

Figure 14.4 shows the major services provided by Frame Relay and ATM at the interfaces. At the UNI interface, the user and network jointly establish procedures for provisioning permanent virtual circuits (PVCs). In addition, the network provides certain options that allow users to obtain bandwidth on demand (more accurately termed *capacity in bps on demand*). The network provides congestion notification to users at this interface, and certain discard options for payload can be executed. Finally, several limited diagnostics are provided by the network to users in the event of unusual problems.

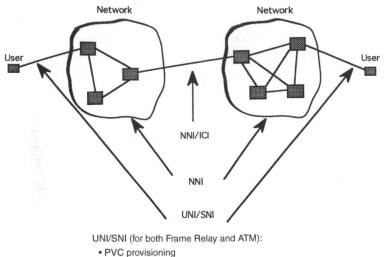

UNI/SNI (for both Frame Relay and ATM):

- PVC provisioning
- SVC
- Bandwidth on demand
- Congestion notification procedures
- Discard elgibility operation
- Limited diagnostics
- Multicasting

NNI/ICI:

- PVC provisioning (Frame Relay)
- Performance requirements (Bellcore for Frame Relay)
- Extensive operations in ATM

NNI:

- Not defined in Frame Relay
- Extensive operations in ATM

Figure 14.4

In Frame Relay, the network-to-network interface (NNI) and inter-carrier interface (ICI) are considerably simpler than the UNI. The principal function at this interface is PVC provisioning and reporting on the status of those PVCs. The NNI for ATM is more complex than Frame Relay. More operations occur between the ATM switches, such as the negotiation of types of traffic (voice, video, and data) and the quality of services associated with the traffic. Likewise, the ATM network-node interface has many operations that deal with connection management, bandwidth analysis, and route discovery.

Private Network-Network Interface (PNNI)

In addition to the operations just described, the ATM Forum has published PNNI. It is a newcomer to ATM and has not yet seen commercial implementation. ITU-T is responsible for publishing the formal ATM standards, but the organization does not concern itself with the operations of private networks. (From ITU-T's perspective, the Internet is considered to be a private network.) Additionally, the ITU-T does not concern itself with the distribution of routing information, route discovery, nor topology analysis. These operations are left to the implementation of individual telecommunication administrations.

This approach is not the case with PNNI. The philosophy behind PNNI is that these important considerations cannot be left to individual implementations. For full interworking to occur in ATM-based networks and ATM switches, there must be standards in place that define how information is distributed between switches in an ATM network.

PNNI consists of two major parts. The first part defines a protocol-to-exchange routing information for route discovery. It defines the operations for distributing topology and routing information between ATM switches, and it allows the switches to compute paths through a network. The second part of PNNI is used for signaling, and defines the procedures to establish point-to-point or point-to-multipoint connections through an ATM network.

PNNI signaling operations are quite similar to many other signaling protocols because they are based on the ITU-T Q.2931 specification. PNNI is not related to IP nor the IP-based route discovery protocols, such as BGP, RIP, and OSPF. It is based on ATM virtual circuit technology.

Operations of IP with Frame Relay and ATM

Figure 14.5 shows the relationship of a user device, such as a workstation, and a Frame Relay network. The same scheme is found in ATM. An important aspect of this relationship is the absence of a Frame Relay interface at the user device. That is, Frame Relay does not operate at the end-user machine. Typically, it resides in a router, which is responsible for encapsulating the user traffic in a Frame Relay frame, and transporting this frame to a Frame Relay switch. The switch relays the traffic to the designation switch that is attached to a LAN where the destination workstation resides.

While Frame Relay and ATM eliminate most of the operations at the network layer, Figure 14.6 illustrates one network layer operation that is essential for Frame Relay and ATM operations: identifying virtual connections. Frame Relay uses a data link connection identifier (DLCI) to identify the destination machine. This 10-bit number corresponds to the virtual circuit number in the network layer protocol, such as an X.25 logical channel number (LCN). ATM uses a 24-bit value called the *virtual path identifier / virtual channel identifier* (VPI/VCI). I will use Frame Relay as the example in this discussion.

In both Frame Relay and ATM networks, the virtual circuit label resides in the Frame Relay or ATM header. This is a layer-2 header,

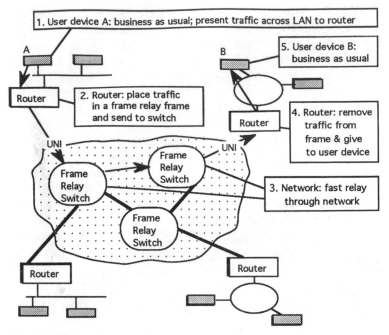

Figure 14.5

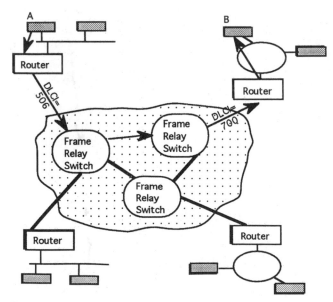

Figure 14.6

which incorporates layers 2 and 3 of older, conventional protocols, notably the virtual circuit label and some traffic management fields.

In a permanent virtual circuit, the DLCIs and VPIs/VCIs are premapped to a destination node. This simplifies the process at the routers because they need only to consult their routing table, check the DLCI or VPI/VCI in the table, and route the traffic to the proper output port based on this address.

Inside the network, the same scheme is used, although Frame Relay switches need not maintain a virtual circuit in the network because Frame Relay does not define the operations within the network "cloud." Connectionless operations can be implemented to allow for dynamic and robust routing between Frame Relay switches. The only requirement is to make certain the frame arrives sequentially at the port designated in the DLCI. However, with ATM, connection-oriented operations are also defined between the switches within the network. ATM does not support proprietary interfaces within the network cloud, and requires the virtual circuit be set up through the network.

Frame Relay and ATM UNI allow multiple users to share a physical link. In Figure 14.7, users A and C are multiplexed onto the UNI by a router, and assigned DLCIs 499 and 506. The traffic is transported to the receiving Frame Relay switch, where it is presented to a router. Note that the DLCIs are translated and mapped into DLCIs

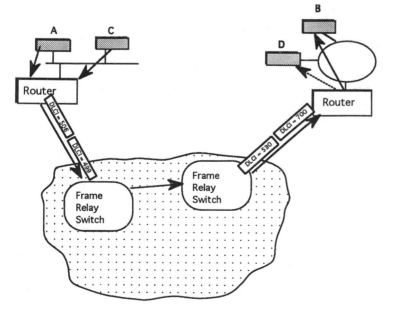

Figure 14.7

700 and 530 at the remote UNI. Once again, the same process occurs with ATM VPIs/VCIs.

Since Frame Relay and ATM are connection-oriented technologies and use labels (DLCIs, VPIs/VCIs) to identify traffic, a router must be able to translate a connectionless address to a label value, and vice-versa. While this operation is not complex, it does require the careful construction of mapping tables at the router. Frame Relay and ATM standards do not describe how this mapping and address translation takes place. Typically, each router has a table that correlates IP addresses to DLCIs and VPIs/VCIs, and vice-versa. This operation is shown in Figure 14.8.

Comparing IP, Frame Relay, and ATM

While I assume that you are now somewhat familiar with Frame Relay and ATM operations (and certainly at ease with IP, after reading this book), it is a good idea to pause briefly and compare some of the major attributes of these three technologies. Table 14.1 makes such a comparison. It consists of four columns: the first is labeled *Attribute* and describes the characteristics (attributes) of the technology in a short phrase. The next three columns, labeled *IP*, *Frame Relay*, and *ATM*, describe how these technologies use or do not use the attribute.

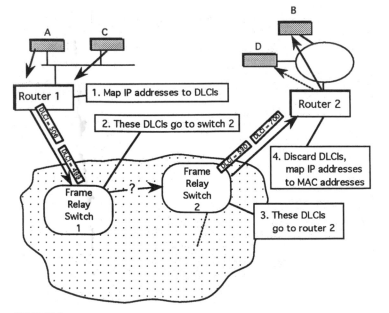

Figure 14.8

TABLE 14.1   Major Attributes of Frame Relay, ATM, and IP

Attribute	IP	Frame Relay	ATM
Application support?	Asynchronous data (with some voice, but not designed for voice)	Asynchronous data (with voice gaining in use, but not designed for voice)	Asynchronous, synchronous voice, video, data
Connection mode?	Connectionless	Connection-oriented	Connection-oriented
Congestion management?	No, replies on other protocols	Yes, congestion notification, traffic tagging (DE bit), and possibly traffic discard	Yes congestion notification, traffic tagging (CLP bit), and possibly traffic discard
Method of identifying traffic?	The IP address	Virtual circuit ID: the DLCI	Virtual circuit ID: the VPI/VCI
PVCs?	No	Yes	Yes
SVCs (connections on demand)?	No	Yes	Yes
Congestion notification technique?	None	The FECN and BECN bits	The CN bits in the PTI field
Traffic tagging technique?	None	The DE bit	The CLP bit
LAN or WAN technology?	Either	WAN-based	Either
PDU size?	Variable (PDU is called a *datagram*)	Variable (PDU is called a *frame*)	Fixed at 48 bytes (PDU is called a *cell*)
Sequencing of traffic?	No	No	Not for cell header, but for payload (it depends on type)
Route discovery responsibility?	No, relies on other protocols	Not defined	Yes, with ATM Forum's PNNI
Routing/switching responsibility?	Yes, using IP address	Not defined	Yes, using VCI/VPI
ACK or NAK retransmissions?	No	No	Only for signaling traffic (SVCs)

Where:

CLP	=	cell loss priority
DE	=	Discard eligibility
DLCI	=	Data link control identifier
FECN	=	Forward explicit congestion notification
LAN	=	Local area network
PDU	=	Protocol data unit
VCI	=	Virtual channel identifier
VPI	=	Virtual path identifier
WAN	=	Wide area network
BECN	=	Backward explicit congestion notification downstream nodes of upstream congestion.

Interworking IP with Frame Relay and ATM Virtual Circuits

Figure 14.9 shows how IP traffic can be transported through an ATM or Frame Relay network. The boundary of the message flow is between a calling user and a called user. In this example, the flow is through interworking units (*IWUs*, in ITU-T terminology). This device is usually called a *router* in internet terms.

The manner in which end-user stations communicate with routers is not defined by ATM or Frame Relay, since the information flow between the end-user station and router is not part of the ATM or Frame Relay UNI. Nonetheless, the user station-to- router operation is well defined in other specifications, discussed in this book. The router need only map the information received from user stations into the ATM or Frame Relay PDU at the originating router. It then performs a complementary (reverse) operation at the terminating router.

Figure 14.9 shows the operations for a LAN-to-LAN transmission with event-by-event notations. The encapsulation headers described in Chapter 3 are employed, such as EtherType and SNAP. The network-level protocol identifier (NLPID or simply PID) is an OSI identifier, which is used in Frame Relay to identify the payload in the frame or cell. In most cases, the PID actually identifies a SNAP header, and the SNAP header is coded to indicate that IP is the protocol family encapsulated in the frame or cell.

Figure 14.10 shows one internetworking scenario between IP, Frame Relay, and ATM. This operation is known as *service interworking* (a Frame Relay Forum term). It means that two dissimilar devices are interworking end to end. At one end is a Frame Relay

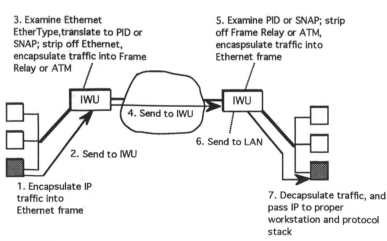

Figure 14.9

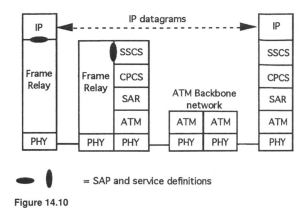

= SAP and service definitions

Figure 14.10

device, and at the other end is an ATM device. Of course, end-to-end IP datagrams are being exchanged, but the service user (the TCP/IP protocol stacks) has no knowledge of the Frame Relay and ATM systems. The Frame Relay service user performs no ATM services, and the ATM service user performs no Frame Relay services. All interworking operations between the user are performed by the IWF.

Figure 14.10 shows the structure of service interworking and the protocol stacks. The location of IWF is not dictated by any standard; it can be placed in a single node or multiple nodes, depending upon the specific topology of an interworking environment.

The service user uses AAL5 operations with message mode and unassured operations. AAL5 SAR is used, as well as AAL5 CPCS and a null SSCS.

The interface between IP and the Frame Relay layer, as well as the interface between the Frame Relay layer and FR-SSCS, occurs through the Frame Relay core SAP (service access point) that is defined in the Frame Relay specifications. Therefore, IWF must accommodate the Frame Relay service definitions at this SAP. These service definitions and SAP are explained in detail in my book *Frame Relay Networks: Specifications and Implementations*, McGraw-Hill, 1995.

In accordance with Frame Relay specifications, the service primitives contain up to five parameters: core user data (the IP datagram), discard eligibility (DE), congestion encountered (CE) backward, congestion encountered (CE) forward, and connection endpoint identifier (CEI).

The *core user data* parameter passes IP datagrams between end users. The datagram is placed into a FR-SSCS PDU at the FR-SSCS layer in the IWU. The DE parameter is sent from the core service user to the service provider (FR-SSCS), and is mapped into the ATM cell loss priority (CLP) bit.

The two congestion parameters supply information about congestion that is encountered in the network. The *congestion encountered forward* parameter indicates that congestion has occurred in transferring data to the receiving user. The *congestion backward parameter* indicates that the network has experienced congestion in transferring these units from the sending user.

The *connection endpoint identifier* parameter further identifies a connection endpoint. For example, this parameter would allow a DLCI to be used by more than one user, and each user would be identified with a connection endpoint identifier value.

Figure 14.11 shows how IP datagrams and Frame Relay frames are segmented into cells. The Frame Relay service-specific convergence sublayer (SSCS), common part convergence sublayer (CPCS), and segmentation and reassembly (SAR) sublayer make up the ATM adaptation layer (AAL). AAL is responsible for segmenting traffic into 48-byte SAR-PDUs at the sending node, and reassembling these SAR-PDUs back to the original traffic at the receiving node.

The ATM layer at the sending node adds a five-byte cell header; at the receiving node, it processes this header and removes it before sending the 48-byte SAR-PDU to AAL. Here is a general description of the operations:

Transmission

1. The destination IP address in the IP datagram is correlated to a Frame Relay DLCI.

2. The IP datagram is encapsulated into the information (I) field of the Frame Relay frame, as a result of passing the traffic through SAP

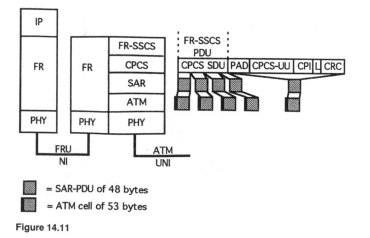

= SAR-PDU of 48 bytes

= ATM cell of 53 bytes

Figure 14.11

to Frame Relay. A PID/SNAP header is placed in the first bytes of the I field to identify the type of traffic that is encapsulated.[1]

3. The encapsulated IP datagram is transported to the IWU across the Frame Relay UNI in the Frame Relay frame.

4. The Frame Relay frame header is translated by the IWU into an ATM cell header, and the IP datagram is segmented into SAR-PDUs. As a general practice, the mapping is as follows:[2]

DLCI → VPI/VCI

DE bit → CLP bit

FECN bit → CN bits

5. The PID/SNAP header is also placed in the bytes of the SAR-PDU, and the SAR-PDU is passed to the ATM layer, which adds the five-byte cell header with its contents established by the mapping operations just described.

6. The cells are passed to the physical layer (say a SONET link) and sent to the next node, eventually reaching the final destination.

Reception

1. If the destination node is a Frame Relay node (not shown in Figure 14.10), then the operations just described are reversed.

2. If the destination node is ATM (as shown in Figure 14.10), no further mapping operations are necessary. The PID/SNAP headers are used to identify the payload (IP) in the SDU and to pass this traffic to the IP module in the destination machine.

The AAL type-5 PDU supports Frame Relay and ATM interworking. The CPI field is not yet defined. The CPCS-UU field is passed transparently by the ATM network. The length field is checked for oversized or undersized PDUs. CRC violations are noted, and a reassembly timer can be invoked at the terminating endpoint.

Using ARP to Correlate IP Addresses with Frame Relay and ATM Virtual Circuits

Address resolution in a Frame Relay network works much the same way as I described for a conventional environment in Chapter 3 of

---

[1]If only the PID is used, it is set to 0xCC to identify IP. If the SNAP header is used, the PID is set to 0x08-00 to identify IP.

[2]The DE (discard eligibility) and CLP (cell loss priority) bits are used to tag traffic when congestion problems occur at the UNI. The forward explicit congestion notification (FECN) and congestion notification (CN) bits inform downstream nodes of upstream congestion.

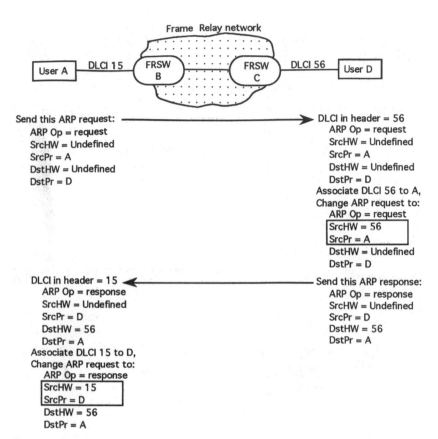

Figure 14.12

this book, with the use of ARP. Figure 14.12 shows how ARP is used with Frame Relay. Be aware that the approach described here does not use ARP in a conventional manner. The hardware address fields in ARP messages contain DLCIs, and pure, modular-OSI layering concepts are not used. Also, with some additional fields, ARP is used in a similar fashion between IP and ATM. Once again, I use Frame Relay as the example, but the ATM operations are quite similar.

To begin the process, user A forms an ARP request message. Since hardware addresses are not used in this process, the hardware address fields are undefined in the request message. The source and destination protocol addresses (for example, IP addresses) are filled in as usual. In this example, the source IP address is A (for user A) and the destination IP address is D (for user D). When user D receives the ARP request, it is encapsulated into the Frame Relay frame, which contains the local DLCI value of 56 (placed into the frame by the Frame Relay network). User D extracts this value from the header and places it in the source hardware address of the incoming ARP request message.

This process allows user D to associate protocol address A (in the source protocol address field) with DLCI 56. The box on the right side of Figure 14.12 shows where the correlation takes place.

Next, user D forms the ARP response message (exchanges the source and destination values in the message), but leaves the destination hardware address undefined (which, of course, becomes defined when the source and destination addresses are exchanged). When user A receives this frame, it has DLCI 15 in the Frame Relay header. Thus, user A extracts this value and places it in the source hardware address field of the message. This operation allows user A to correlate DLCI 15 to protocol address D. Once again, the two boxes in this figure highlight where the correlations take place.

IP Switching

Before I leave the subject of IP, Frame Relay, and ATM, I should discuss the subject of IP switching. Traditional IP routing makes routing decisions on each datagram that comes into a router. In so doing, the router consults a routing table (at each node) and makes a routing decision on the datagram. Since this approach entails considerable processing and can result in delays, several vendors have been working on schemes that speed up the relaying of traffic through an internet.

One approach is called *IP switching* and, although the exact operations differ among implementations, the idea is to build a path through an internet to eliminate the node-by-node routing done with traditional methods. Some of the systems that use IP switching are really using ATM and running IP over the ATM backbone. The switching is performed with the ATM header (VPI and VCI).

Other implementations distinguish IP switching by the user of hardware instead of software for the bulk of the IP address translations and table lookups. Still others distinguish IP switching by the nature of how the switching fabric in the router is designed.

Another similar approach is *tag switching*. This operation is distinguished by the fact that routing tables contain complete information about the path from the sender to the receiver. A pointer in the data unit is used to index into the routing table to identify the best route.

Carefully check the design (and throughput) of these new routers before making any acquisition decisions. There is a considerable amount of marketing hyperbole associated with this subject.

Summary

Frame Relay has assumed an important position in the data communication network industry. It is the technology of choice for many private and public networks. ATM is viewed by some as the eventual successor to Frame Relay, but the latter's success and position in the marketplace make that scenario unlikely in the near future.

Frame Relay and ATM are quite different from IP. They operate at layer 2 with a connection-oriented architecture and are not installed (presently) in end-user stations. IP is connectionless, operates at layer 3, and must operate in the end-user equipment. IP will continue to operate as the preferred layer-3 routing protocol and will continue to "run on top" of Frame Relay and ATM networks.

Management Considerations

This chapter classifies several of the ITU-T and International Standards Organization (ISO) protocols as OSI, which is not actually correct, although it is common in the industry to do so. These protocols instead use the OSI model as a foundation for their design. Strictly speaking, the number of defined OSI protocols are very few, because the intent of OSI is to provide a model first and define protocols second.

I would also like to state (I am sure I am one of the few people in the industry who has this opinion) that, as a model, OSI has been very successful. Its major problem is that the OSI architects made the mistake of embedding actual protocols into the model. Unfortunately, most people do not distinguish between the OSI protocols and the OSI model.

Vendor Strategies with Internet-Based Products

By 1990, enterprises such as commercial banks, insurance companies, and government departments had either written a plan to migrate to OSI standards or were planning to write such a plan. Indeed, the U.S. Government, which was the chief architect and sponsor of the Internet, issued a directive for government agencies to migrate to GOSIP (the U.S. Government OSI Profile), which is an implementation of OSI.

The use of internet standards has overwhelmed OSI, but OSI is hanging on and a number of my clients are now using OSI or are planning to migrate to it. In any case, it appears that in the future users must deal with vendor-specific protocols, internet protocols, and OSI protocols.

Without question, every major communications vendor is planning to support one or both of the following scenarios: either migrating away from vendor-specific products toward the OSI and/or TCP/IP suites or maintaining vendor-specific layers and providing interfaces between these layers and the OSI/TCP/IP suites.

The following scenario is *not* what vendors and manufacturers are openly espousing: that vendor-specific protocols are the best approach, and their product lines are built strictly on specific customer requirements (i.e., tailored to the individual customer).

I should emphasize that a company tasked with designing, manufacturing, and selling computer and communications products must frequently produce a system that is tailored to a specific user environment. In a situation in which the environment does not fit the OSI or TCP/IP framework, what is to be done?

The answer is obvious: Build the product to meet the customer's needs, and try to design "hooks" into and out of the OSI and TCP/IP worlds. A number of manufacturers are adapting to this approach with considerable success. Moreover, it is not contradictory to the spirit of OSI. TCP/IP standards do not address this issue. OSI does not care what the system does in its internal operations, nor does it care how the system does it. OSI stipulates only that a given and standardized input into *any* system must produce a predictable and standardized output from that system.

Vendors react to the marketplace

It might prove useful to move back in time and examine what was going on during the embryonic stages of the integration of computers and communications. During the 1970s, several manufacturers realized that they could not afford to continue operating in an unorganized and ill-structured communications environment, even within their own product lines. Consequently, they began to develop a more coherent approach to their own products and embarked on efforts to build a structured framework (architecture) for their communication protocols.

The implementation of vendor-specific architectures alleviated the incompatibility problem of products within vendors' product lines; but it did nothing to address the serious problem of incompatibility between different vendors' computers, terminals, and other equipment. If anything, the development of vendor-specific systems made matters worse, because each manufacturer embarked on a separate course to invent a "better mousetrap."

At this time, several standards groups became active. The ISO began work in 1979 on OSI, and the OSI model was published in 1984 to serve as a standard model for computer communications.

Of course, you have learned that internet standards served as pioneers to some of the OSI protocols. Moreover, TCP and IP served as a valuable foundation for "launching" all the internet standards. Without question, many dollars have been saved by the U.S. government and private industry because of internet standards.

So what about the future? Does it make sense to maintain both OSI and TCP/IP? Is one better than the other? Should users care? With these questions in mind, let me describe some of the activities in the computer and communication standards arena and develop some answers.

A Simplified Comparison of TCP/IP and OSI Stacks

Figure 15.1 shows the relationship of the OSI (more accurately the ITU-T/ISO) stack to the TCP/IP stack. Several organizations and people have stated that some of these layers are functionally equivalent. Numerous reports and articles have been published stating that the transmission control protocol (TCP) and transport protocol, class 4 (TP4), as well as Internet Protocol (IP) and connectionless network protocol (CLNP), do the same things. It should be stated categorically, however, that the OSI and Internet Protocols perform similar functions, but there is definitely not a one-to-one mapping of their services. The following discussion compares the stacks and analyzes the mapping the functions of one stack to the other.

The lower two layers of these two protocol stacks do not present any serious compatibility problems. Indeed, the top five layers can rest somewhat transparently over the bottom two. Both stacks use

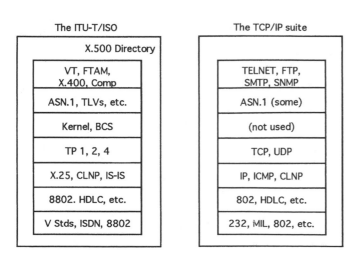

Figure 15.1 Comparison of ITU-T/ISO and TCP/IP Suites.

existing international standards. For example, at the physical layer, the ubiquitous EIA-232-E standard is used in both stacks, although the OSI stack cites the use of V Series Recommendations. EIA-232-E is compatible with its counterparts in the V Series (V.24 and V.28), and also aligns with ISO 2110 for the physical connection.

X.21 or X.21*bis* can also be applied to both stacks at the physical layer. The physical level LAN standards, as published by the IEEE 802 standards, apply to both stacks. The Integrated Services Digital Network (ISDN) physical layer is applicable to both stacks, and the ISO publishes these standards under the 8802 numbers.

The data link layer presents no major problems since most vendors have adapted a version of high-level data link control (HDLC), such as link access procedures balanced (LAPB) in X.25-based networks, PPP for dial-up links to and from ISPs, link access procedure for the D channel (LAPD) in ISDNs for the control channel, and LAPM for error-correcting modems. LAN standards use compatible, physical data link protocols with the media access control (MAC) sublayer of the 802 standards. Moreover, the IEEE 802.2 logical link control (LLC) standard works well with both stacks. To be accurate, there are no actual OSI protocols defined at layers one and two, and none of these standards just discussed are OSI protocols.

Mapping problems occur at the upper five layers and especially the upper three layers. As Figure 15.1 illustrates, at layer three, the OSI stack contains X.25 and CLNP. Admittedly, the functions of CLNP and IP closely parallel each other. However, CLNP is more functionally rich than IP.

No correlation exists between X.25 and the TCP/IP stack. X.25 is designed as a connection-oriented network interface. Some of the functions supported in X.25 are carried in TCP and to some extent in the Internet Control Message Protocol (ICMP).

Then why can't we use X.25 as a functional equivalent to TCP and ICMP? First, the mapping would be horrendous. Some of the functions do not map, and others are contradictory to the intent of the protocols. Second, TCP is designed to be a very reliable end-to-end protocol. X.25 is designed to be a reliable protocol, but it does not have the graceful close features of TCP; X.25 gives the network the option of discarding packets in certain situations (reset and restart). Third, ICMP carries a number of diagnostic and status messages, but it does not support the number and type of diagnostic packets that X.25 supports.

So what is to be done with X.25 in relation to TCP/IP? The answer is that nothing prevents the network manager from mapping TCP/IP over an X.25 network, as you learned in Chapter 11. Moreover, it is technically feasible to use CLNP in place of IP and place it between TP and X.25. TP4 is overkill for the X.25-based network, and TP2 is a more likely candidate at the transport layer for the X.25/CLNP stack.

TCP/IP does not have any comparable protocols to OSI in the session and presentation layers. Abstract Syntax Notation One (ASN.1) is finding its way into internet network management standards (for example, in the simple network management protocol or SNMP), but it is not used to the extent it is used in OSI. TCP/IP does not have the OSI transfer syntax protocol, which is shown in Figure 15.1 as TLV (type, length, value notation). Nothing precludes a user from employing TLV with internet protocols, as long as each end of the communications channel knows how to use it. Some internet implementations use the External Data Representation (XDR) protocol, which is quite similar to but incompatible with TLV.

The session layer presents vexing problems. Its services are required by almost all the OSI application layer protocols, so it is not easy to bypass if a user is accessing an OSI application layer protocol. TCP/IP does not have a session layer, although several of the TCP/IP application layer protocols perform session services.

Other mapping problems occur in the applications layer, where the TCP/IP protocol stack is best known for the file transfer protocol (FTP), SMTP, Telnet, browsers, and web applications. The OSI stack contains very elaborate protocols with file transfer and access management (FTAM), X.400 message handling system (MHS), and the virtual terminal (VT). Certain of the functions can be mapped on a limited scale, but the TCP/IP application-layer protocols simply do not perform the many services of their counterparts in the OSI stack, and vice-versa.

For example, FTP permits third-party transfers and FTAM does not. On the other hand, FTAM allows considerable manipulation of objects within a file and FTP does not have this level of granularity. FTP permits two logical connections between two FTP clients and control servers: a control connection and a data connection. This concept does not exist in FTAM.

The OSI environment relies heavily on the ISO OSI network management standards and the Common Management Information Protocol (CMIP). The Internet has made great progress in this arena with SNMP. Presently, the concept of X.500 does not exist in the TCP/IP suite, although the Domain Name System (DNS) is an ideal application for placing into an X.500 directory.

IP and CLNP

I have pointed out a number of times that CLNP and IP are quite similar, but they are not compatible. Figure 15.2 shows the protocol data units of CLNP and IP; obviously, the formats are quite different.

ISO CLNP PDU

Protocol identifier
Length indicator
Version/protocol ID extension
Lifetime
Segment/more/error report/type code
Segment length
Checksum
Destination address length
Destination address
Source address length
Source address
Data unit identifier
Segmentation offset
Total PDU length
Options
Data

IP DATAGRAM

Version	Header length
Type of service	
Total length	
Identifier	
Flags	Fragment offset
Time to live	
Protocol	
Header checksum	
Source address	
Destination address	
Option and padding	
Data	

Figure 15.2 ISO CLNP PDU and IP Datagram.

TP4 and TCP

TCP is similar to many of the ISO/ITU-T transport layer operations. Many of their support functions, such as port/TSAP multiplexing, end-to-end acknowledgment, and timer operations are designed to achieve the same goals. However, the two protocols differ in many of their features, and in several instances the capabilities in one protocol do not exist in the other. Figure 15.3 compares the formats of the two data units.

TP4 does not use port identifiers. Its identifiers are the destination and source reference fields and transport service access points (TSAPs, located in the variable part of the transport protocol data unit, or TPDU).

Both protocols support sliding window concepts, TP4 with the credit (CDT) field and TCP with the window field. The variable part field of TP4 can be coded to negotiate many services, such as throughput and delay. This capability does not exist in TCP. The OSI transport protocol is organized around five classes of protocols, each providing a specific set of services. One of these classes is TP4. TCP has no such capability.

I have read a number of articles stating that TCP is more efficient than TP4. This finding is not surprising. TP4 provides more services, but function rarely comes without cost. Several options now exist that allow users to run TP0 and TCP (see Chapter 11). The principal differences between TP4 and TCP are summarized in Table 15.1.

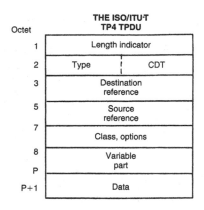

Figure 15.3 Comparison of TP4 TPDU and TCP TPDU.

TABLE 15.1 Comparison of TP4 and TCP

TP class 4	TCP
Connection-oriented	Connection-oriented
Complex, with many functions	Simple, relatively few functions
Complex and varied TPDU	One format for segment
Data placed in specific SDUs from upper layer and sent as TPDUs	Data sent on a stream basis from upper layer and sent as segments
Expedited data can arrive out of sequence with earlier data	Urgent data stays in order within the stream and segment
Uses OSI service access point (SAP)	Uses the IP 32-bit address and the port number to achieve a socket
Push function nonexistent	Uses push function to force transfer
Supports multiple classes (0–4)	Does not use class concept
Uses OSI-based service definitions	Uses TCP-specific primitives
Uses TP-specific timers and state diagrams	Uses TCP-specific timers and state diagrams
No graceful close	Supports a graceful close

Summary

The TCP/IP and OSI standards are garnering the most support for use as international data communication network standards. They are rich in function, and they offer many options. However, they are also incompatible. Presently, TCP/IP has "out-distanced" OSI protocols in the protocol race and will most likely increase that distance. Nonetheless, OSI, as a model, has been a very valuable tool for network designers and programmers. The OSI model's architecture is found in Frame Relay, SONET, ATM, and many other architectures. Therefore, TCP/IP and OSI-based systems will most likely coexist and internetwork with each other for many years to come.

Index

ABOUT THE AUTHOR

Uyless Black is President of Information Engineering Inc., a Virginia-based telecommunications consulting firm. He has designed and programmed a wide range of data communications systems, as well as voice and data networks. Previously he was a senior officer for the Federal Reserve, where he managed numerous large-scale data communications systems. Mr. Black has served as an advisor and consultant to many companies, including AT&T, Bell Northern Research, and Bellcore. He is the author of more than twenty books on telecommunications and networks.